Inclusive Smart Museums

James Hutson • Piper Hutson

Inclusive Smart Museums

Engaging Neurodiverse Audiences and Enhancing Cultural Heritage

James Hutson
Professor of Art History and
Visual Culture
Lindenwood University
Saint Charles, MO, USA

Piper Hutson
Art History and Visual Culture
Lindenwood University
St Charles, MO, USA

ISBN 978-3-031-43614-7   ISBN 978-3-031-43615-4   (eBook)
https://doi.org/10.1007/978-3-031-43615-4

© The Editor(s) (if applicable) and The Author(s), under exclusive licence to Springer Nature Switzerland AG 2024

This work is subject to copyright. All rights are solely and exclusively licensed by the Publisher, whether the whole or part of the material is concerned, specifically the rights of translation, reprinting, reuse of illustrations, recitation, broadcasting, reproduction on microfilms or in any other physical way, and transmission or information storage and retrieval, electronic adaptation, computer software, or by similar or dissimilar methodology now known or hereafter developed.

The use of general descriptive names, registered names, trademarks, service marks, etc. in this publication does not imply, even in the absence of a specific statement, that such names are exempt from the relevant protective laws and regulations and therefore free for general use.

The publisher, the authors, and the editors are safe to assume that the advice and information in this book are believed to be true and accurate at the date of publication. Neither the publisher nor the authors or the editors give a warranty, expressed or implied, with respect to the material contained herein or for any errors or omissions that may have been made. The publisher remains neutral with regard to jurisdictional claims in published maps and institutional affiliations.

This Palgrave Macmillan imprint is published by the registered company Springer Nature Switzerland AG.

The registered company address is: Gewerbestrasse 11, 6330 Cham, Switzerland

Paper in this product is recyclable.

This book is dedicated to our incredible children, Bishop and Aurora, who have been the true inspiration behind its creation. Your endless curiosity, open minds, and compassionate hearts have reminded us of the importance of preserving and celebrating our cultural heritage for future generations. Through your innocent eyes and inquisitive spirits, you have sparked a desire in us to create a more inclusive and accessible world of cultural heritage.

Your unwavering belief in the power of diversity and your eagerness to embrace different perspectives have fueled our commitment to ensuring that every individual, regardless of their background, can find their voice and place within our shared history.

With this dedication, we express our deepest hopes for a more inclusive tomorrow. We envision a world where cultural heritage is not just preserved but actively celebrated and understood by all. A world where every person's story is valued and appreciated, and where diversity is cherished as the vibrant tapestry that enriches our collective human experience.

As you grow and navigate the complexities of the world, we hope that this book will serve as a guiding light, reminding you of the importance of empathy, understanding, and respect for all cultures and perspectives. May it ignite your passion for exploration, inspire you to be ambassadors of inclusivity, and empower you to shape a future where everyone's heritage is recognized and cherished.

With all our love and unwavering belief in your potential to make a difference.

Acknowledgments

We would like to extend our sincere gratitude to the individuals who have contributed to the creation of this book and supported us throughout this journey.

First and foremost, we would like to thank Dr. Katherine Herrell for her pioneering efforts in piloting the decentered collaborative interdisciplinary author model alongside Dr. James Hutson during the challenging times of the COVID-19 pandemic in 2020. Her innovative approach and unwavering dedication to collaboration have greatly influenced the development of this work.

We are immensely grateful to Dr. Kathi Vosevich, Dean of the College of Arts and Humanities, for her unwavering support and encouragement for the research that has culminated in this text. Her guidance and belief in our scholarly pursuits have been instrumental in shaping this book.

We would also like to express our appreciation to Drs. Sara Bagley and Colleen Biri for their expertise and background in psychology, social science research, and statistical modeling. Their valuable insights and contributions have greatly enhanced the depth and rigor of our work.

Our heartfelt thanks go to Wells Fargo for providing Dr. Piper Hutson with the invaluable curatorial experience that has broadened her understanding of cultural heritage institutions. Their support has enabled her to better serve these institutions through research and consultation.

We would like to acknowledge Provost Dr. Bethany Alden-Rivers for her dedication in guiding the future of Lindenwood University. Her leadership and vision have created an environment that fosters innovation, collaboration, and academic excellence.

Lastly, we want to express our deep appreciation to Terri Edwards for instilling a sense of wonder and encouraging a pursuit of a career in the arts for Dr. Piper Hutson. Her unwavering support and belief in her abilities have been instrumental in shaping her passion for cultural heritage and the arts.

To all those mentioned above and to the countless others who have supported us along the way, we offer our heartfelt thanks. Your contributions have been invaluable, and we are forever grateful for your presence in our lives.

Contents

1 **Introduction: Building Inclusive Museums**   1
   1.1 *Cultural Heritage*   1
   1.2 *Neurodiversity in Museums*   5
   1.3 *Sensory Days*   25
   1.4 *Identification Matters*   27
   1.5 *Children's Museums*   28
   1.6 *Staff Training Programs*   32
   1.7 *Inclusive Smart Museums*   34
   1.8 *Summary of Chapters*   38
      Chapter 2: Storytelling   38
      Chapter 3: Inclusivity and Environment   39
      Chapter 4: Gamification   39
      Chapter 5: Immersive Technologies   40
      Chapter 6: Conclusion: Future Directions for Neuro-inclusivity in Museums and Heritage Sites   40
   References   41

2 **Storytelling**   49
   2.1 *Digital Storytelling and Museums*   50
   2.2 *Personal Narratives*   63
   2.3 *Social Stories and Museums*   67
   2.4 *Community Storytelling*   70
   References   76

3 Inclusivity & Environment 85
- 3.1 Sensory Kits 85
- 3.2 Wayfinding and Sensory Maps 90
  - Wayfinding Technologies 90
- 3.3 Immersive Storymaps 108
- References 115

4 Gamification 127
- 4.1 Gamification and Game-Based Learning 128
- 4.2 Gamification and Accessibility 132
- 4.3 Treasure Hunts 137
- 4.4 Gamified Digital Storytelling 142
- References 146

5 Immersive Technologies 153
- 5.1 Adaptive Extended Reality 154
- 5.2 Avatars and Inclusivity 165
- 5.3 Digital Twins 171
- 5.4 Wearables, Neuroscience, and Exhibition Design 182
  - Wearables and Exhibition Design 182
- 5.5 Artificial Intelligence and Museums 202
- References 212

6 Conclusion: Future Directions for Neuro-inclusivity in Museums and Heritage Sites 229
- 6.1 Apprenticeships and Residencies 229
- 6.2 Looking Ahead 232
- References 238

Index 241

About the Authors

James Hutson is an administrator and researcher in higher education specializing in artificial intelligence, neurodiversity, immersive realities, digital humanities, and gamification of education. He received his BA in Art from the University of Tulsa, his MA in Art History from Southern Methodist University, and his PhD in Art History from the University of Maryland, College Park. He has also received his MA in Leadership and MA in Game Design at Lindenwood University and is now pursuing his PhD in Artificial Intelligence at Capitol Technology University. Dr. Hutson has taught at five universities across the country since 2006 and has served as chair of Art History and program manager of Pre-Art Therapy and Pre-Art Conservation, Assistant Dean of Graduate and Online Programs for the School of Arts, Media, and Communication, and now serves as Lead XR Disruptor and Department Head of Art History and Visual Culture for the College of Arts and Humanities. His scholarship focuses on the intersections of art, culture, and technology.

Piper Hutson has over 16 years of experience curating at galleries across the country and has co-curated over 40 exhibitions during her multiple positions, as well as head-curating ten shows in the past five years. She completed her EdD at Lindenwood University with her dissertation work entitled The Role of Education in the Art Viewing Experience, comparing the evolution of learning in museums and corporate art collections. With a focus on nineteenth-century British art, she is also an adjunct professor, having taught a variety of courses for eight years, both online and on the ground. Her current work involves improving inclusivity in cultural heritage collections for neurodiverse populations. She has co-authored several works on inclusivity in the workplace and best practices on supporting neurodiversity in cultural heritage institutions.

List of Figures

Fig. 1.1	Autism puzzle in the head	25
Fig. 1.2	Indianapolis Children's Museum, August 5, 2015. Photograph by Josh Grenier	29
Fig.1.3	Astronaut Steve Bowen with Children's Museum visitor, Boston Children's Museum. August 19, 2012	31
Fig. 2.1	Building map, a visit to the museum, Betty Brinn Children's Museum	51
Fig. 2.2	Interactive display, Maritime Experiential Museum & Aquarium. October 6, 2011	52
Fig. 2.3	Museum of London Interactive. August 18, 2010	53
Fig. 2.4	Parking map, Lewisburg Children's Museum	55
Fig. 2.5	Map of National Railway Museum premises, South Australia	55
Fig. 2.6	The National Museum of the Marine Corps' interactive website	58
Fig. 2.7	Canadian Museum for Human Rights	73
Fig. 3.1	Verbal communication card, Columbia River Maritime Museum, Astoria	88
Fig. 3.2	MTA launches app to assist blind and low-vision bus riders	90
Fig. 3.3	Quiet and less-crowded spaces, sensory-friendly map of The Metropolitan Museum of Art for visitors on the autism pectrum, 2015	95
Fig. 3.4	Sensory-friendly sessions, a visit to the museum, Betty Brinn Children's Museum	96
Fig. 3.5	Sensory symbols, a visit to the museum, Betty Brinn Children's Museum	98
Fig. 3.6	Spaces with natural light, sensory-friendly map of The Metropolitan Museum of Art for visitors on the autism spectrum, 2015	106

xiii

… LIST OF FIGURES

Fig. 3.7	Journey Through Hallowed Ground Byway, Catoctin Furnace	112
Fig. 3.8	Catchments along the Great Barrier Reef, State of Queensland	113
Fig. 4.1	Exploratorium, May 2008	142
Fig. 4.2	Dinosaur Hall, Natural History Museum, July 14, 2009	143
Fig. 5.1	Night of Museums, Muséum national d'Histoire naturelle. (May 11, 2011)	164
Fig. 5.2	Charlette Proto, Second Life	165
Fig. 5.3	REACTOR, The Foundation of the Hellenic World (FHW). (May 28, 2001)	173
Fig. 5.4	After Frans Hals, *Portrait of a Man*. (Kremmer Collection, between 1627 and 1630)	174
Fig. 5.5	Buddhist paintings from the important silk-road temples of Dun Huang	176
Fig. 5.6	Bust of Nefertiti, Neues Museum, Berlin	183
Fig. 5.7	Holocube, DLR German Aerospace Center	184
Fig. 5.8	Sensory Map, Columbia River Maritime Museum, Astoria	188
Fig. 5.9	Topographical organization of human emotions in the body from Nummenmaa et al. (2020 Proceedings of the National Academy of Sciences of the United States of America (PNAS))	199
Fig. 5.10	Eye-tracking algorithm using visible light	200
Fig. 5.11	Anatomically defined default mode network (DMN)	201

LIST OF TABLES

Table 1.1	Self-reported diagnoses of survey participants	12
Table 1.2	Reasons neurodiverse populations avoid museums	14
Table 1.3	Pre-visitation considerations for neurodiverse population	15
Table 1.4	Themes of negative museum experiences reported by neurodiverse participants	17
Table 1.5	Helpful accommodations and features reported by neurodiverse participants	19
Table 1.6	Recommendations for improving museum experience for neurodiverse visitors	21
Table 1.7	Recommendations for enhancing accessibility and inclusivity in museums	24
Table 2.1	Recommendations for enhanced accessibility in pre-visitation maps	56
Table 2.2	Benefits of digital storytelling in museums	57
Table 2.3	Examples of digital storytelling in museums	57
Table 2.4	Examples of personal narratives in museums	64
Table 2.5	Examples of social stories in museums	67
Table 2.6	Examples of community storytelling in museums	71
Table 3.1	Standard contents of a sensory kit for neurodiverse visitors	87
Table 3.2	Best practices for wayfinding design	91
Table 3.3	Elements for consideration in sensory maps	97
Table 3.4	Sensory processing subtypes	104
Table 3.5	Examples of immersive storymaps	109
Table 3.6	Elements of immersive storymaps	115
Table 4.1	Elements of gamification and game-based learning	129
Table 4.2	Elements of gamification and accessibility	133
Table 4.3	Examples of accessible gamification	135

Table 4.4	Best practices and considerations for treasure hunt design	138
Table 4.5	Elements of gamified digital storytelling	144
Table 5.1	Benefits of adaptive extended reality in museums	155
Table 5.2	Examples of adaptive extended reality in museums	157
Table 5.3	Benefits of digital twins in museums and cultural heritage	172
Table 5.4	Examples of digital twins in museums and cultural heritage	178
Table 5.5	Methods for personalized museum experiences	195
Table 5.6	Neuroscience and museums	197
Table 5.7	Artificial intelligence and museums	203
Table 5.8	Reducing bias with AI systems in museums	205
Table 5.9	Use cases of ChatGPT for museums	208
Table 6.1	Recommendations for action	236

CHAPTER 1

Introduction: Building Inclusive Museums

The intersection of cultural heritage, neurodiversity, and inclusivity in museum settings are crucial considerations to engage the public at large. The increasing use of emerging technologies like extended reality (XR) and virtual museums (VM) to engage neurodiverse populations and promote inclusivity also benefits a general audience. Therefore, the need to address the unique needs of neurodiverse visitors by combining existing approaches like social stories and sensory maps with XR experiences results in greater impact in museums overall. The impact of the COVID-19 pandemic on museums, leading to a shift towards digital experiences and the potential of XR and digital twin technologies in creating immersive virtual experiences, has opened up new pathways for engagement with the public. The importance of considering sensory sensitivities and providing staff training programs to support neurodiverse individuals can optimize these new pathways.

1.1 Cultural Heritage

Over the past two decades, museums have increasingly sought to build connections with the community and increase inclusivity of visitors. At the same time, emerging technologies, such as extended reality (XR) and virtual museums (VM) are increasingly adopted to engage with different generational expectations but also for the purposes of supporting inclusivity and neurodiverse populations. First, such technologies were adopted to

© The Author(s), under exclusive license to Springer Nature Switzerland AG 2024
J. Hutson, P. Hutson, *Inclusive Smart Museums*,
https://doi.org/10.1007/978-3-031-43615-4_1

augment exhibitions in the physical museum space for edutainment. Since then, XR has expanded from room-size environments (CAVEs) and augmented exhibitions to the creation of entire virtual museums, such as The Museum of Pure Form and The Virtual Museum of Sculpture. Digital twins of museums are increasingly common, along with UNESCO World Heritage Sites. Such virtual experiences can be leveraged to prepare neurodiverse visitors prior to visiting a museum. This chapter will outline how existing approaches to social stories and sensory maps may be combined with XR experiences to support neurodiverse visitors and their families. While onsite, immersive technologies can be used both for engagement and to provide accommodations for greater inclusivity and diversity (Hutson & Hutson, 2023a).

In times of public health crises when travel becomes restricted, public spaces close, and anxiety over an uncertain future spreads, institutions must adopt an agile mindset to continue to engage with their constituents in innovative ways. At the same time, such events as the global spread of COVID-19, which the World Health Organization (WHO) classified a pandemic on March 11, 2020, promote human resilience and spur innovative solutions to emerging problems that find application beyond their immediate intended use cases. Such was the case for cultural heritage institutions, which had to quickly pivot to find new ways for the public to engage with their collections. The call to stay home and limit large gatherings of people led museums, galleries, and cultural heritage sites to close around the globe almost overnight. For instance, the Smithsonian announced all 19 of its related institutes, museums, and even the National Zoo would close to the public on March 14, 2020 (AP, 2020; Daher, 2020).

At first, front-of-house staff were repurposed in other areas, such as helping to catalogue and digitize collections (Cobley et al., 2020). But as the pandemic wore on, there was increased pressure for furloughs and then layoffs among museum staff and educators (Krantz & Downey, 2021). To stave off further loss of human capital and retain public engagement with sites and collections across the globe, many museums turned to emerging technologies. For instance, The Louvre in Paris spent much of the year digitizing and then releasing over 480,000 pieces from its collection in 2021 on their platform, while the work began in 2017 for digitizing UNESCO World Culture Heritage Sites would provide remote access to global locations cut off by border closures and travel bans in 2020 (Longhi-Heredia & Marcotte, 2021; Wildgans, 2022).

An unprecedented investment in research and development followed with companies such as Facebook (now Meta) to make extended reality (XR) – including augmented reality (AR), mixed reality (MR), and virtual reality (VR) – commercially available, user-friendly, and affordable. The launch of the all-in-one head-mounted display (HMD) Oculus Quest 2 (released on October 13, 2022) represents a watershed moment for immersive experiences and the ability to engage the public (Raja & Priya, 2021). At the same time, advancements were made in digital twin technologies. While previous photogrammetric techniques would require thousands of individual photographs painstakingly stitched together manually to create 3D models of objects or spaces, the latest generation of software compiles millions of individual images automatically (Brennan & Christiansen, 2018). The latest hand-held scanners, such as Scantech, can also be used to produce high-resolution digital twins of objects, complete with precise colors and textures (Harrington et al., 2022). Both VR HMD and digital twin systems are now highly portable, user-friendly, and affordable. These technologies are now poised to work in tandem to create high-fidelity recreations of objects and historical sites and view in an immersive environment anywhere in the world.

The advances in technology coupled with the demand for virtual experiences accelerated by the global pandemic have led to an unprecedented effort to digitize museum collections and create digital twins of locations globally. The initial impetus for such projects was to allow for access to locations that were closed to promote social distancing and to incentivize future tourism in general (Franczuk et al., 2022). However, as this chapter will outline, the availability of digital versions of spaces and objects contained within and the hardware to view prior to and during visitation can now be leveraged to support inclusivity and accessible efforts for neurodiverse populations in cultural heritage institutions. Efforts to support diverse populations with a variety of needs have dominated scholarship on museum studies since the last millennium. With an estimated 10% of the world's population (650 million people) living with a disability, museums have introduced many strategies to promote accessibility. For instance, audio and visual aids have seen widespread adoption, including audio guides, captioning, and sign language interpretation for visitors who are blind, deaf, or hard of hearing. Accessible facilities include wheelchair ramps and elevators, as well as accessible restrooms and parking for those with mobility restrictions. And inclusive programming showcases underrepresented perspectives to celebrate diverse cultures and communities.

However, the unique needs of neurodiverse visitors have only recently begun garnering attention (Hutson & Hutson, 2022; Sokoloff & Schattschneider, 2022).

The integration of emerging technologies, such as extended reality (XR) and virtual museums (VM), into the cultural heritage landscape has enhanced inclusivity efforts and enhanced the engagement of diverse audiences. The global pandemic accelerated the adoption of these technologies, allowing museums to digitize collections and create virtual experiences accessible to global audiences (Gatto et al., 2021). The advancements in XR, including augmented reality (AR), mixed reality (MR), and virtual reality (VR), along with digital twin technologies, have made immersive experiences more accessible, user-friendly, and affordable. The availability of digital twins and portable VR headsets has opened up new possibilities for supporting neurodiverse visitors and their families (Yin et al., 2023). By combining existing strategies like social stories and sensory maps with XR experiences, museums can provide inclusive accommodations and prepare neurodiverse visitors before their physical visit (Moufahim et al., 2023). The transformative potential of these technologies can further be illustrated with specific ways museums can support and engage individuals with neurodiverse conditions, ensuring a more inclusive and enriching museum experience for all.

In order to best facilitate the use of emerging technologies to support inclusive experiences, a neurohumanities methodology and approach should be employed. Neurohumanities integrates insights from neuroscience and the humanities to gain a deeper understanding of human behavior and cognition. This interdisciplinary approach supports cultural heritage institutions by applying neuroscientific methods to explore the neural mechanisms underlying perception, engagement with art and historical narratives, aesthetic experiences, storytelling, empathy, and cultural identity formation (Carew & Ramaswami, 2020). By incorporating these insights, institutions can enhance interpretation, design more engaging exhibits, tailor educational programs, and foster a deeper connection between visitors and cultural heritage. The collaboration between scholars from diverse fields and the integration of scientific methodologies enriches our understanding of cultural heritage and facilitates a greater appreciation for it across diverse populations.

1.2 Neurodiversity in Museums

Despite the progress made in promoting diversity, equity, accessibility, and inclusion (DEAI) in museums, there has been a significant gap in attention and support for neurodiverse individuals. The American Alliance of Museums (AAM) commissioned a study to review how inclusivity efforts were being implemented across institutions, as well as perceptions of such programming by both regular museum attendees and the public in general during the pandemic (Cuyler, 2020). The results of the study were used to develop resources and strategies for museums, including primers for professionals to support efforts to promote diversity, equity, accessibility, and inclusion (DEAI). Support for such efforts has gained momentum with museum administrators and researchers, especially in addressing physical disabilities; however, the same call to action for supporting neurodiversity has yet to be headed. The lack of attention paid to this marginalized community becomes clear when reviewing AAM primers, which do not even mention neurodiversity. Therefore, while advances in inclusivity efforts have been made with regard to ethnicity, culture, physical disability, race, religion, and gender, there remains a significant percentage of the population not considered (Andermann & Arnold-de Simine, 2012; Ariese & Wróblewska, 2022; Pohawpatchoko et al., 2017). With an estimated 15–20% of the global population considered to be neurodiverse, greater attention needs to be paid to the specific needs of this group (Ott et al., 2022). The population is also estimated to be growing. In 2022, the Centers for Disease Control and Prevention (CDC) reported that 1 in 44 children were diagnosed with autism spectrum disorders (ASD). The rate of diagnosis makes this population one of the largest among those with disabilities (CDC, 2022).

Individuals diagnosed with ASD are classified as having neurodevelopmental conditions, which may include autism, ADHD, ADD, and dyslexia as the most common co-occurring diagnoses. The different types and levels of social and intellectual abilities of the group require the diagnosis to use the term "spectrum disabilities" due to the way in which they can manifest (CDC, 2022). However, it is important to note that the term "disability" may not accurately reflect the experiences and abilities of individuals within this community. Instead, the concept of a "spectrum" is employed to capture the diverse ways in which individuals with autism spectrum condition (ASC) – as will be the preferred term in this book moving forward – process sensory stimuli and navigate social and intellectual dimensions. The use of the term "spectrum condition" recognizes the unique manifestation and variation of abilities within this community, highlighting the different types and levels of social and intellectual functioning present (Bargiela et al., 2016; Su et al., 2022). Embracing this understanding allows for a more inclusive and comprehensive perspective that acknowledges the diversity of experiences and strengths within the autism spectrum condition (Manjra & Masic, 2022).

Regardless of such diversity in experiences, abilities, and how individuals process the world around them, there are certain physiological considerations for museum professionals to consider when designing experiences that are inclusive. For example, those with ASC can find navigating museum spaces challenging given crowds, unexpected audio modulation, and/or lighting intensities (Nisticò et al., 2022). Furthermore, museum challenges can include unforeseen vestibular sensory input from interactive exhibitions, the close proximity of large crowds, and an overactive visual field.

The average museum going public may not experience stressors with sensory stimuli common in museums, such as noise, waiting in lines, crowds, or exhibition lighting, but those with sensory sensitivity may. Moreover, the 2001 Council for Museums, Archives, and Libraries identified that a fully accessible program should include many considerations associated with access, such as social, financial, emotional, attitudinal, cultural, and/or educational (Hooper-Greenhill, 2004). Notably absent were sensory considerations of access. Therefore, Schwartzman and Knowles (2022) recently recommended readjusting the list to expand considerations of the sensory needs of visitors. Sensory sensitivities dissuade not only those with ASC from visiting certain locations but also their families due to the potential negative social behaviors that might arise.

When exploring the intersection of neurodiversity and museum experiences, it becomes evident that there is a significant gap in research specifically addressing the experiences of self-identified and/or diagnosed neurodiverse individuals in museum and cultural heritage settings (Sokoloff & Schattschneider, 2022). As noted, neurodiversity refers to the natural variation in neurological traits and cognitive processes present among individuals, including but not limited to autism, attention deficit hyperactivity disorder (ADHD), dyslexia, and other neurological differences (Shah et al., 2022). Understanding and addressing the unique needs, preferences, and experiences of neurodiverse individuals in the context of museums is crucial for creating inclusive and accessible cultural spaces.

Despite the growing recognition of the importance of neurodiversity and accessibility in museums, empirical research focusing on the experiences of neurodiverse individuals in these settings remains limited. While some studies have explored accessibility measures and general visitor experiences, few have specifically targeted the perspectives and needs of neurodiverse individuals (Han et al., 2020; Kelly & Orsini, 2021). For instance, the longest-running study of its kind on general accessibility has been conducted in the UK, The Euan's Guide Access Survey (https://www.euansguide.com/). The survey conducted on accessibility in various venues revealed significant findings that shed light on the experiences and perspectives of disabled individuals. The responses from the participants highlight the challenges they face when seeking accurate accessibility information and the impact it has on their decision-making process and overall experience (Hutson & Hutson, 2022).

A striking 72% of the participants reported encountering misleading, confusing, or inaccurate accessibility information on a venue's website. This alarming statistic highlights the urgent need for venues to ensure that their online accessibility information is clear, reliable, and up to date. Inaccurate information can lead to false expectations and frustration, ultimately hindering individuals with disabilities from fully participating in activities and events (Ma, 2022).

The survey also revealed that 74% of the respondents have experienced disappointment during their trips or had to change their plans due to poor accessibility. This unfortunate reality underscores the ongoing barriers and obstacles that individuals with disabilities encounter in their daily lives. Inaccessible venues not only restrict their ability to fully engage in cultural and social experiences but also lead to feelings of exclusion and disappointment (Yang, 2022).

However, the survey also provided some encouraging insights. Among the participants, 51% expressed that reviews from other disabled people improve their confidence when visiting new places. This indicates the value and impact of peer reviews and shared experiences in shaping decisions and fostering a sense of reassurance for individuals with disabilities. It emphasizes the importance of platforms like EuansGuide.com, where 46% of the respondents stated they have visited new places after reading reviews. These platforms play a crucial role in providing reliable and firsthand information about accessibility, enabling individuals to make informed choices and explore new venues with confidence (Anshari et al., 2022).

An overwhelming 91% of the participants acknowledged actively seeking disabled access information before visiting a new place. This high percentage highlights the proactive approach taken by individuals with disabilities to gather relevant information and plan their visits. It underscores the significance of accessible information in facilitating inclusive experiences and ensuring equal opportunities for participation. Furthermore, the survey revealed that 58% of the respondents avoid visiting venues that have not shared their disabled access information, assuming that they are inaccessible. This response indicates the detrimental impact of incomplete or absent accessibility information on potential visitors' decisions. It emphasizes the need for venues to be transparent and proactive in sharing their accessibility details, as it directly influences the choices of individuals with disabilities (Leverton et al., 2022).

The Euan's Guide Access Survey has provided valuable insights into the challenges individuals with disabilities encounter when seeking accurate information and navigating various venues. These findings emphasize the significance of reliable accessibility information, the role of peer reviews in building confidence, and the proactive approach taken by individuals to gather information. However, it is important to recognize that the survey's focus on overall accessibility does not fully capture the unique experiences and needs of neurodiverse individuals in museums and cultural heritage settings.

To address this gap, further research specifically focusing on neurodiversity is crucial. Such research would enable a deeper understanding of the specific challenges neurodiverse individuals may encounter in museums, including difficulties in processing information, sensory sensitivities, and navigating social interactions (King et al., 2021). By exploring the experiences of this subset of the population, museums can gain insights into the barriers that may hinder their engagement with exhibits and cultural offerings.

Moreover, research on neurodiversity in museum settings can inform the development of targeted interventions and accommodations. Understanding the specific needs of neurodiverse individuals can guide the implementation of sensory-friendly experiences, social narratives, and accessible communication strategies (Gudi et al., 2022). By creating inclusive environments that cater to the diverse needs of neurodiverse visitors, museums can ensure that they can fully participate, learn, and enjoy the cultural and educational offerings.

Conducting research that centers on the experiences of neurodiverse individuals in museums and cultural heritage settings is essential for several reasons. First, it allows us to gain insights into the unique challenges they may face when engaging with exhibits, interpreting information, or navigating the physical environment (King et al., 2021). By understanding these challenges, museums can implement targeted interventions and accommodations to ensure that neurodiverse individuals can fully access and enjoy the cultural offerings (Gudi et al., 2022).

Second, research in this area can shed light on the specific interests, preferences, and modes of engagement of neurodiverse individuals. By identifying the types of exhibits, activities, or interpretive methods that resonate with them, museums can create more inclusive and appealing experiences that cater to a diverse range of visitors (Letourneau et al., 2021). This understanding can lead to the development of innovative and effective strategies that not only support neurodiverse individuals but also enhance the experiences of all visitors (Fletcher et al., 2023).

Third, research focusing on neurodiverse individuals can contribute to broader discussions surrounding the value of inclusion and accessibility in cultural institutions (Limas et al., 2022). By highlighting the experiences and perspectives of neurodiverse individuals, museums can advocate for the importance of accommodating diverse needs, challenging preconceptions, and promoting inclusivity in the cultural heritage sector. This research can inspire positive change and encourage other institutions to prioritize accessibility and embrace the principles of universal design (Morrow, 2022).

The current lack of research specifically focusing on the experiences of self-identified and/or diagnosed neurodiverse individuals in museum and cultural heritage settings is a significant gap in our understanding of accessibility and inclusion. Addressing this gap through rigorous and inclusive research is essential for creating meaningful and equitable museum experiences for neurodiverse individuals (Cruz et al., 2023). By actively involving neurodiverse communities and fostering interdisciplinary collaborations, museums can bridge this gap, develop evidence-based practices, and embrace the principles of neuro-inclusivity (Sokoloff & Schattschneider, 2022). Through research, museums can lead the way in fostering truly inclusive cultural spaces that celebrate and accommodate the diverse needs and experiences of all visitors (Poulopoulos & Wallace, 2022).

In recognition of the limited research on the experiences of neurodiverse individuals in museum and cultural heritage settings, the researchers of this study have undertaken an empirical investigation specifically focused on addressing this gap. By conducting a comprehensive study, the researchers aim to shed light on the unique needs, preferences, and experiences of neurodiverse individuals within the context of museums. Employing a mixed methods approach, the study aimed to gather comprehensive data on the needs, preferences, and experiences of neurodiverse individuals within the context of museums (Hutson & Hutson, 2023b). To ensure the inclusion of diverse perspectives and authentic representation of neurodiverse individuals, a participatory approach was adopted. Throughout the research process, neurodiverse individuals were actively involved as collaborators and co-researchers, contributing their insights and shaping the study design. The study utilized a combination of qualitative and quantitative research methods to capture a holistic understanding of the experiences of neurodiverse individuals. In-depth surveys were conducted to delve into the lived experiences, challenges, and aspirations of participants during museum visits.

In order to reach a diverse and representative sample, the study employed a targeted recruitment strategy. The survey and study information were directly distributed to closed neurodiversity groups via social media platforms. This approach aimed to ensure the involvement of individuals who self-identified and/or were diagnosed as neurodiverse, creating a safe and inclusive space for their voices to be heard. The direct distribution of the study to closed neurodiversity groups via social media platforms allowed for a more focused and specific recruitment process. By reaching out to these communities, the researchers aimed to engage participants who have firsthand experiences of navigating museums as neurodiverse individuals. This approach fostered a sense of trust and understanding, enabling participants to share their insights openly and honestly.

The utilization of a mixed methods approach, combined with the targeted distribution of the study to closed neurodiversity groups, strengthens the validity and applicability of the findings. The comprehensive data gathered through this methodology provides a rich understanding of the experiences, challenges, and aspirations of neurodiverse individuals in museum and cultural heritage settings. The researchers acknowledge that the study's methodology may have certain limitations, such as potential self-selection bias among participants and the inherent challenges of generalizing findings across diverse neurodiverse populations. However, by prioritizing the voices of neurodiverse individuals and employing a participatory research approach, the study strives to capture the nuanced and diverse experiences within this community.

To gain a comprehensive understanding of the participants' backgrounds and characteristics, demographic information was collected as part of the study. This information provides valuable insights into the diverse profiles of the individuals involved. The study utilized a mixed methods methodology and distributed the survey directly to closed neurodiversity groups via social media platforms, ensuring a targeted and representative sample. The participants were asked about various demographic aspects, including age, gender identity, Hispanic/LatinX ethnicity, and race/ethnic heritage. Let's delve into the findings to gain a deeper understanding of the participants' demographics. First, the study examined the age distribution of the participants. The data revealed a wide range of age groups represented, indicating a diverse mix of participants. The age groups spanned from 18 to 64 years old, with participants evenly distributed across different age brackets. This diverse age range ensures that insights from participants of various life stages and experiences are captured in the study.

The study also sought to understand the gender identities of the participants. The findings showcased a rich tapestry of gender diversity, with individuals identifying as male, female, non-binary/third gender, and some participants choosing not to disclose their gender identity. This inclusion of diverse gender identities contributes to a more nuanced understanding of the experiences of neurodiverse individuals across the gender spectrum. Furthermore, the study explored the participants' Hispanic/LatinX ethnicity. The majority of participants identified as non-Hispanic/LatinX, indicating a predominantly non-Hispanic/LatinX sample. However, it is important to note that there were a small number of participants who identified as Hispanic/LatinX, allowing for some insights into the experiences of individuals from this background. Finally, the study examined the race/ethnic heritage of the participants. The findings highlighted a predominance of individuals identifying as White/Caucasian, followed by participants from various racial and ethnic backgrounds, including Black or African-American, Asian, and Other. This diversity in race and ethnicity ensures that multiple perspectives and experiences are represented in the study.

The collection of demographic information in this study offers a robust foundation for understanding the unique experiences and perspectives of self-identified and/or diagnosed neurodiverse individuals in museum and cultural heritage settings. By considering the diversity within the sample, researchers can analyze how factors such as age, gender identity, ethnicity, and race may intersect with neurodiversity to shape individuals' experiences in these settings. This comprehensive understanding is vital for developing inclusive and tailored approaches to engage and support neurodiverse audiences in cultural heritage institutions.

The study included a diverse group of 92 participants who self-identified and/or were diagnosed with various neurodiverse conditions (Table 1.1). Their demographic information and self-reported diagnoses were collected to gain insights into the experiences of neurodiverse individuals in museum and cultural heritage settings.

Regarding the participants' self-identified diagnoses, the study found that a range of neurodiverse conditions were represented in the sample. Four participants (4.35%) reported having dyslexia, a learning disorder that affects reading and writing skills. Two participants (2.17%) identified with dysgraphia, a condition characterized by difficulties in writing.

Table 1.1 Self-reported diagnoses of survey participants

Diagnosis	Percentage	Count
Childhood Disintegrative Disorder	0.00%	0
Kanner's Syndrome	0.00%	0
Dyslexia	4.35%	4
Dysgraphia	2.17%	2
ADHD	28.26%	26
PMDD	3.26%	3
PTSD	11.96%	11
Autism Spectrum Disorder (ASD)	23.91%	22
Other (please specify)	4.35%	4
Autism	5.43%	5
Pervasive Developmental Disorder (PDD-NOS)	3.26%	3
Asperger's Syndrome	13.04%	12
Total	100%	92

ADHD, a neurodevelopmental disorder associated with attention difficulties, was reported by 26 participants (28.26%).

Additionally, three participants (3.26%) disclosed having PMDD (Premenstrual Dysphoric Disorder), a severe form of premenstrual syndrome that affects mood and behavior. Eleven participants (11.96%) reported having PTSD (Post-Traumatic Stress Disorder), which can result from experiencing or witnessing a traumatic event. Twenty-two participants (23.91%) identified with Autism Spectrum Disorder (ASD), a condition characterized by social and communication challenges.

Four participants (4.35%) mentioned having other neurodiverse conditions that were not specified in the options provided. Five participants (5.43%) specifically identified with the diagnosis of autism, while three participants (3.26%) reported having Pervasive Developmental Disorder-Not Otherwise Specified (PDD-NOS). Twelve participants (13.04%) disclosed having Asperger's Syndrome, a condition on the autism spectrum associated with difficulties in social interaction.

The diverse range of self-identified diagnoses in the study highlights the importance of understanding the experiences of individuals with different neurodiverse conditions in museum and cultural heritage settings. By including participants with various diagnoses, the study aimed to capture a wide range of perspectives and experiences within the neurodiverse community.

It is important to note that the diagnoses reported by the participants were self-identified and may not have been clinically diagnosed in all cases. Nonetheless, their participation provides valuable insights into the experiences of neurodiverse individuals and contributes to a better understanding of how museums and cultural heritage institutions can cater to the needs and preferences of this diverse population.

The study examined the participants' visitation patterns to museums and explored their experiences in these cultural settings. The data revealed a range of frequencies in museum visits among the participants. However, out of all participants, none of them reported never visiting museums, indicating that all participants had at least some level of engagement with museums. With a frequency of once a year or less, 9.09% stated that they rarely visit museums. Twenty (56.82%) mentioned that they visit museums occasionally, ranging from 2 to 4 times a year, while 34.09% reported frequent museum visits, with a frequency of 5 or more times a year. These findings indicate that the majority of participants had a moderate level of engagement with museums, either visiting occasionally or frequently. The data suggests that neurodiverse individuals have an interest in and actively engage with museums, seeking out these cultural experiences to varying degrees.

Among the participants who did state that they had not visited museums, several reasons were identified for their lack of engagement (Table 1.2). These reasons reflect the barriers and challenges that neurodiverse individuals may face when considering museum visits. Firstly, a lack of interest was cited by 11.76% as the primary reason for not visiting museums. This suggests that museums may not always align with the personal preferences or interests of neurodiverse individuals, potentially indicating a need for more diverse and inclusive programming to cater to a broader range of interests.

Sensory issues emerged as a significant barrier, with 35.29% reporting challenges related to noise, lighting, crowds, and other sensory stimuli commonly encountered in museum environments. For individuals with sensory sensitivities, these factors can be overwhelming or overstimulating, making museum visits a challenging experience. Creating sensory-friendly spaces and providing accommodations to mitigate sensory triggers could greatly enhance the accessibility of museums for neurodiverse individuals.

Accessibility concerns, including physical and cognitive barriers, were reported by 7.84%. This highlights the need for museums to prioritize inclusivity and ensure that their spaces, exhibits, and programs are accessible to individuals with diverse needs. Addressing physical accessibility, providing clear signage and wayfinding, and offering alternative formats

Table 1.2 Reasons neurodiverse populations avoid museums

Reason	Percentage	Count
Lack of interest	11.76%	6
Sensory issues (noise, lighting, crowds, etc.)	35.29%	18
Accessibility concerns (physical, cognitive, etc.)	7.84%	4
Cost	9.80%	5
Distance or transportation issues	29.41%	15
Lack of inclusive programming or accommodations	3.92%	2
Other (please specify)	1.96%	1
Total	100%	51

for information dissemination can significantly improve the museum experience for neurodiverse visitors.

Cost was identified as a barrier by 9.80%. Financial considerations can limit the ability of neurodiverse individuals to access museums, especially when tickets or memberships are prohibitively expensive. Implementing accessible pricing options, such as reduced admission fees or free admission days, can help make museums more financially inclusive.

Distance and transportation issues were reported by 29.41%. This suggests that the proximity of museums and the availability of accessible transportation options can significantly impact the likelihood of neurodiverse individuals being able to visit these cultural institutions. Collaborations with local transportation authorities and providing information on accessible transportation options can help overcome these challenges.

Lastly, two participants (3.92%) mentioned a lack of inclusive programming or accommodations as a reason for not visiting museums. This highlights the importance of developing inclusive programming that considers the diverse needs and interests of neurodiverse individuals, as well as providing accommodations such as quiet spaces, sensory-friendly exhibits, and trained staff to support visitors with specific requirements.

Along with general reasons for lack of engagement with cultural heritage institutions, participants were asked if they had ever decided not to visit a museum due to certain pre-visitation considerations. Table 1.3 presents the percentages and counts for each response option and provides ways museums can preempt issues before a visit even occurs.

These findings suggest that a significant number of participants have encountered barriers related to pre-visitation considerations, leading them to decide not to visit museums. Unclear directions to the location and a lack of clearly identified parking on the museum's website were cited as

Table 1.3 Pre-visitation considerations for neurodiverse population

Pre-visitation consideration	Percentage	Count
Directions to the location unclear	34.78%	16
Parking not clearly identified on website	30.43%	14
Maps of the structure unavailable	17.39%	8
Virtual walkthrough unavailable	8.70%	4
Other (please specify)	8.70%	4
Total	100%	46

the most common reasons for not visiting. The unavailability of maps of the structure and virtual walkthroughs were also mentioned as factors contributing to the decision not to visit. Additionally, a small percentage of participants specified other reasons for not visiting, indicating the presence of additional barriers that were not covered in the response options provided.

These results highlight the importance of addressing pre-visitation considerations and providing clear and accessible information to potential visitors. Improving the availability of directions, parking information, maps, and virtual walkthroughs can help alleviate barriers and encourage individuals to visit museums. By addressing these concerns, cultural institutions can enhance their accessibility and attract a wider range of visitors, including those who may have previously been deterred by these pre-visitation considerations.

Participants were then asked a free-response question as to what else may have negatively impacted their museum experience if they did, in fact, attend a visit (Table 1.4). The participants' responses to the question about negative museum experiences provide valuable insights into the specific situations that affected their visits. These experiences can be grouped into several thematic categories, shedding light on the challenges faced by neurodiverse individuals in museum settings.

Sensory overload and noise emerged as a common issue mentioned by participants. Crowded spaces with loud sounds were reported to be overwhelming and caused a loss of attention. One noted, "Heat, crowds meaning sounds and movements, bright lights, all make for a very suffocating and draining experience." Participants expressed difficulties in reading information due to excessive noise, which hindered their ability to engage with the exhibits. One respondent noted, "Sensory issues – usually noise-related where I can't focus on reading or listening to information due to other noise from other patrons." Bright lights and a multitude of sensory stimuli were described as suffocating and draining, preventing participants from immersing themselves in the art.

Overcrowding and a lack of personal space were also significant concerns. Some participants felt uncomfortable with people standing too close, finding it unnerving and distracting. For instance, one noted: "During a tour, they packed everyone into each room, and I felt trapped." The experience of being trapped in crowded rooms during guided tours was mentioned, leaving participants longing for more freedom and the option of self-guided exploration. One participant noted, "Despite timed

Table 1.4 Themes of negative museum experiences reported by neurodiverse participants

Theme	Quotations
Sensory overload and noise	"Crowd, loud sound."
	"Sensory overload, loss of attention despite finding it interesting."
	"Very noisy so was not able to read the information on the displays."
	"Heat, crowds meaning sounds and movements, bright lights, all make for a very suffocating and draining experience."
	"Sensory issues – usually noise-related where I can't focus on reading or listening to information due to other noise from other patrons."
	"Sensory issues – sound, usually from other visitors."
Overcrowding and lack of personal space	"Too busy with people standing too close."
	"Despite timed entry, the next group was being let in to the space while the previous group was still crowded."
	"During a tour, they packed everyone into each room, and I felt trapped."
	"Crowds are very distracting to me. The feeling of people close behind me is unnerving."
	"Too crowded, no seating, lines too long."
Lack of accessibility and accommodations	"Lack of understanding of the impact of cues."
	"The descriptions for artworks were not written in plain language."
	"Poorly curated so that exhibits including sound or flashing lights are placed in close proximity to 2D visual work."
Organization and direction	"Several exhibitions that have had a 'path' that does not have a quick way off."
	"Unclear directions for the route around the museum cause anxiety."
	"Despite timed displays, which don't have clearly marked starts and ends, are frustrating."
Emotional and mental well-being	"Sensory overwhelm led me to seek out the quietest space to decompress."
	"Having to be there, putting up with other people, is even more stressful."

(*continued*)

Table 1.4 (continued)

Theme	Quotations
	"Sensory issues – usually noise-related where I can't focus on reading or listening to information due to other noise from other patrons." "Lack of understanding by staff and mocking."

entry, the next group was being let in to the space while the previous group was still crowded." Lack of seating and long lines further contributed to a sense of discomfort and hindered enjoyment.

Accessibility and accommodations played a crucial role in shaping participants' experiences. The lack of understanding of cues and the absence of plain language descriptions for artworks were mentioned as barriers to comprehension and engagement. Participants expressed frustration when exhibits with sound or flashing lights were placed too close to two-dimensional visual work, causing sensory discomfort. Mocking and a lack of understanding from staff members added to the challenges faced by participants, emphasizing the need for improved staff training and sensitivity.

Issues related to organization and direction were highlighted as well. Participants expressed anxiety when faced with unclear directions for navigating the museum or when exhibitions lacked a clear pathway for exiting. One noted, "Unclear directions for the route around the museum cause anxiety." Timed displays without clear start and end markers were also mentioned as frustrating, leading to confusion and a sense of being rushed. For instance, another participant noted that "Despite timed displays, which don't have clearly marked starts and ends, are frustrating."

Emotional and mental well-being emerged as important factors influencing participants' experiences. Sensory overwhelm often led participants to seek out quieter spaces for decompression, resulting in a limited exploration of the museum and reduced enjoyment. Additionally, the stress of navigating crowded spaces and the need to tolerate other visitors affected participants' overall experience.

These quotations, gathered from participants, provide a narrative illustration of the challenges faced by neurodiverse individuals in museum settings. They underscore the importance of museums addressing sensory sensitivities, providing clear directions and accessible information, creating inclusive exhibits, and fostering understanding and empathy among staff members. By taking these considerations into account and implementing appropriate accommodations, museums can strive to create more welcoming and inclusive environments that enhance the experiences of neurodiverse visitors.

The participants were asked about specific accommodations or features that they found helpful during their museum visits. The responses provide insights into the types of support that can enhance the museum experience for neurodiverse individuals (Table 1.5). The data collected is summarized in the following table.

The most commonly mentioned accommodation was quiet rooms or designated quiet times, with 42.86% of participants finding this feature helpful. This highlights the importance of providing spaces where individuals can retreat to when they need a break from sensory stimulation. Sensory-friendly programming or events were also mentioned by 14.29% of participants, indicating the value of creating inclusive programs that consider the sensory needs of neurodiverse individuals.

Additionally, 8.57% of participants mentioned the usefulness of social stories or sensory maps. These tools can help individuals prepare for their museum visit by providing visual and descriptive information about the space and exhibits, reducing anxiety, and promoting a sense of familiarity. Staff trained in neurodiversity awareness were identified as helpful by 5.71% of participants, emphasizing the significance of providing staff who understand and can support the specific needs of neurodiverse visitors.

A smaller percentage of participants, 2.86%, mentioned the benefit of adaptive or assistive technology, indicating the potential value of incorporating technological solutions to enhance accessibility in museums. Lastly,

Table 1.5 Helpful accommodations and features reported by neurodiverse participants

Answer	%	Count
Quiet rooms or designated quiet times	42.86%	15
Sensory-friendly programming or events	14.29%	5
Social stories or sensory maps	8.57%	3
Staff trained in neurodiversity awareness	5.71%	2
Adaptive or assistive technology	2.86%	1
Other (please specify)	25.71%	9
Total	100%	35

25.71% of participants provided other suggestions or accommodations not listed in the options, reflecting the diverse range of individual needs and preferences within the neurodiverse population.

These findings highlight the importance of considering and implementing various accommodations and features that cater to the specific requirements of neurodiverse individuals. By providing quiet spaces, sensory-friendly programming, social stories, trained staff, and technological adaptations, museums can create inclusive environments that enhance the museum experience for neurodiverse visitors.

The participants were asked to provide their insights and suggestions regarding additional accommodations or features that museums could implement to enhance the experience for neurodiverse visitors. These responses offer valuable perspectives and shed light on the specific needs and preferences of this population (Table 1.6).

One recurring theme in the participants' suggestions is the importance of sensory considerations. They emphasized the need for quiet rooms or designated quiet times within the museum, as well as soft and low lighting in certain areas. The participants also highlighted the significance of reducing noise levels and providing noise-canceling-compatible audio guides to create a more comfortable and accessible environment for individuals with sensory sensitivities. These recommendations align with the goal of minimizing sensory overload and creating a sensory-friendly atmosphere within museums (Tobias, 2021).

Clear and accessible communication was another prominent theme among the participants' suggestions. They emphasized the importance of informative websites that provide relevant details about the museum, such as directions, parking information, and even busy periods analysis. Participants also suggested the use of social stories or sensory maps to help visitors navigate the museum and prepare for their visit in advance. They stressed the need for consistent and informative image descriptions for art pieces, ensuring that they are written in plain language and providing audio options through headphones for individuals who may benefit from audio descriptions.

The participants also emphasized the significance of staff training in neurodiversity awareness. They suggested that museum staff and volunteers should receive comprehensive training to enhance their understanding of the needs and experiences of neurodiverse visitors. Additionally, participants recommended the implementation of allocated quiet times or

Table 1.6 Recommendations for improving museum experience for neurodiverse visitors

Theme	Recommendations
Sensory considerations	• Provide virtual tour headsets, with advanced notice for busy periods. • Designate quiet areas and use soft, low lighting. • Offer noise-canceling compatible audio guides. • Reduce overall noise levels. • Create sensory guides for exhibits and allocate quiet visit time slots. • Provide seats in silent areas.
Clear communication and directions	• Ensure clear and accessible information on directions and parking. • Use plain language and bionic reading for lengthy texts. • Develop informative websites with exhibit details and accessibility features. • Provide visual maps or graphics for navigation.
Staff training and awareness	• Conduct more training for staff and volunteers on neurodiversity awareness. • Give advance warnings about areas that may provoke overstimulation. • Foster understanding and implement less restrictive rules and open activity areas.
Enhancing engagement and interactivity	• Develop immersive and interactive exhibitions to enhance visitor engagement. • Limit the number of people in exhibits and dim lights to reduce sensory overload. • Increase knowledge transfer through non-verbal methods, speech, images, and graphic storyboards.
Audio and visual accessibility	• Offer headphones/earplugs, free audio guides, and alternative "quiet" routes. • Improve image descriptions for art pieces to ensure consistency and informativeness. • Provide audio options through headphones for artwork audio descriptions.

specific time slots for quiet visits, enabling individuals to have a more relaxed and comfortable experience within the museum.

The suggestions put forth by the participants reflect a commitment to inclusivity and accessibility. They highlight the importance of providing a range of accommodations, such as sensory-friendly spaces, clear communication, immersive exhibitions, and reduced crowd sizes. By implementing these suggestions, museums can create environments that cater to the diverse needs of neurodiverse visitors, ensuring a more inclusive and enriching experience for all.

These recommendations reflect the importance of considering a range of accommodations and features to create a more inclusive and welcoming environment for neurodiverse visitors. By implementing these suggestions, museums can provide sensory-friendly spaces, clear communication, engaging exhibits, and accessible resources, fostering a positive and enriching experience for all visitors. It is crucial for museum professionals and researchers to take into account these valuable insights when designing and planning exhibitions and programs. By incorporating the suggested accommodations and features, museums can create more accessible and welcoming spaces that embrace the diversity of their visitors, fostering meaningful engagement and enhancing the overall museum experience.

Addressing the needs of the neurodiverse population of visitors to museums has only recently entered the accessibility conversation. The broadest adoptions regarding accommodations in institutions remain confined to physical accessibility with considerations for those with ASC emerging in the United Kingdom (UK) in large and established museums with resources (Barclay, 2022). Those programs that do exist that support accessibility for neurodiverse populations commonly use the following strategies. Providing sensory-friendly experiences is an important aspect of creating inclusive museum environments. Many museums recognize the needs of visitors who may be sensitive to loud noises and bright lights, and they offer sensory-friendly experiences or designated "quiet hours" to cater to their specific needs. These dedicated times allow visitors to explore the museum in a more relaxed and comfortable environment (Upson, 2021).

To further enhance accessibility, some museums provide sensory maps that highlight sensory-friendly areas and features within the museum. These maps can help visitors identify quiet spaces, areas with low lighting, and exhibits that offer tactile experiences (Fletcher et al., 2023). Additionally, they can alert visitors to areas that may be overwhelming due to larger crowds or loud noises, enabling them to plan their visit accordingly. Museums are also utilizing technology to improve accessibility. Audio guides and other forms of accessibility technology, such as mobile apps, are being offered to visitors (Vaz et al., 2020). These tools allow individuals to navigate the museum and access information in a way that suits their sensory needs. By modulating sensory input and providing personalized experiences, museums are ensuring that visitors can engage with the exhibits comfortably (Vi et al., 2017). In an effort to support visitors with autism and other neurodiverse conditions, museums are also providing social stories and visual schedules. These resources help individuals prepare for their museum visit by offering information about what to expect, the layout of the museum, and steps to follow during their visit (Coffey, 2018). By providing clear and visual guidance, museums promote a sense of familiarity and reduce anxiety for these visitors. Recognizing the importance of staff knowledge and awareness, many museums are investing in training programs on neurodiversity. Staff members are educated on various neurological conditions and learn how to provide support and assistance to visitors with different sensory needs (Silberman, 2015). This training ensures that staff members can create a welcoming and inclusive environment for all visitors. Finally, museums are expanding their range of accessible materials. Large print materials, audio descriptions, and other alternative formats are being offered to make exhibits and events more accessible to individuals with sensory processing differences (Wates, 2014). These resources enable visitors to engage with the museum's content in a way that suits their sensory preferences and enhances their overall experience (Table 1.7).

A holistic approach to accessibility is being considered that addresses pre-visit planning and resources to familiarize visitors with sensory information and routes through unfamiliar locations (Brule et al., 2016; Cho & Jolley, 2016). Support onsite can include accessibility maps, museum social stories, sunglasses, headphones, and even therapy putty (Fletcher et al., 2018). Engaging a sensory sensitive audience now includes integrating kinesthetic or tactile exhibits and including "cool down" spaces with sensory modalities that allow individuals who are overstimulated to regulate their cognitive flexibility and extended the duration of the stay. Such areas are often equipped with therapy balls, mats, mood lighting, and sound modulation. In certain programs, trained occupational therapy students run special sensory activities and act as personal tour guides to support visitors and foster exhibit interactions (Sokoloff & Schattschneider, 2022). Given that parents with children with autism report 70% higher rates of anxiety, isolation, and depression, the sense of well-being and belonging in the museum experience is significant and impactful (Silverman et al., 2012).

With considerations for neurodiverse populations in museums receiving limited attention compared to other DEAI efforts, and the significant

Table 1.7 Recommendations for enhancing accessibility and inclusivity in museums

Recommendation	Description
Providing sensory-friendly experiences	Many museums offer sensory-friendly experiences or designated "quiet hours" to accommodate visitors who are sensitive to loud noises or bright lights.
Providing sensory maps	Some museums provide sensory maps that highlight specific areas within the museum that are sensory-friendly, such as quiet spaces, exhibits with low lighting, and tactile experiences.
Offering audio guides and accessibility technology	Museums offer audio guides and other accessibility technologies, such as apps, to help visitors modulate sensory input and navigate the museum.
Providing social stories and visual schedules	Museums provide social stories and visual schedules to assist visitors with autism in preparing for their museum visit.
Training staff on neurodiversity	Many museums prioritize training programs to educate their staff on neurodiversity and how to best support visitors with neurological conditions.
Providing alternative format materials	Museums offer alternative format materials, such as large print, audio descriptions, and multimedia experiences, to make exhibits and events more accessible.

estimated percentage of the global population affected, it is imperative to address the specific needs of this population. Museum professionals must consider the diverse experiences and abilities within the neurodiverse community when designing inclusive experiences in order to truly support the entire community. Sensory considerations, such as noise, crowds, lighting, and sensory sensitivities, play a significant role in the museum experience for individuals with ASC. Efforts to accommodate neurodiverse visitors have started to emerge, including sensory-friendly experiences, sensory maps, accessibility technology, social stories, staff training, and alternative format materials. A holistic approach to accessibility, including pre-visit planning and on-site support, is being adopted to create a welcoming and accommodating environment for neurodiverse visitors. The focus on addressing sensory needs and providing supportive resources is pivotal in ensuring the well-being and sense of belonging for neurodiverse individuals and their families. With this understanding, a cautionary tale of past attempts for inclusivity should be discussed.

1.3 Sensory Days

Unfortunately, the current approach to inclusivity in museums for individuals with autism spectrum condition (ASC) often revolves around sensory days. These events, such as early open events or special extended hours, aim to minimize crowds and create a more relaxed experience (Fletcher et al., 2018). Sensory hours may be implemented during these events, where lights are dimmed, and noise levels are reduced to accommodate those with sensory sensitivities. Measures such as shutting off hand dryers in restrooms or lowering the volume of interactive features and triggered audio are also taken into consideration. However, there is a growing criticism of these "token" autism inclusion days, particularly when they coincide with World Autism Awareness Day on April 2 (Matson & Boisjoli, 2009). The origins of this day in 2007 were centered around well-intentioned individuals who focused on "cures" and "combat" messaging, which led to the perception of exclusion rather than inclusion. The limited invitation to visit museums during off-hours can inadvertently reinforce feelings of seclusion. Additionally, the use of outdated symbols like puzzle pieces (Fig. 1.1) to represent ASC efforts can further

Fig. 1.1 Autism puzzle in the head

contribute to a sense of something being missing or an inability to function "normally." It is crucial for institutions to actively engage in discussions with their autistic communities to navigate these challenges and make informed choices regarding language and associations (Praslova, 2022).

These sensory days, while well-intentioned, have garnered criticism for their limited scope and tokenistic nature. By designating specific days or hours for individuals with ASC, museums inadvertently create a sense of segregation rather than true inclusion (Hughes, 2015). The practice of scheduling these events around World Autism Awareness Day, which historically focused on "cures" and "combat" messaging, further reinforces the notion that individuals with ASC are somehow separate from the rest of society (O'Laughlin, 2023). The use of puzzle piece symbols, often associated with "ASD," can perpetuate the idea that something is missing or that individuals with ASC are incomplete (Woods, 2016).

In order to truly foster inclusivity, museums must actively engage with their autistic communities and adopt more comprehensive approaches. It is important to move beyond sensory days and consider the specific needs of individuals with ASC throughout the museum experience (Parsons et al., 2020). This involves providing sensory-friendly environments beyond designated times, such as dimming lights and reducing noise levels, to accommodate individuals with sensory sensitivities (Sadatsafavi et al., 2022). Inclusive practices can also include measures like eliminating sudden audio triggers or adjusting the volume of interactive features to create a more comfortable and accessible environment (Kinzig et al., 2013).

Moreover, language and symbolism play a crucial role in promoting a sense of belonging for individuals with ASC. Museums should strive to use language that emphasizes acceptance, neurodiversity, and the unique strengths of individuals on the autism spectrum (Krcek, 2013). Moving away from the puzzle piece symbols and embracing more inclusive imagery and messaging can contribute to a more positive and empowering experience for individuals with ASC and their families (Atherton et al., 2021).

To navigate these challenges and make informed choices, museums need to actively involve autistic individuals and their families in decision-making processes. By listening to their experiences, needs, and preferences, museums can develop more effective strategies and programs that truly meet the diverse requirements of the autistic community (Hummerstone & Parsons, 2022). This collaborative approach ensures that museums create a welcoming and inclusive environment that celebrates the contributions and perspectives of individuals with ASC (Schofield et al., 2020).

Having discussed the limitations of sensory days and the need for more inclusive approaches in museums for individuals with ASC, it is evident that identification plays a crucial role in creating meaningful and inclusive experiences. Understanding the specific needs and preferences of individuals on the autism spectrum is essential for designing tailored programs and accommodations. The importance of identification and how museums can create an environment that respects and supports the diverse needs of these individuals should now be considered. We will explore the significance of person-first language, the role of self-identification, and the strategies for effectively identifying and addressing the unique requirements of individuals with ASC in cultural heritage institutions. By recognizing the importance of identification, museums can take significant strides towards creating a more inclusive and accessible space for individuals on the autism spectrum.

1.4 Identification Matters

The importance of identification cannot be overstated when it comes to creating inclusive museum experiences for individuals with autism spectrum condition (ASC). Recent studies have highlighted the preferences of neurodiverse adults regarding the use of identity-first language, which emphasizes their autism as an inherent part of their identity rather than a separate condition (Vivanti, 2020; Botha et al., 2021). This shift in language aligns with the broader movement of marginalized communities reclaiming their identities and challenging the use of person-first language (Fraser, 2022; Williams et al., 2022). Similarly, the choice of symbols and colors used in autism awareness efforts has evolved. The use of infinity or butterfly symbols in gold, multicolor, red, or tan tones is favored over the traditional blue puzzle piece, which has been associated with stereotypes and misconceptions about autism (Praslova, 2022; CDC, 2022).

It is crucial to recognize that many existing museum initiatives targeting individuals with ASC have primarily focused on children and have been designed from the perspective of neurotypical parents, resulting in limited and exclusionary activities (Reilly, 2022). These efforts often revolve around quiet hours and segregated activities, which deviate from the normal museum experience and may inadvertently reinforce the notion of difference and separation. Additionally, the use of time-specific events can be counterintuitive to the free-choice, informal learning ethos of museums, creating a sense of rush and potentially overwhelming neurodiverse visitors. Instead, the aim should be to integrate sensory inclusion within regular museum operations, ensuring that all visitors can engage at their own pace and in their own time (Hladik & Ausderau, 2022). While special sensory hours can still play a valuable role, they should be seen as supplementary rather than the primary approach to inclusion.

By understanding and embracing the preferences and needs of individuals with ASC, museums can adopt a more inclusive and respectful approach to identification. This involves using identity-first language, selecting symbols and colors that reflect the community's desires, and designing programs that align with the principles of universal design and free-choice learning (Parsons et al., 2020). In the next section, we will explore practical strategies for museums to effectively identify and address the unique requirements of individuals with ASC, fostering an environment that celebrates diversity, empowers self-advocacy, and promotes meaningful engagement with cultural heritage.

Understanding the significance of identification and the importance of inclusive practices for individuals with ASC, the next section explores the specific context of children's museums. Children's museums play a crucial role in providing interactive and educational experiences for young visitors, including those with diverse abilities. These institutions have the opportunity to create inclusive spaces that cater to the unique needs of children with ASC and promote their engagement and learning. By examining the strategies and approaches employed by children's museums, we can gain insights into effective practices that can be applied more broadly across cultural heritage institutions.

1.5 Children's Museums

Children's museums hold immense potential for creating inclusive and enriching experiences for children on the autism spectrum. These institutions have long been recognized as ideal settings for informal learning, providing children with open environments where they can interact with each other and engage with a wide range of learning materials and subjects (Fig. 1.2). The hands-on, open-ended, and sensory-rich nature of children's museums caters to diverse learning styles, making them conducive

Fig. 1.2 Indianapolis Children's Museum, August 5, 2015. Photograph by Josh Grenier

to supporting children with autism in their educational journeys (Jeffery-Clay, 1998).

Special hours or sensory-friendly events are often organized, providing quieter and less crowded environments for children with ASC and their families to enjoy the museum experience. Sensory kits, containing tools and materials to support sensory regulation, are made available to visitors, enabling children with ASC to engage with the exhibits more comfortably (Fletcher et al., 2022). In addition, staff training programs focused on disability awareness and inclusive practices have been implemented to ensure that museum staff can provide effective support and facilitate learning for children with ASC (Fletcher et al., 2022).

Several children's museums have implemented these strategies to cater to autistic populations. For example, the Children's Museum of Pittsburgh offers sensory-friendly hours where the museum environment is modified to reduce sensory stimuli. They also provide sensory kits equipped with noise-canceling headphones, fidget toys, and visual schedules to support sensory regulation. The Children's Museum of Houston has developed a program called "Sensory Friendly Day" that offers a low-sensory environment, specialized activities, and trained staff to accommodate the needs of children with autism and other sensory sensitivities (Varner, 2015).

Children's museums have been at the forefront of creating inclusive and enriching experiences for children on the autism spectrum. These institutions have long been recognized as ideal settings for informal learning, offering open environments where children can interact and engage with various learning materials and subjects (Ferrari, 2015). The hands-on, open-ended, and sensory-rich nature of children's museums naturally caters to diverse learning styles, making them conducive to supporting children with autism in their educational journeys (Jeffery-Clay, 1998).

However, despite the inherent inclusivity of children's museums, there are still barriers that prevent children with autism spectrum condition (ASC) from fully benefiting from these spaces. Sensory considerations, such as large crowds, unfamiliar lights, smells, and sounds, can pose challenges for individuals, and the lack of trained staff who understand the specific needs of this population further exacerbates the issue (Hladik & Ausderau, 2022). Recognizing the importance of creating accessible experiences, many children's museums have implemented strategies to address these barriers.

One such example is The Children's Museum of Indianapolis, which organizes "Sensory Friendly Saturdays." During these events, the museum creates a quieter and less crowded environment, adjusting lighting and sound levels to accommodate children with ASC. They also provide sensory kits that include tools and materials to support sensory regulation, allowing children with ASC to engage with the exhibits more comfortably (Fletcher et al., 2022).

The Please Touch Museum in Philadelphia also embraces inclusivity by hosting "Play Without Boundaries" events. These events offer a sensory-friendly experience for children with autism and other special needs, featuring reduced lighting, quiet spaces, and specialized programming. Sensory kits, equipped with noise-canceling headphones, fidget tools, and social stories, are made available to further support children's sensory needs during their visit (Haas, 1997).

Additionally, the Boston Children's Museum (Fig. 1.3) offers the Morningstar Access Program with sessions specifically designed for children with autism and their families. These sessions provide a low-stimulus environment with reduced crowds, quiet areas, and modified exhibits. Sensory bags, containing items such as noise-canceling headphones,

Fig. 1.3 Astronaut Steve Bowen with Children's Museum visitor, Boston Children's Museum. August 19, 2012

weighted lap pads, and visual supports, are also provided to enhance the museum experience for children with autism (Alper, 2021).

By prioritizing sensory considerations, providing targeted support, and fostering staff awareness, children's museums are taking significant steps towards creating inclusive environments that cater to the unique needs of children with autism spectrum condition (ASC). These efforts demonstrate a commitment to accessibility and ensure that children with ASC can fully engage and participate in the museum experience (Coffey, 2018). The implementation of sensory-friendly events, the availability of sensory kits, and the provision of staff training programs focused on disability awareness all contribute to making children's museums more welcoming and accommodating for children with ASC. These initiatives not only address the specific challenges faced by individuals with sensory sensitivities but also promote a greater understanding and acceptance of neurodiversity among all visitors.

Through these inclusive practices, children's museums are fostering an environment where children with ASC can explore, learn, and play alongside their peers, without feeling excluded or overwhelmed (McGillicuddy & O'Donnell, 2014). By actively addressing the barriers that may hinder the participation of children with ASC, these museums are creating opportunities for meaningful engagement and empowering children with ASC to develop their skills, confidence, and social connections. Moreover, the impact of these efforts extends beyond the individual experiences of children with ASC. By embracing inclusivity and promoting awareness of neurodiversity, children's museums contribute to a more inclusive society where differences are celebrated and valued (Bogle, 2019). Visitors of all ages and abilities can benefit from the enriched environments that prioritize accessibility and ensure that everyone can participate and enjoy the educational and interactive opportunities offered by children's museums (Gong et al., 2020).

The efforts made by children's museums to cater to the needs of children with ASC reflect a commitment to creating inclusive spaces that embrace neurodiversity. By prioritizing sensory considerations, providing targeted support, and fostering staff awareness, children's museums are paving the way for a more inclusive and accepting society. Through these initiatives, children with ASC can engage with confidence, learn, and thrive, while promoting understanding, empathy, and inclusivity among all visitors.

1.6 Staff Training Programs

Staff training programs have become instrumental in creating inclusive and accessible museum experiences, extending beyond children's museums to encompass cultural institutions worldwide, including those in the United Kingdom (Theriault & Ljungren, 2022). These programs prioritize autism awareness and empathy training for staff, equipping them with the knowledge and skills to better assist children with ASC and improve interactions with all museum patrons (NAS, 2022). By proactively responding to the needs of groups requiring accommodations, public-facing positions such as docents and visitor services staff can anticipate challenges and provide assistance to parents navigating the facilities. Seeking advice and support from organizations like the Autism Society or local communities not only opens the door to building trust but also demonstrates the institution's commitment to actively participating in the discussion (Kotowski & Zybert, 2020).

Effective training equips staff to recognize and interact with neurodiverse individuals by familiarizing them with potential physical attributes, such as limited eye control and the use of self-soothing techniques like rocking or repetitive gestures. Additionally, staff are made aware of the challenges neurodiverse individuals may face in understanding non-direct language, emphasizing the importance of clear and direct communication (Sheply & McGinnis, 2020). In cases where on-site training is limited by financial constraints, some institutions have enlisted the assistance of local universities to hire staff members already trained in extensive accessibility knowledge. This ensures that the museum has personnel well-versed in creating inclusive experiences for neurodiverse visitors (Kennedy, 2006). Moreover, the museum community's altruistic inclinations have led to the availability of online training materials, allowing institutions to access and learn from best practices shared by others (Restrepo-Harner et al., 2021; Ghadim & Daugherty, 2021).

For example, the National Autistic Society (NAS) in the United Kingdom offers training programs specifically designed for museum staff. These programs focus on increasing awareness and understanding of autism, providing insights into the unique challenges faced by individuals with ASC, and offering practical strategies to enhance communication and engagement (Dawson-Squibb et al., 2019). By participating in these training programs, staff members are better prepared to anticipate the needs of neurodiverse visitors and create a more inclusive environment (Cutress & Muncer, 2014).

In addition to formal training programs, museums often seek advice and support from organizations like the Autism Society or local communities. This collaboration allows museums to gain valuable insights and perspectives from individuals with lived experiences, ensuring that their initiatives and practices align with the needs and expectations of the neurodiverse community (Long, 2013). Building these relationships not only fosters trust but also demonstrates the institution's commitment to actively participating in the ongoing dialogue surrounding accessibility and inclusion.

Furthermore, various museums around the world have implemented staff training programs to enhance the inclusivity and accessibility of their spaces. For instance, The Metropolitan Museum of Art (The Met) in New York City offers training programs for its staff, covering topics such as sensory sensitivities and communication strategies, to effectively engage with visitors on the autism spectrum (Freed-Brown, 2010). The Science Museum in London provides staff training focused on supporting visitors with Autism Spectrum Condition (ASC), fostering a culture of inclusivity and understanding (Matson & Sturmey, 2011). Additionally, the Museum of Science and Industry (MSI) in Chicago has developed a comprehensive training program called "Autism Awareness for Museum Professionals," ensuring its staff is well-prepared to engage with visitors on the autism spectrum (Zhang & Epley, 2012). These examples highlight the commitment of museums to prioritize staff training and create a supportive and inclusive environment for neurodiverse individuals.

In cases where on-site training is limited by financial constraints, some institutions have sought the assistance of local universities to hire staff members already trained in extensive accessibility knowledge (Hackler & Saxton, 2007). This ensures that the museum has personnel well-versed in creating inclusive experiences for neurodiverse visitors. Moreover, the museum community's altruistic inclinations have led to the availability of online training materials, allowing institutions to access and learn from best practices shared by others. These resources enable museums to tap into a wealth of knowledge and expertise, ultimately enhancing their staff's capacity to provide inclusive and welcoming experiences for neurodiverse individuals.

Through comprehensive staff training programs, museums demonstrate their commitment to creating inclusive spaces that cater to the needs of neurodiverse individuals. By investing in autism awareness and empathy training, institutions empower their staff to provide a supportive and understanding environment for all visitors. Proactive measures, such as reaching out to relevant organizations and communities for guidance, contribute to building trust and fostering meaningful engagement. With a trained and empathetic staff, museums can better recognize and respond to the unique needs of neurodiverse individuals, ultimately enhancing the overall museum experience for everyone (Theriault & Ljungren, 2022; NAS, 2022).

1.7 Inclusive Smart Museums

Facilitating a positive museum experience for neurodiverse individuals and their families begins with ensuring preparedness for the visit. Research emphasizes the importance of families feeling prepared and gathering information beforehand, as it greatly influences the quality of the experience (Coffey, 2018). The Internet serves as a valuable tool for accessing information, as museums' websites, social media pages, and advocacy organizations provide valuable resources to learn about the institution and the neurodiverse programming available. With approximately 35% of museums offering mobile applications (apps), the channels for disseminating information and facilitating social sharing are evident. This dialogical relationship between museums and visitors creates a personal story through interactions before, during, and after a visit (Dal Falco & Vassos, 2017).

However, accessibility goes beyond overcoming the anxiety of visiting an unknown location and addressing potential sensory processing issues. It also involves comprehending the educational material presented, which can pose additional challenges for individuals with ASC who may have co-occurring learning disorders or difficulties (Giri et al., 2022; Madge, 2021; Mammarella et al., 2022). Fortunately, museums have resources available to support diverse learners. Online resources and digital access provide remote access to collections, exhibitions, and educational materials. On-site, virtual tours, digital audio guides, and other interactive digital experiences further enhance understanding of curated content (Hawkey, 2004).

Designing for sensory processing considerations is indeed a crucial aspect of creating inclusive museum experiences for neurodiverse individuals. By incorporating elements that accommodate various sensory needs, such as lighting, sound, and spatial design, museums can create environments that are more comfortable and accessible. However, it is equally important to go beyond sensory considerations and embrace a broader understanding of neurodiversity (Varriale et al., 2022).

One powerful way to achieve this is through curating exhibitions that highlight neurodiverse experiences as valuable and diverse perspectives, rather than focusing solely on disability. An exemplary exhibition that demonstrates this approach is the *Dyslexic Design* curated by Jim Rokos as part of the London Design Festival in 2016 (https://rokos.com/blogs/exhibitions/dyslexic-design). This exhibition showcased the work of dyslexic designers and aimed to challenge the traditional narrative around dyslexia. Rather than portraying dyslexia as a disability, the exhibition celebrated it as another frame of mind and an asset that can bring unique creativity and innovation to the design field (Maragiannis, 2021).

The exhibition not only featured the work of dyslexic designers but also provided a platform for dialogue and understanding through a series of talks exploring the challenges and experiences of dyslexic individuals. By showcasing the talents and perspectives of dyslexic designers, the exhibition challenged stereotypes and highlighted the richness and diversity of neurodiverse experiences. It aimed to shift the narrative from one of deficit to one of appreciation and recognition (Walkowiak, 2021).

Incorporating exhibitions like *Dyslexic Design* into the museum landscape helps promote inclusivity and raises awareness about the contributions of neurodiverse individuals. It encourages visitors to see neurodiversity as a valuable part of the human experience, fostering a more inclusive and accepting society. By curating exhibitions that showcase neurodiverse experiences as just another type of experience, museums can play a vital role in breaking down barriers and promoting a more inclusive and diverse cultural landscape (Bérubé, 2021).

Therefore, by considering both how technology can be leveraged to serve a broader population, and how messaging of exhibitions is designed for that audience, a more inclusive experience can be created. Furthermore, while the digitization efforts undertaken during the pandemic were not initially intended to create inclusive experiences, they can be reconfigured and combined with other strategies for inclusivity. Digital resources, such as online collections and digital twin mapping of museum spaces, can be leveraged to assist individuals in understanding the site they will visit and societal expectations. By incorporating expanded digital storytelling techniques, museums can enhance the accessibility of their content for neurodiverse visitors, providing a more inclusive and engaging experience (Nicolaou, 2023).

Inclusive smart museums embrace the power of technology and digital resources to cater to the needs of neurodiverse individuals. By leveraging online platforms, mobile apps, and digital experiences, museums can ensure that information is accessible, comprehensible, and engaging for all visitors. The ongoing dialogue between museums and visitors, facilitated by technology and social media, fosters a personalized and inclusive museum experience. Furthermore, the digitization efforts undertaken during the pandemic present an opportunity to reimagine and reconfigure digital resources to meet the specific needs of neurodiverse individuals, enabling them to fully understand and appreciate the cultural heritage presented in museums (Dumitru, 2023).

As an introductory case study, the Postal Museum offers an overview of the recommendations to come. The group of Ambitious About Autism Youth Patrons played a pivotal role in providing valuable insights and perspectives on the needs of autistic individuals, those with learning disabilities, and different sensory sensitivities when visiting museums. Through their collaborative efforts with the Postal Museum, a range of initiatives has been developed to ensure a more inclusive experience for these audiences (PMT, 2021).

One significant development is the creation of comprehensive visual stories that serve as essential preparation tools for autistic individuals visiting the museum sites. These visual stories provide detailed information and guidance, enabling visitors to familiarize themselves with the museum environment and understand what to expect during their visit.

To further enhance the experience, the Postal Museum offers sensory kits called "post satchels" filled with information and sensory toys. These kits are thoughtfully designed and color-coded, ensuring that each visitor's specific needs and preferences are addressed. By providing these resources, the museum aims to create a more comfortable and engaging experience for individuals with different sensory sensitivities. Recognizing the importance of planning ahead, the museum has also developed a pre-visit video that offers valuable information to help visitors effectively plan their trip to The Postal Museum. Social stories and sensory maps ensure a planned experience is possible taking into consideration various sensory processing conditions. This resource assists in familiarizing individuals with the layout, exhibits, and facilities, ensuring they can navigate and enjoy their visit with confidence.

To facilitate communication and navigation, the Postal Museum provides non-verbal communication cards. These cards serve as a helpful tool for individuals who may prefer or require non-verbal communication methods, guiding them around the museum and fostering a seamless and inclusive experience. In addition, the museum organizes relaxed morning events specifically catered to autistic and neurodiverse audiences. These events provide a more tranquil and accommodating environment, allowing visitors to engage with the exhibits at their own pace and comfort level.

To ensure that all staff members are equipped with the necessary skills and knowledge to support and accommodate autistic visitors, the museum has made a commitment to train all front-of-house staff. This training emphasizes the importance of understanding and responding to the unique needs and experiences of autistic individuals, promoting a welcoming and inclusive atmosphere. These initiatives and commitments demonstrate a strong dedication to inclusivity and accessibility for diverse audiences. By actively involving the insights and suggestions the community and neurodiverse individuals and organizations, the museum has taken important steps to create a more engaging and inclusive museum experience for individuals with autism, learning disabilities, and different sensory sensitivities.

These past examples highlight the critical importance of inclusive museum practices and their role in creating enriching experiences for diverse audiences. It is evident that past efforts to support inclusivity in cultural heritage institutions have laid a solid foundation for further advancements in accommodating neurodiverse populations. As our understanding of neurodiversity improves and diagnoses become more accurate, it becomes increasingly vital to extend inclusive practices beyond specific groups and encompass the general population at large. By building upon the knowledge and experiences gained from supporting neurodiverse individuals, museums can enhance their accessibility and inclusivity for all visitors. This includes developing innovative strategies, implementing inclusive design principles, and fostering a culture of empathy and understanding. As we move forward, it is crucial to continue engaging with experts, collaborating with communities, and staying abreast of emerging research to ensure that museums evolve as inclusive spaces that celebrate diversity and provide meaningful experiences for everyone.

1.8 Summary of Chapters

Chapter 2: Storytelling

The power of storytelling should be leveraged for the realm of cultural heritage. The key takeaway is the utilization of digital storytelling techniques to enrich and enhance cultural heritage experiences. By employing immersive and interactive narratives, cultural heritage institutions can captivate visitors and create deeper connections to history and culture. The chapter highlights the importance of personal narratives and their role in contributing to our collective understanding of the past. Techniques for collecting and preserving these narratives are explored, recognizing their value in preserving diverse perspectives and experiences. Moreover, the chapter emphasizes the significance of community engagement in cultural heritage and showcases effective methods for facilitating community storytelling. By fostering a sense of belonging and shared history, collective narratives play a vital role in promoting inclusivity and a stronger connection to cultural heritage. Overall, this chapter underscores the transformative power of storytelling in creating meaningful and engaging cultural heritage experiences for visitors.

Chapter 3: Inclusivity and Environment

Creating inclusive and accessible environments within cultural heritage institutions necessitates careful attention to environmental design. The key focus is on strategies and tools that enhance inclusivity for diverse visitors. The chapter examines the use of sensory kits, which are designed to support individuals with sensory sensitivities, and provides examples of successful projects that have implemented these kits in heritage contexts. It also explores the utilization of sensory maps, which visually represent sensory features within a space, facilitating better navigation and engagement for visitors with sensory sensitivities. Additionally, the chapter delves into the design and implementation of immersive storymaps, showcasing their potential to create engaging and immersive experiences that foster a deeper connection between visitors and the cultural heritage they encounter. By exploring these innovative approaches, the chapter emphasizes the importance of creating environments that cater to the diverse needs of visitors, promoting inclusivity and accessibility within cultural heritage institutions.

Chapter 4: Gamification

In the realm of cultural heritage, gamification techniques have emerged as powerful tools for engaging visitors. This chapter focuses on the application of gamification in cultural heritage institutions, highlighting its effectiveness in creating immersive and interactive experiences. It explores the principles and practices of game-based learning, showcasing how this approach enhances the understanding and appreciation of cultural heritage through real-world examples. Additionally, the chapter delves into the captivating world of treasure hunts and their ability to engage audiences with heritage, presenting case studies that highlight their transformative impact. Furthermore, it explores the integration of gamified digital storytelling, discussing the design and implementation of interactive narratives that enhance visitor engagement and immersion. By examining the potential of gamification in cultural heritage, this chapter emphasizes the importance of innovative and interactive approaches to enrich the visitor experience.

Chapter 5: Immersive Technologies

Immersive technologies have revolutionized the way visitors experience and engage with cultural heritage institutions. This chapter delves into the transformative potential of adaptive extended reality, avatars, digital twins, and wearable devices. It explores how adaptive extended reality, including virtual, augmented, and mixed reality experiences, create immersive and customizable environments that cater to individual visitor needs. Additionally, the chapter examines the use of avatars to interact with virtual characters in heritage contexts and the concept of digital twins that provide realistic simulations of physical assets or environments. It also explores the use of wearable devices, such as smart glasses and haptic feedback devices, to enhance the visitor experience through augmented reality and sensory feedback. Through examples and case studies, this chapter highlights the power of immersive technologies in creating inclusive, engaging, and memorable experiences for diverse audiences in cultural heritage institutions.

Chapter 6: Conclusion: Future Directions for Neuro-inclusivity in Museums and Heritage Sites

Creating inclusive and accessible environments is essential for engaging diverse audiences. The chapters have highlighted the power of storytelling, gamification, and immersive technologies in enhancing cultural heritage experiences. These approaches have demonstrated their efficacy in fostering deeper connections with heritage, engaging visitors of all abilities, and creating meaningful and impactful experiences. However, the journey towards neuro-inclusivity is ongoing, and future directions for research and advancements in the field are crucial. Emerging technologies hold immense potential, and collaborations between museums, researchers, and neurodiverse communities can further drive innovation and progress. Additionally, the findings from this study have broader implications for policy and practice within the heritage sector. The importance of fostering neuro-inclusivity cannot be overstated, as it ensures that cultural heritage experiences are accessible and enriching for all visitors. By embracing neuro-inclusivity, museums and heritage sites can truly become spaces that celebrate diversity and create lasting connections between individuals and their shared heritage.

REFERENCES

Alper, M. (2021). Critical media access studies: Deconstructing power, visibility, and marginality in mediated space. *International Journal of Communication, 15*, 22.

Andermann, J., & Arnold-de Simine, S. (2012). Museums and the educational turn: History, memory, inclusivity. *Journal of Educational Media, Memory, and Society, 4*(2), 1–7.

Anshari, M., Hamdan, M., Ahmad, N., Ali, E., & Haidi, H. (2022). COVID-19, artificial intelligence, ethical challenges and policy implications. *AI & Society*, 1–14.

Ariese, C., & Wróblewska, M. (2022). *Practicing decoloniality in museums: A guide with global examples* (p. 106). Amsterdam University Press.

Associated Press (AP). (2020). Coronavirus spreads to over 60 countries; France closes the Louvre. *New Zealand Herald*, 2 March. https://www.nzherald.co.nz/world/news/article.cfm?c_id=2&objectid=12312989

Atherton, G., Edisbury, E., Piovesan, A., & Cross, L. (2021). Autism through the ages: A mixed methods approach to understanding how age and age of diagnosis affect quality of life. *Journal of Autism and Developmental Disorders*, 1–16.

Barclay, D. M. (2022). *Traveling different: Vacation strategies for parents of the anxious, the inflexible, and the neurodiverse*. Rowman & Littlefield.

Bargiela, S., Steward, R., & Mandy, W. (2016). The experiences of late-diagnosed women with autism spectrum conditions: An investigation of the female autism phenotype. *Journal of Autism and Developmental Disorders, 46*, 3281–3294.

Bérubé, P. (2021). From institutional to representational critique: Museum's contribution to the disability imagery. *The International Journal of the Inclusive Museum, 14*(2), 95.

Bogle, D. E. (2019). *Building bridges: Curricula notes: The arts, equity, democracy and inclusion community curriculum for transitional kindergarten*. Archway Publishing.

Botha, M., Hanlon, J., & Williams, G. L. (2021). Does language matter? Identity-first versus person-first language use in autism research: A response to Vivanti. *Journal of Autism and Developmental Disorders*, 1–9.

Brennan, M., & Christiansen, L. (2018). Virtual materiality: A virtual reality framework for the analysis and visualization of cultural heritage 3D models. *Digital Heritage*.

Brule, E., Bailly, G., Brock, A., Valentin, F., Denis, G., & Jouffrais, C. (2016, May). MapSense: Multi-sensory interactive maps for children living with visual impairments. In *Proceedings of the 2016 CHI conference on human factors in computing systems* (pp. 445–457).

Carew, T. J., & Ramaswami, M. (2020). The neurohumanities: An emerging partnership for exploring the human experience. *Neuron, 108*(4), 590–593.

Centers for Disease Control and Prevention (CDC). (2022). What is autism spectrum disorder? (ASD). https://www.cdc.gov/ncbddd/autism/facts.html

Cho, H., & Jolley, A. (2016). Museum education for children with disabilities: Development of the nature senses traveling trunk. *Journal of Museum Education, 41*(3), 220–229.

Cobley, J., Gaimster, D., So, S., Gorbey, K., Arnold, K., Poulot, D., et al. (2020). Museums in the pandemic: A survey of responses on the current crisis. *Museum Worlds, 8*(1), 111–134.

Coffey, C. S. (2018). *Creating inclusive experiences in children's museums for children with autism spectrum disorder* (Doctoral dissertation, The University of Wisconsin-Milwaukee).

Cruz, R. A., Firestone, A. R., & Love, M. (2023). Beyond a seat at the table: Imagining educational equity through critical inclusion. *Educational Review*, 1–27.

Cutress, A. L., & Muncer, S. J. (2014). Parents' views of the national autistic society's EarlyBird Plus programme. *Autism, 18*(6), 651–657.

Cuyler, A. C. (2020). Looking Beyond What We've Done Before: Minding Potential Blind Spots in Diversifying United States Museums. *International Journal of the Inclusive Museum, 13*(4).

Daher, N. (2020). Smithsonian museums to close amid coronavirus outbreak. *SmithsonianMag.com*, 12 March. https://www.smithsonianmag.com/smithsonian-institution/smithsonian-museums–close-amid-coronavirus-outbreak-180974399/

Dal Falco, F., & Vassos, S. (2017). Museum experience design: A modern storytelling methodology. *The Design Journal, 20*(sup1), S3975–S3983.

Dawson-Squibb, J. J., Davids, E. L., & de Vries, P. J. (2019). Scoping the evidence for EarlyBird and EarlyBird Plus, two United Kingdom-developed parent education training programmes for autism spectrum disorder. *Autism, 23*(3), 542–555.

Dumitru, C. (2023). Distance learning and higher education hybridization: Opportunities and challenges for students with disabilities. *Advances in Distance Learning in Times of Pandemic*, 237–271.

Ferrari, A. N. (2015). *Developing audiences: Programs for individuals with disabilities in children's museums* (Doctoral dissertation, San Francisco State University).

Fletcher, T. S., Wiskera, E. S., Wilbur, L. H., & Garcia, N. M. (2022). The sensory totes programme: Sensory-friendly autism program innovations designed to meet COVID-19 challenges. *World Federation of Occupational Therapists Bulletin, 78*(1), 44–52.

Fletcher, T., Chen, A., Norris, A., Pizarro, E., Tran, J., & Tripp, M. (2023). Guidelines for sensory havens in autism and sensory-friendly events. *Teaching Exceptional Children*.

Fletcher, T. S., Blake, A. B., & Shelffo, K. E. (2018). Can sensory gallery guides for children with sensory processing challenges improve their museum experience? *Journal of Museum Education, 43*(1), 66–77.

Franczuk, J., Boguszewska, K., Parinello, S., Dell'Amico, A., Galasso, F., & Gleń, P. (2022). Direct use of point clouds in real-time interaction with the cultural heritage in pandemic and post-pandemic tourism on the case of Kłodzko Fortress. *Digital Applications in Archaeology and Cultural Heritage, e00217*.

Fraser, J. (2022). Museum languages. *Curator: The Museum Journal, 65*(2), 229–230.

Freed-Brown, E. A. (2010). *A different mind: Developing museum programs for children with autism.* Metropolitan Museum of Art.

Gatto, C., D'Errico, G., Paladini, G. I., & De Paolis, L. T. (2021). Virtual reality in Italian museums: A brief discussion. In *Augmented reality, virtual reality, and computer graphics: 8th International Conference, AVR 2021, Virtual Event, September 7–10, 2021, Proceedings 8* (pp. 306–314). Springer International Publishing.

Ghadim, M. R., & Daugherty, L. (Eds.). (2021). *Museum-based art therapy: A collaborative effort with access, education, and public programs.* Routledge.

Giri, A., Aylott, J., Giri, P., Ferguson-Wormley, S., & Evans, J. (2022). Lived experience and the social model of disability: Conflicted and inter-dependent ambitions for employment of people with a learning disability and their family carers. *British Journal of Learning Disabilities, 50*(1), 98–106.

Gong, X., Zhang, X., & Tsang, M. C. (2020). Creativity development in preschoolers: The effects of children's museum visits and other education environment factors. *Studies in Educational Evaluation, 67*, 100932.

Gudi, A., Shah, S., Raja, S., & Sanak, S. (2022, September). Museums and neurodiversity. *11th Inclusive Design Conference Helen Hamlyn Centre for Design Conference Proceedings* (p. 35).

Haas, N. T. (1997). Project explore: How children are really learning in children's museums. *The Visitor Studies Association, 9*, 63–69.

Hackler, D., & Saxton, G. D. (2007). The strategic use of information technology by nonprofit organizations: Increasing capacity and untapped potential. *Public Administration Review, 67*(3), 474–487.

Han, D. I. D., Weber, J., Bastiaansen, M., Mitas, O., & Lub, X. (2020). Blowing your mind: A conceptual framework of augmented reality and virtual reality enhanced cultural visitor experiences using EEG experience measures. *International Journal of Technology Marketing, 14*(1), 47–68.

Harrington, M. C., Jones, C., & Peters, C. (2022, July). Virtual nature as a digital twin botanically correct 3D AR and VR optimized low-polygon and photogrammetry high-polygon plant models: A short overview of construction methods. *ACM SIGGRAPH 2022 Educator's Forum* (pp. 1–2).

Hawkey, R. (2004). *Learning with digital technologies in museums, science centres and galleries* (Vol. 9). Nesta Futurelab.

Hladik, L., & Ausderau, K. (2022). Stakeholder collaboration to develop an evaluation tool to assess the accessibility of cultural institutions for families with children with autism. *The American Journal of Occupational Therapy, 76*(Supplement_1).

Hooper-Greenhill, E. (2004). Measuring learning outcomes in museums, archives and libraries: The Learning Impact Research Project (LIRP). *International Journal of Heritage Studies, 10*(2), 151–174.

Hughes, J. M. (2015). *Changing conversations around autism: A critical, action implicative discourse analysis of US neurodiversity advocacy online* (Doctoral dissertation, University of Colorado at Boulder).

Hummerstone, H., & Parsons, S. (2022). Co-designing methods with autistic students to facilitate discussions of sensory preferences with school staff: Exploring the double empathy problem. *International Journal of Research & Method in Education*, 1–13.

Hutson, J., & Hutson, P. (2023a). Museums and the metaverse: Emerging technologies to promote inclusivity and engagement. In L. Župčán (Ed.), *Application of modern trends in museums.* IntechOpen. https://doi.org/10.5772/intechopen.110044

Hutson, J., & Hutson, P. (2023b). *Inclusive smart museums study* [Data Set]. Lindenwood University.

Hutson, P., & Hutson, J. (2022). Neurodivergence and inclusivity in cultural institutions: A review of theories and best practices. *Creative Education, 13*(9), 3069–3080.

Jeffery-Clay, K. R. (1998). Constructivism in museums: How museums create meaningful learning environments. *Journal of Museum Education, 23*(1), 3–7.

Kelly, C., & Orsini, M. (2021). Beyond measure? Disability art, affect and reimagining visitor experience. *Studies in Social Justice, 15*(2), 288–306.

Kennedy, J. (2006). *Inclusion in the museum: A toolkit prototype for people with autism spectrum disorder* (Doctoral dissertation, University of Oregon, Arts and Administration Program).

King, E., Smith, M. P., Wilson, P. F., & Williams, M. A. (2021). Digital responses of UK museum exhibitions to the COVID-19 crisis, March–June 2020. *Curator: The Museum Journal, 64*(3), 487–504.

Kinzig, A. P., Ehrlich, P. R., Alston, L. J., Arrow, K., Barrett, S., Buchman, T. G., et al. (2013). Social norms and global environmental challenges: The complex interaction of behaviors, values, and policy. *BioScience, 63*(3), 164–175.

Kotowski, R., & Zybert, E. (Eds.). (2020). *Museotherapy: How does it work? Museums as a place of therapy.* The National Museum in Kielce.

Krantz, A., & Downey, S. (2021). The significant loss of museum educators in 2020: A data story. *Journal of Museum Education, 46*(4), 417–429.

Krcek, T. E. (2013). Deconstructing disability and neurodiversity: Controversial issues for autism and implications for social work. *Journal of Progressive Human Services, 24*(1), 4–22.

Letourneau, S. M., Bennett, D., McMillan Culp, K., Mohabir, P., Schloss, D., Liu, C. J., & Honey, M. (2021). A shift in authority: Applying transformational and distributed leadership models to create inclusive informal stem learning environments. *Curator: The Museum Journal, 64*(2), 363–382.

Leverton, M., Samsi, K., Woolham, J., & Manthorpe, J. (2022). Lessons learned from the impact of Covid-19 on the work of disability support organisations that support employers of social care personal assistants in England. *Health & Social Care in the Community, 30*(6), e6708–e6718.

Limas, J. C., Corcoran, L. C., Baker, A. N., Cartaya, A. E., & Ayres, Z. J. (2022). The impact of research culture on mental health & diversity in STEM. *Chemistry—A European Journal, 28*(9), e202102957.

Long, S. (2013). Practicing civic engagement: Making your museum into a community living room. *Journal of Museum Education, 38*(2), 141–153.

Longhi-Heredia, S. A., & Marcotte, P. (2021). The attractiveness of Quebec's heritage sites in the era of Covid-19. *VISUAL REVIEW. International Visual Culture Review/Revista Internacional de Cultura Visual, 8*(2), 151–165.

Ma, G. Y. K. (2022). An ecological approach to self-reflections on the inaccessibility of arts and cultural activities to wheelchair users. *Disability & Society*, 1–21.

Madge, C. (2021). Autism in museums: Welcoming families and young people. Kids in Museums. *Museum Next*. https://www.museumnext.com/article/how-can-museums-increase-accessibility-for-neurodiverse-audiences/?adlt=strict

Mammarella, I. C., Cardillo, R., & Semrud-Clikeman, M. (2022). Do comorbid symptoms discriminate between autism spectrum disorder, ADHD and non-verbal learning disability? *Research in Developmental Disabilities, 126*, 104242.

Manjra, I. I., & Masic, U. (2022). Gender diversity and autism spectrum conditions in children and adolescents: A narrative review of the methodologies used by quantitative studies. *Journal of Clinical Psychology, 78*(4), 485–502.

Maragiannis, A. (2021). *Diversity and inclusivity by design*. Multicomponent Submission/School of Design, University of Greenwich, London.

Matson, J. L., & Boisjoli, J. A. (2009). The token economy for children with intellectual disability and/or autism: A review. *Research in Developmental Disabilities, 30*(2), 240–248.

Matson, J. L., & Sturmey, P. (Eds.). (2011). *International handbook of autism and pervasive developmental disorders*. Springer Science & Business Media.

McGillicuddy, S., & O'Donnell, G. M. (2014). Teaching students with autism spectrum disorder in mainstream post-primary schools in the Republic of Ireland. *International Journal of Inclusive Education, 18*(4), 323–344.

Morrow, P. (2022). *Cultural inclusion for young people with SEND: Practical strategies for meaningful inclusion in arts and culture*. Taylor & Francis.

Moufahim, M., Heath, T., O'Malley, L., Casey, K., Denegri-Knott, J., Kuruoglu, A., et al. (2023). Teaching note–Critical pedagogies: Practical examples from the marketing classroom. *Journal of Marketing Management, 39*(1–2), 149–165.

National Autistic Society (NAS). (2022). *Communication tools*. Retrieved August 5, 2022, from https://www.autism.org.uk/advice-and-guidance/topics/communication/communication-tools/social-stories-and-comic-strip-coversations

Nicolaou, C. (2023). The secret power of digital storytelling methodology: Technology-enhanced learning utilizing audiovisual educational content. In *Enhancing education through multidisciplinary film teaching methodologies* (pp. 235–246). IGI Global.

Nisticò, V., Faggioli, R., Tedesco, R., Giordano, B., Priori, A., Gambini, O., & Demartini, B. (2022). Brief report: Sensory sensitivity is associated with disturbed eating in adults with autism spectrum disorders without intellectual disabilities. *Journal of Autism and Developmental Disorders*, 1–6.

O'Laughlin, C. A. (2023). *Acts of resilience and resistance: Persistence by autistic college students* (Doctoral dissertation, Saint Louis University).

Ott, D. L., Russo, E., & Moeller, M. (2022). Neurodiversity, equity, and inclusion in MNCs. *AIB Insights, 22*(3), 1–5.

Parsons, S., Yuill, N., Good, J., & Brosnan, M. (2020). 'Whose agenda? Who knows best? Whose voice?'Co-creating a technology research roadmap with autism stakeholders. *Disability & Society, 35*(2), 201–234.

Pohawpatchoko, C., Colwell, C., Powell, J., & Lassos, J. (2017). Developing a native digital voice: Technology and inclusivity in museums. *Museum Anthropology, 40*(1), 52–64.

Postal Museum Team (PMT). (2021). *Delivering accessibility at The Postal Museum*. 25 June. https://www.postalmuseum.org/blog/delivering-accessibility-at-the-postal-museum/

Poulopoulos, V., & Wallace, M. (2022). Digital technologies and the role of data in cultural heritage: The past, the present, and the future. *Big Data and Cognitive Computing, 6*(3), 73.

Praslova, L. (2022). Your "Autism Awareness Day" might be excluding autistic people. *Harvard Business Review*. Retrieved August 5, 2022, from https://hbr.org/2022/04/your-autism-awareness-day-might-be-excluding-autistic-people

Raja, M., & Priya, G. G. (2021). Conceptual Origins, Technological Advancements, and Impacts of Using Virtual Reality Technology in Education. *Webology, 18*(2).

Reilly, J. (2022). *What if we looked at museums and neurodiversity differently? The Neurodiverse Museum*. Retrieved August 5, 2022, from https://theneurodiversemuseum.org.uk/uncategorized/what-if-we-looked-at-museums-and-neurodiversity-differently/

Restrepo-Harner, C., Marsico, K., & Kerr, M. M. (2021). Young tourists with disabilities: Considerations and challenges. In *Children, young people and dark tourism* (pp. 82–98). Routledge.

Sadatsafavi, H., Vanable, L., DeGuzman, P., & Sochor, M. (2022). Sensory-friendly emergency department visit for patients with autism spectrum disorder—A scoping review. *Review Journal of Autism and Developmental Disorders*, 1–15.

Schofield, J., Scott, C., Spikins, P., & Wright, B. (2020). Autism spectrum condition and the built environment: New perspectives on place attachment and cultural heritage. *The Historic Environment: Policy & Practice, 11*(2–3), 307–334.

Schwartzman, R., & Knowles, C. (2022). Expanding accessibility: Sensory sensitive programming for museums. *Curator: The Museum Journal, 65*(1), 95–116.

Shah, P. J., Boilson, M., Rutherford, M., Prior, S., Johnston, L., Maciver, D., & Forsyth, K. (2022). Neurodevelopmental disorders and neurodiversity: Definition of terms from Scotland's National Autism Implementation Team. *The British Journal of Psychiatry, 221*(3), 577–579.

Sheply, E., & McGinnis, R. (2020). *Advancing disability inequality through cultural institutions*. University of Leicester.

Silberman, S. (2015). *Neurotribes: The legacy of autism and the future of neurodiversity*. Penguin.

Silverman, F., Bartley, B., Cohn, E., Kanics, I. M., & Walsh, L. (2012). Occupational therapy partnerships with museums: Creating inclusive environments that promote participation and belonging. *International Journal of the Inclusive Museum, 4*(4).

Sokoloff, R. L., & Schattschneider, E. (2022). *The fight to connect: Making museums accessible to neurodiverse communities* (Doctoral dissertation, Brandeis University).

Su, W. C., Culotta, M., Tsuzuki, D., & Bhat, A. (2022). Cortical activation during cooperative joint actions and competition in children with and without an autism spectrum condition (ASC): An fNIRS study. *Scientific Reports, 12*(1), 5177.

Theriault, S., & Ljungren, R. (2022). Attending to each other: Centering neurodivergent museum professionals in attentive facilitation. *Journal of Museum Education, 47*(2), 238–250.

Tobias, A. (2021). *Museum access and disabilities: A critical examination of web-based museum resources for children with autism spectrum disorder* (Doctoral dissertation, State University of New York at Buffalo).

Upson, L. D. (2021). *Online information for visitors about the accessibility of museums in New Zealand* (Doctoral dissertation, Auckland University of Technology).

Varner, R. (2015). *Museums and visitors with autism: An overview of programs*. Children's Museum of Pittsburgh.

Varriale, L., Cuel, R., Ravarini, A., Briganti, P., & Minucci, G. (2022). Smart and inclusive museums for visitors with autism: The app case "A Dip in the Blue". In *Sustainable digital transformation: Paving the way towards smart organizations and societies* (pp. 133–152). Springer International Publishing.

Vaz, R., Freitas, D., & Coelho, A. (2020). Blind and visually impaired visitors' experiences in museums: Increasing accessibility through assistive technologies. *The International Journal of the Inclusive Museum, 13*(2), 57.

Vi, C. T., Ablart, D., Gatti, E., Velasco, C., & Obrist, M. (2017). Not just seeing, but also feeling art: Mid-air haptic experiences integrated in a multisensory art exhibition. *International Journal of Human-Computer Studies, 108*, 1–14.

Vivanti, G. (2020). Ask the editor: What is the most appropriate way to talk about individuals with a diagnosis of autism? *Journal of Autism and Developmental Disorders, 50*(2), 691–693.

Walkowiak, E. (2021). Neurodiversity of the workforce and digital transformation: The case of inclusion of autistic workers at the workplace. *Technological Forecasting and Social Change, 168*, 120739.

Wates, N. (2014). *The community planning handbook: How people can shape their cities, towns and villages in any part of the world*. Routledge.

Wildgans, J. (2022). IP issues relating to cultural heritage platforms and new business models. In *Research handbook on intellectual property and cultural heritage* (pp. 480–501). Edward Elgar Publishing.

Williams, K., Foulser, A. A., & Tillman, K. A. (2022). Effects of language on social essentialist beliefs and stigma about mental illness. *Proceedings of the Annual Meeting of the Cognitive Science Society, 44*(44).

Woods, P. (2016). *Exploring the use of an autobiographical account in diagnostic assessment of Autism Spectrum Disorder with a young child* (Doctoral dissertation, University of Leicester).

Yang, L. (2022). Deconstructing social exclusions: The practice of digital activities among disabled people in China. *Media, Culture and Society, 44*(8), 1588–1601.

Yin, Y., Zheng, P., Li, C., & Wang, L. (2023). A state-of-the-art survey on Augmented Reality-assisted Digital Twin for futuristic human-centric industry transformation. *Robotics and Computer-Integrated Manufacturing, 81*, 102515.

Zhang, Y., & Epley, N. (2012). Exaggerated, mispredicted, and misplaced: When "it's the thought that counts" in gift exchanges. *Journal of Experimental Psychology: General, 141*(4), 667.

CHAPTER 2

Storytelling

The transformative power of storytelling in the realm of cultural heritage has remained one of the most potent tools of human communication throughout history. Now, digital storytelling techniques can be harnessed to convey the past in newly innovative and engaging ways. The following highlights the profound impact of digital storytelling in enhancing cultural heritage experiences by creating immersive narratives that bridge the gap between past and present. The chapter showcases real-world case studies of successful digital storytelling projects implemented in museums and heritage sites, illustrating their ability to make historical narratives more accessible, interactive, and compelling. Furthermore, it emphasizes the pivotal role of personal narratives in cultural heritage, exploring techniques for collecting and preserving these invaluable accounts to ensure their accessibility for future generations. The chapter presents case studies that demonstrate how personal narratives enrich the visitor experience by establishing intimate and personal connections to the past. Additionally, it underscores the significance of community engagement, outlining effective methods for facilitating community storytelling and celebrating the diverse voices within a heritage context. By actively fostering strong connections with communities, museums and heritage sites contribute to a more inclusive, dynamic, and vibrant cultural heritage landscape.

© The Author(s), under exclusive license to Springer Nature Switzerland AG 2024
J. Hutson, P. Hutson, *Inclusive Smart Museums*,
https://doi.org/10.1007/978-3-031-43615-4_2

2.1 Digital Storytelling and Museums

The use of storytelling as a method to convey information is an inherently human strategy and is counted among the oldest of social practices for communication and learning (Howard, 1991; Hymes, 2003). Throughout history, individuals and communities have used storytelling as a means to share knowledge, pass down cultural traditions, and create connections between generations. Stories have the power to captivate and engage audiences, evoking emotions and making information more memorable. The art of storytelling involves the skillful use of narrative elements such as characters, plot, and setting to convey messages and convey meaning (Anglin et al., 2023). It allows for complex ideas and concepts to be communicated in a relatable and accessible way. In the realm of cultural heritage, storytelling plays a crucial role in preserving and transmitting the stories, experiences, and values of a particular community or society (Echavarria et al., 2022). It allows for the exploration of historical events, cultural practices, and personal journeys, providing a window into the past and shaping our understanding of the present (Dias, 2022).

With the expansion of digital technology, the way in which stories are delivered and received has been transformed and conceptualized into digital storytelling through various digital communication tools (Roza & Rustam, 2023). Digital storytelling techniques harness the power of technology to convey captivating narratives of the past. By utilizing multimedia elements and interactive features, digital storytelling enhances cultural heritage experiences, bridging the gap between history and contemporary audiences (Okanovic et al., 2022). Real-world case studies shall be called upon to demonstrate the effectiveness of digital storytelling in creating immersive and engaging experiences. Additionally, the chapter emphasizes the importance of accessibility in digital storytelling, ensuring that diverse audiences can access and connect with cultural heritage. The preservation of personal narratives and community engagement are also highlighted as integral aspects of storytelling in cultural heritage, fostering inclusivity and enriching the visitor experience. Through the transformative potential of digital storytelling, cultural heritage institutions can create meaningful connections between audiences and the stories that shape our collective history.

Instead of one medium used to tell a story, such as a speech, text, or video, digital storytelling often combines video, text, audio narration, and more into a multimodal experience. With the latest generation of emerging technologies in XR supported by artificial intelligence (AI), multimedia digital communication tools and hypermedia-supported tools can expand the limits of storytelling for museum goers and support neurodiverse populations (Matsiola et al., 2018; Pilgrim & Pilgrim, 2021). This approach does not require investment in infrastructure or a radical reworking of current educational content to be effective.

Most institutions already provide accessible resources through a variety of mechanisms including their websites, social media accounts, digital applications, or traditional printed handouts of maps or museums guides. These resources are being coupled with mobility-enhancing systems using interactive digital storytelling, personalization and adaptability, and mixed media (Fig. 2.1) (Zhong et al., 2019). The new, enhanced experiences have the potential to improve the attractiveness of not only cultural heritage sites and museums but also act as a new conduit for interpretation, analysis, and cultural knowledge for diverse communities. Additionally, the innovative use of new digital technologies will provide new forms of

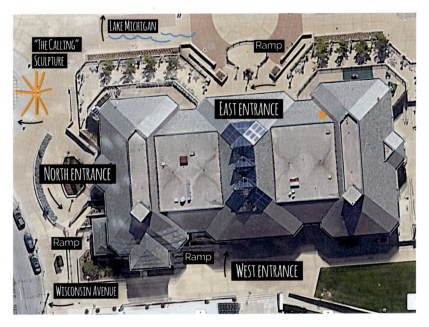

Fig. 2.1 Building map, a visit to the museum, Betty Brinn Children's Museum

cultural interactive experiences that are comfortable, sensory-friendly, and comprehensible to neurodiverse audiences.

In the realm of user experience design for inclusivity, it is essential to prioritize inclusive design principles from the early stages of digital storytelling. By incorporating neuroinclusive elements into the design, digital accessibility can be enhanced, making the content more accessible to a wider range of users (Hadley, 2022). One approach to improving accessibility is by incorporating responsive hover elements into the design. For example, buttons that change color or provide visual cues when interacted with can enhance the usability of the digital experience (Fig. 2.2). These visual indicators can assist users, including those with neurodiverse conditions, in understanding the interactive elements and navigating through the content more effectively (Terrado et al., 2022).

Another design consideration is the use of tabs that minimize, resembling a paperclip. These collapsible tabs can help organize content and

Fig. 2.2 Interactive display, Maritime Experiential Museum & Aquarium. October 6, 2011

make it more accessible, especially for individuals who may benefit from a more structured presentation of information (Fig. 2.3). By allowing users to expand or collapse sections of content, it provides a more manageable and customizable experience based on individual preferences and cognitive abilities (Li et al., 2022).

Incorporating these inclusive design elements not only enhances accessibility but also contributes to a more engaging and user-friendly digital storytelling experience for all users (Izzo & Bauer, 2015). By considering the diverse needs and preferences of users, designers can create interfaces that are more intuitive, adaptable, and inclusive (Pattison & Stedmon, 2006). This approach ensures that individuals with varying cognitive abilities and sensory sensitivities can navigate and engage with the content in a way that suits their unique needs, promoting a more inclusive and meaningful digital experience (King & Lord, 2015).

One recommendation for inclusive digital design is the use of digital screen labeling. The North Carolina Museum of Art implemented this approach to address the challenges posed by non-traditional display formats. Digital labeling allows visitors to pinch the screen and zoom in on

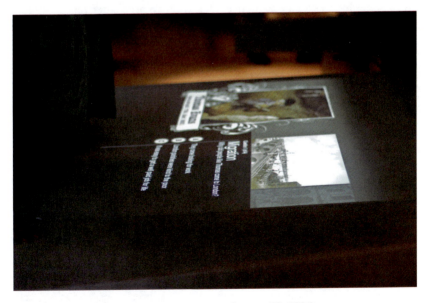

Fig. 2.3 Museum of London Interactive. August 18, 2010

high-resolution photographs of artworks, enabling them to examine the details more closely than they would from a distance or through a protective glass screen (Harrell & Kotecki, 2015). Additionally, digital labels can include video content, such as interviews with artists and curators, to provide context and interpretive narratives. The inclusion of a "related artwork" feature further guides visitors to other pieces by the same artist or in a similar style elsewhere in the gallery. Moreover, digital labels have the potential to track engagement and provide information on the conservation history of artworks. By addressing the provenance of pieces and detailing how they have been cared for over time, visitors gain a deeper understanding of the artworks' significance and preservation efforts (Arts et al., 2015).

The ongoing development of digital labels includes the integration of analytics tools to gather valuable insights. By understanding how visitors interact with the labels, which features are most popular, and how much time is spent on specific content, museums can continuously improve the user experience and tailor their offerings to meet the diverse needs and preferences of their audience (Lanir et al., 2013). By prioritizing inclusive design in digital storytelling, museums and cultural institutions can create engaging and accessible experiences that cater to a broader range of visitors, ensuring that everyone has the opportunity to connect with and appreciate the artistic and cultural heritage on display (Black, 2005; Mortara et al., 2014).

While existing accessibility resources seek greater inclusivity in visitor experience, new considerations delivered via digital storytelling can serve to address obstacles for neurodiverse individuals. In general, inclusivity seeks to provide equal access to opportunities and resources for potentially marginalized populations. In order to be truly inclusive, these individuals must feel welcomed not only on location through accommodations but also prior to the visit (Fig. 2.4). An understanding of the travel logistics, parking, desired paths mapped by curatorial staff, sensory-friendly areas, and more can reduce the anxiety of the unknown for those with ASC and assist with sensory processing hindrances before even entering the physical space of a museum itself (Fig. 2.5 and Table 2.1).

Providing such information through existing technology and digital assets facilitated with expanded digital experiences leads to a better experience and retention of educational material presented on-site during regular operating hours (Holcombe-James, 2022). While "Sensory Days" seek to offer experiences tailored to those with ASC, they inadvertently

2 STORYTELLING   55

Parking can be found in 2 places, either off of Rt 15 or Market Street.

Our Entrance is through the courtyard in the front of the building and up the stairs or elevator.

Fig. 2.4 Parking map, Lewisburg Children's Museum

Fig. 2.5 Map of National Railway Museum premises, South Australia

segregate the population from the general public and imply that "normal" visiting hours are not for them (Fletcher et al., 2022). Through expanded digital experiences, a sense of belonging can be created where regular visiting hours are welcoming (Black, 2012). In addition, the ability afforded through virtual walkthroughs and digital recreations of the location provides an opportunity to revisit the site, review educational materials provided, and encourage post-visit interactions through sharing experiences on the institution's social media platforms (Charitonos et al., 2012). All of this instills conceptual anchors of memory and subsequent reinforcement of institutional messaging. Digital storytelling offers multiple ways to access information, catering to diverse learning styles and abilities. Through the use of text, audio, and video, visitors can choose the format

Table 2.1 Recommendations for enhanced accessibility in pre-visitation maps

Recommendation	Description
Access details	Provide detailed information about accessibility features, such as the number of steps, width of doorways, ramps, or elevators.
Route information	Highlight accessible routes within the site, indicating wheelchair-friendly pathways or pathways with fewer obstacles.
Restroom facilities	Clearly mark locations of accessible restrooms, specifying features like grab bars, accessible sinks, and sufficient maneuvering space.
Parking and drop-off points	Include information on accessible parking spaces and designated drop-off points for visitors with disabilities.
Sensory considerations	Provide information about sensory considerations, such as areas with low ambient noise, quiet spaces, or specific lighting conditions.

that best suits their needs, ensuring that information is accessible to all (Hur & Suh, 2012). This approach enhances engagement by providing interactive experiences that allow visitors to explore and learn at their own pace. Digital storytelling creates a safe and inclusive environment, particularly for individuals with neurodiverse needs, by incorporating accessible and inclusive design principles. Visitors have control over their engagement, enabling them to customize their experience and feel empowered during their museum visit. Moreover, digital storytelling can be enriched with accessibility features such as closed captioning, audio description, and sign language interpretation, ensuring that individuals with different abilities can fully engage with the content and have a meaningful museum experience (Montagud et al., 2020) (Table 2.2).

Digital storytelling can thus allow visitors to personalize their experiences by providing a wide range of options tailored to their specific needs, interests, and preferences, making the experience more engaging and inclusive (Katifori et al., 2020). In a technology-driven age, museums are seeking a variety of these tools, including immersive realities, to stay current with the ways their visitors are engaging with the world in their daily lives. The ways in which museums are seeking to tell stories with technology include digital tour guides, AR and Bluetooth technologies, and smart museums (Table 2.3). The integration of digital tour guides is becoming more commonplace, and companies are looking to support this adoption (Verde et al., 2022).

Examples such as Mobile Tour app (Fig. 2.6) and Digital Guide System are digital solutions that allow museums to embed their own images,

Table 2.2 Benefits of digital storytelling in museums

Recommendation	Description
Providing multiple ways to access information	Digital storytelling can offer text, audio, and video formats, accommodating different learning styles and abilities and ensuring that information is accessible to all visitors.
Enhancing engagement	Interactive digital stories create immersive and personalized experiences, allowing visitors to explore and learn at their own pace. It enhances engagement by providing an interactive and captivating learning environment.
Creating a safe and inclusive environment	Digital storytelling fosters a safe and inclusive environment for visitors with neurodiverse needs. It incorporates accessible design principles, empowering visitors to control their engagement and interact with content comfortably.
Accessibility features	Digital storytelling can be enriched with accessibility features such as closed captioning, audio description, and sign language interpretation. These features support visitors with different abilities and ensure inclusive access to the content.

Table 2.3 Examples of digital storytelling in museums

Museum	Digital storytelling example
The British Museum	The British Museum offers a virtual tour that allows visitors to explore its collection and learn about the history and significance of various artifacts through interactive storytelling.
The Louvre	The Louvre provides a mobile app that offers audio-guided tours with engaging narratives, enabling visitors to delve into the stories behind iconic artworks and historical artifacts.
The National Museum of Natural History	The National Museum of Natural History features interactive exhibits with digital storytelling elements, such as touchscreens and multimedia displays, to engage visitors and provide in-depth information about natural history and biodiversity.
The Museum of Modern Art	The Museum of Modern Art (MoMA) offers a digital storytelling platform called MoMA Learning, which provides online resources, activities, and videos that explore art concepts, artists, and exhibitions, enhancing visitors' understanding and engagement.
The Smithsonian Institution	The Smithsonian Institution utilizes digital storytelling in various museums under its umbrella, such as the National Air and Space Museum, to present immersive narratives and multimedia experiences that bring science, history, and culture to life.

Fig. 2.6 The National Museum of the Marine Corps' interactive website

videos, and audio of their collections for visitors to experience (Podsukhina et al., 2022). The multimedia component allows for greater memory retention than traditional storytelling by addressing different learning styles (Manik et al., 2022). This new form of content delivery combines participation commonly seen with computer or video games complete with automatic story generation and narration. For example, the British Museum uses AR in their mobile game *A Gift for Athena* (2014) for the Parthenon gallery using tablets that can be checked out. The game tasks visitors with finding specific statues based on an outline and rewards them with more information about the works prior to assigning another task to explore (Sabiescu & Charatzopoulou, 2015). Furthermore, these digital tours need not be solely in person. Virtual experiences can also represent inclusive alternatives to traditional museum visits through the digital embodiment of historical characters and their stories that may also blend physical artifacts with the immersive experience. In such a way, visitors can experience the rich tapestry of stories in museum collections prior to visiting (if at all) and have a greater understanding on-site (Cecilia, 2021).

Along the same lines as digital tour guides, smart museums are also eliminating physical barriers to their collections by allowing technological advancements to remove sensory barriers as well. Smart museums, such as the Smart Museum of Art (Chicago), bring together traditional exhibitions with emerging technologies, where the use of immersive technology seeks to enhance how material on complex cultural heritage is delivered to visitors (Dohoney, 2020). The use of technology to enhance the visitor experience can include interactive exhibits, virtual reality experiences, and mobile apps that provide additional information and resources. Smart museums may also use technology to collect data on visitor behavior and preferences and to improve the overall management and operation of the museum. Overall, the goal of a smart museum is to make the museum visit more engaging, interactive, and personalized for visitors. The transition to becoming "smart" refers to the heterogeneous technologies allowing museum environment to become more interactive, innovative, and accessible (Korzun et al., 2016).

In the ever-evolving landscape of technology and digital innovation, museums are finding new ways to engage their visitors and enhance the overall experience. One such approach is the concept of creating location-aware institutions, where mobile apps and digital platforms are utilized to provide contextually relevant information based on the visitor's physical location within the space (Krishnasamy et al., 2020). Spotzer Digital, a notable player in this field, has made significant strides in creating location-aware experiences for cultural institutions (https://spotzerdigital.com/) (Burdick et al., 2016). Founded in early 2014, Spotzer has collaborated with institutions such as the Neue Galerie in New York and the Boston Athenaeum, one of the oldest independent libraries and cultural institutions in the country. Through their app, Spotzer provides a seamless and immersive experience that adapts to the visitor's location and preferences.

When a museum visitor downloads apps like that developed by Spotzer and enters the museum, the app utilizes geolocation technology to detect the visitor's proximity to different artworks or exhibits. As the person walks up to a specific work of art, the app automatically pulls up relevant information, providing insights, historical context, and even multimedia content related to the artwork. This real-time access to curated information enhances the visitor's understanding and appreciation of the piece (Hoffman et al., 2008; Spitzer et al., 2018). Moreover, such apps are designed to learn from the visitor's preferences and behaviors, allowing for a more personalized experience. As the visitor moves towards another collection or exhibit, the app can dynamically adjust the content and recommendations based on the individual's interests, providing a tailored and engaging journey through the museum or library (Vrettakis et al., 2023).

By incorporating location-aware technologies, museums and other cultural heritage institutions can add a new layer of proximity and contextual awareness to their physical spaces. This integration of technology with the physical environment allows for a seamless blending of the digital and real-world experiences. Visitors can navigate the space more effectively, discovering hidden gems and gaining deeper insights into the collections as they explore (Michalakis & Caridakis, 2022). The implementation of location-aware technologies also opens up possibilities for interactive and immersive experiences. For instance, augmented reality (AR) overlays can be integrated into the app, enabling visitors to view virtual objects or visualizations directly in the physical space. This enhances the visitor's connection to the exhibits, enabling them to see beyond the surface and delve into a deeper understanding of the subject matter (Parker et al., 2021).

As museums and libraries continue to embrace the digital era, the concept of creating location-aware experiences is gaining momentum. By leveraging the power of mobile apps, geolocation technology, and personalized content delivery, institutions can transform the visitor experience, offering a seamless blend of the physical and digital realms. The apps and other similar solutions pave the way for more interactive, immersive, and contextually rich experiences, ensuring that museums and libraries remain vibrant and relevant in the digital age (Dionisio & Nisi, 2021).

Therefore, the infrastructure and ability to move past the elimination of mere physical barriers for museum accessibility exists. The developments support the call for greater attention to neurodiverse accessibility as only addressing physical disabilities and accessibility will no longer suffice (Zallio & Clarkson, 2022). The new multisensory approach afforded by digital storytelling and smart museums is essential to remove barriers to learning as part of the museum experience (Eardley et al., 2016). Once sensory obstacles have been removed and/or minimized, personalized learning experiences can be tailored to each individual and material and spaces delivered by way of storytelling (Clouder et al., 2020). At the same time, engaging visitors through multisensory approaches and considerations can bolster learning, for stories are not limited to oral communication and are critical for the creation of an atmosphere through the senses (Kelly et al., 2021).

The elicitation of emotions such as empathy enriches stories, maintaining the attention of the audience while also creating memorable experience one can become invested in (Cañas-Bajo, 2020). Storytelling supports other cognitive factors that improve learning, including improving attention and time on task by keeping the listener engaged, and empathy through emotional identification with the subject providing a cognitive framework to help understand and retain new information (Pujol et al., 2012). Drawing upon previous research, the following proposes leveraging the engaging nature of storytelling delivered through new immersive and interactive digital experiences to mitigate various ASC symptoms that would prohibit access to and appreciation of cultural heritage in museums. The educational resources of social stories and sensory maps that have been created to support neurodiverse visitors with various sensory processing disorders (SPD) should be digitized. The proposed "storymap" combination can then be transformed into a digital expression and experience through digital storytelling strategies. Taken together, this *digital storymap* can provide support prior to the visit, on-site, and engage diverse audiences with personalized, story-driven narratives of museum collections, while supporting multisensory experiences (Langran & DeWitt, 2020).

The raising of awareness highlights the crucial role of incorporating sensory maps, visualscapes, soundscapes, smellscapes, and touchscape maps in cultural planning for the restoration and preservation of deteriorated heritage sites (El-Sayyad, 2019). While many studies primarily focus on improving the visual aspects of a place, it is essential to recognize that places offer a multitude of sensory experiences that foster a connection between the past and present (Fakfare et al., 2021; Gretzel & Koo, 2021). Sensory experiences are shaped by the interplay between the physical environment, human behavior, and the surrounding ambiance. Any changes in the urban landscape can result in the reshaping of the sensory landscape as new sensory connections are formed. The senses not only have a biological dimension but also contribute to the cultural character of places and objects, imbuing them with meaning and value (Mazzocchi, 2022).

Smells, for example, have the power to evoke emotions, trigger memories, and influence well-being. Designers can harness the potential of scents to create atmospheres that soothe, energize, or evoke specific associations. Urban smellscape wheels provide a framework for understanding and utilizing smells in the urban environment (Rodriguez & Kross, 2023; Roe & McCay, 2021). Likewise, the field of environmental noise control has also gained significant attention in recent years, raising awareness of the detrimental effects of excessive noise exposure (Liu et al., 2020; Torija & Clark, 2021). Soundscapes can be regarded as the auditory counterpart of visualscapes. They refer to the acoustic environment of a place and serve as a tool for understanding the significance of sounds in preserving the authenticity of a heritage site (Qiu et al., 2021). Historical soundscapes may include the ringing of bells, the sound of water from fountains, the reverberation of wooden staircases, and the footsteps on cobblestone streets (Jordan & Fiebig, 2020). Therefore, by incorporating sensory elements into the planning and design of cultural spaces, we can enhance the overall experience and ensure the preservation of the sensory heritage of a place. This holistic approach considers the diverse ways in which our senses shape our perception and understanding of the built environment, creating immersive and meaningful encounters with heritage sites (Gao et al., 2022).

When it comes to implementing strategies that enhance visitor engagement, including these sense components and mapping to create immersive experiences, institutions have several solutions at their disposal. One such solution is Curio interactive exhibition software. This user-friendly digital storytelling software empowers institutions to design and publish their own interactive exhibitions, providing every visitor with a unique and engaging experience. With Curio, institutions can easily create multimedia-rich exhibitions that incorporate elements like audio, video, images, and interactive features (Giglitto, 2014). By utilizing this software, institutions can craft personalized and immersive experiences that captivate their visitors, fostering deeper connections with the content and enhancing their overall museum experience (https://www.curiopublisher.com/).

The use of storytelling as a method to convey information is deeply ingrained in human culture and history. It has been utilized as a powerful tool for communication and learning, allowing individuals and communities to share knowledge, preserve cultural traditions, and foster connections across generations. The advent of digital technology has revolutionized storytelling, enabling innovative and immersive experiences that bridge the gap between the past and present. Digital storytelling techniques harness the power of multimedia elements, interactive features, and personalized narratives to enhance cultural heritage experiences. Through real-world case studies, this chapter has demonstrated the effectiveness of digital storytelling in engaging audiences and making historical narratives more accessible and engaging. Moreover, the chapter has emphasized the importance of accessibility, personal narratives, and community engagement in cultural heritage storytelling. By leveraging the transformative potential of digital storytelling, cultural heritage institutions can create meaningful connections between audiences and the stories that shape our collective history. The integration of emerging technologies, such as AR and smart museum concepts, further expands the possibilities for immersive and inclusive storytelling experiences. As the field continues to evolve, the future of storytelling in cultural heritage holds great promise in fostering neuro-inclusivity and providing enriching experiences for diverse audiences.

2.2 Personal Narratives

Personal narratives play a pivotal role in cultural heritage, offering a unique and intimate perspective that contributes to our collective understanding of history and culture (Coenen et al., 2013). These narratives provide a glimpse into the lived experiences, memories, and emotions of individuals, offering a personal connection to the past. The significance of personal narratives lies in their ability to humanize historical events and cultural practices, giving them context and meaning (Phoenix, 2022). There are a variety of strategies to collect, preserve, and disseminate these personal stories given the range of collective human experiences and museums demonstrate that diversity in their presentations (Table 2.4).

One technique for collecting and preserving personal narratives is oral history. Oral history involves the recording and preservation of firsthand accounts through interviews and conversations with individuals who have experienced or witnessed significant events (Swaminathan & Mulvihill, 2022). These interviews capture personal stories, reflections, and insights that might not be found in traditional historical records or documents. Through oral history, cultural heritage institutions can actively collect and preserve narratives that might otherwise be lost to time (Calabria, 2019).

Preserving personal narratives for future generations is crucial for maintaining a comprehensive understanding of our history and culture (Ladson-Billings, 2021). Archival practices, such as digitization and transcription, ensure the accessibility and longevity of personal narratives. Digitization allows for easy dissemination and sharing of personal narratives, making them accessible to a wider audience. Transcription of oral

Table 2.4 Examples of personal narratives in museums

Museum	Personal narrative example
The National Museum of African American History and Culture	The National Museum of African American History and Culture features personal narratives shared by individuals who have experienced significant events in African American history, providing firsthand accounts and perspectives.
The Holocaust Memorial Museum	The Holocaust Memorial Museum collects and presents personal narratives of Holocaust survivors, allowing visitors to hear their stories of resilience, survival, and remembrance, creating a powerful connection to the history and impact of the Holocaust.
The Ellis Island Museum	The Ellis Island Museum showcases personal narratives of immigrants who passed through Ellis Island, sharing their experiences, challenges, and dreams as they arrived in the United States and offering a glimpse into the immigrant experience.
The 9/11 Memorial and Museum	The 9/11 Memorial and Museum includes personal narratives of survivors, witnesses, and family members affected by the September 11 attacks, offering a deeply personal and emotional connection to the tragic events and their aftermath.
The International Slavery Museum	The International Slavery Museum presents personal narratives of individuals who were enslaved or impacted by the transatlantic slave trade, sharing their stories to educate visitors about the history and legacies of slavery around the world.

histories into written form not only facilitates searchability and analysis but also enables individuals with hearing impairments to engage with these narratives (Shopes, 2019).

Case studies of personal narrative projects in heritage contexts demonstrate the power of these initiatives in enriching the visitor experience. One compelling case study is the Smithsonian Institution's Civil Rights History Project (CRHP), which collected oral histories from individuals who participated in the Civil Rights Movement (https://nmaahc.si.edu/explore/initiatives/civil-rights-history-project). This initiative allowed visitors to hear firsthand accounts of this transformative period in American history, connecting them to the personal experiences and emotions of those involved. By doing so, the project created a deeper and more meaningful engagement with the history of the Civil Rights Movement, fostering empathy and understanding among visitors (Shankar, 2022).

Similarly, the United States Holocaust Memorial Museum's Oral History project collects and preserves the testimonies of Holocaust survivors, liberators, and other witnesses (https://www.ushmm.org/collections/the-museums-collections/about/oral-history). Through audio and video recordings of interviews, the project captures the vivid memories and emotions of individuals who lived through one of the darkest periods in human history. By sharing these personal stories, the project not only provides a historical account of the Holocaust but also humanizes the experiences of those directly affected, fostering empathy and understanding among visitors (Filov, 2012).

Another noteworthy example is the StoryCorps project, an oral history initiative that aims to record and preserve the diverse stories of individuals from all walks of life (https://storycorps.org/). StoryCorps sets up recording booths in various locations, inviting participants to have meaningful conversations with their loved ones or friends. These conversations are then archived in the Library of Congress and made available to the public. By capturing and sharing these stories, StoryCorps promotes empathy, understanding, and the preservation of individual voices within the broader cultural narrative (Pozzi-Thanner, 2005).

The Australian State Library of New South Wales Oral History and Sound Collection project is another compelling initiative that focuses on collecting personal narratives from South Sudanese Australians. This project explores their migration experiences, cultural heritage, and contributions to Australian society. Utilizing various storytelling methods, including interviews, photographs, and audiovisual recordings, the project documents and shares these narratives. By amplifying the voices and experiences of South Sudanese Australians, the project challenges stereotypes, promotes cultural understanding, and celebrates the diverse heritage within Australian society (Whitebeach, 2014).

The Unsung Heroes Project at the Lowell Milken Center is another impactful case study that seeks to empower students and educators to uncover and share the stories of individuals who have made significant contributions to history but have often been overlooked or forgotten (https://www.lowellmilkencenter.org/programs/projects). Through these projects, young people are inspired to take action and make a positive impact on their communities. The Unsung Heroes serve as role models, teaching values such as courage and compassion while also fostering important academic and life skills necessary for success in the twenty-first century. For educators, the opportunity to engage in a shared discovery process with their students brings about profound and lasting change in individuals, schools, communities, and the world at large. By delving into the stories of Unsung Heroes, students gain a deeper understanding of diversity and respect, recognizing the importance of embracing different perspectives and strengthening the bonds that unite humanity. The Unsung Heroes Projects bridge the gap between generations, connecting the past to the present and offering moral lessons that resonate with society (Goodson & Ralph, 2020).

Lastly, another notable example is the *My Story, My Tattoo* traveling exhibition at the Wellington Museum in New Zealand. This project collected 31 personal stories and photographs of individuals with tattoos, exploring the meanings and cultural significance behind their body art (https://www.wellington.ca/en/discover/mus-mystorymytattoo.aspx). The exhibition not only showcased the diversity of tattoo culture but also highlighted the personal narratives and journeys of the individuals, fostering empathy and understanding among visitors (Ngarimu-Cameron, 2019).

These are but some examples that demonstrate the power of personal narratives in cultural heritage. They provide a means to humanize historical events, challenge dominant narratives, promote empathy and understanding, celebrate diverse voices, and honor the contributions of individuals and communities (Harter et al., 2021). By incorporating personal narratives into cultural heritage initiatives, museums and heritage sites create immersive and engaging experiences that connect visitors to the past in deeply personal and relatable ways (Olaz et al., 2022).

As demonstrated in the examples above, personal narratives are a vital component of cultural heritage, contributing to our collective understanding of history and culture (Henderson, 2019). Techniques such as oral history, archival practices, and digitization ensure the preservation and accessibility of personal narratives for future generations. Case studies of personal narrative projects demonstrate their potential to enrich the visitor experience and foster a deeper connection to cultural heritage. By incorporating personal narratives into exhibitions and educational programs, cultural heritage institutions can create a more inclusive and relatable experience, allowing individuals to see themselves in the stories of the past.

2.3 Social Stories and Museums

Building upon the exploration of personal narratives in cultural heritage, the next section delves into the use of social stories in museums. Social stories are narrative tools that provide individuals, particularly those on the spectrum, with a structured framework for understanding and navigating social situations (Beck, 2020). In the context of museums, social stories serve as valuable resources to prepare visitors for their museum experience and support their sensory and social needs. This section examines the role of social stories in creating inclusive and accessible museum environments, highlighting their potential to enhance the visitor experience for neurodiverse individuals (Schwartzman & Knowles, 2022). It explores effective strategies for developing and implementing social stories in museums, showcasing case studies that demonstrate their positive impact in fostering a sense of familiarity, reducing anxiety, and promoting engagement among visitors with ASC (Table 2.5).

Table 2.5 Examples of social stories in museums

Museum	Social story example
The Children's Museum of Indianapolis	The Children's Museum of Indianapolis provides social stories to help prepare children with autism for their visit. These stories outline what to expect during the visit, including details about exhibits, sensory experiences, and expectations for behavior, helping children feel more comfortable and prepared.
The Science Museum, London	The Science Museum in London offers social stories that guide individuals with autism through specific exhibits, explaining the interactive elements, potential sensory experiences, and expected behaviors. These stories aim to support visitors in navigating the museum and engaging with the exhibits.
The Museum of Natural History, New York	The Museum of Natural History in New York creates social stories that introduce children with autism to the museum's dinosaur exhibit. These stories provide visual narratives that outline the visit, highlighting key features and providing information about the exhibits to help children with autism prepare for their visit.
The Art Institute of Chicago	The Art Institute of Chicago develops social stories to assist individuals with autism in exploring specific art collections. These stories introduce selected artworks, provide sensory information, and offer guidance on appropriate behaviors, ensuring a positive and inclusive experience for visitors with autism.
The British Museum, London	The British Museum in London offers social stories that prepare visitors with autism for their visit to the museum. These stories include information about the layout of the museum, exhibits of interest, and guidance on managing sensory experiences, fostering a supportive and inclusive environment for individuals with autism.

Similar to personal narratives, social stories play a crucial role in providing a social narrative within museum and cultural heritage settings. Coined and trademarked by Carol Gray in 1991, social stories are concise descriptions of specific situations or activities, such as visiting a museum. These narratives prove to be valuable resources for individuals with ASC and other developmental conditions, as they offer a clear and predictable explanation of what to expect during a museum visit (Walker & Smith, 2015). The intention behind social stories is not to change the behavior of visitors, but rather to enhance their understanding of the events and expectations they may encounter.

Initially, social stories were designed without visual stimuli, focusing solely on the narrative aspect. However, as research and understanding evolved, the inclusion of visual imagery became more prominent in the development of social stories. For instance, in 2006, Ricciardelli noted that visual elements were incorporated to enhance the effectiveness of the tool. This adaptation was based on a deeper comprehension of the needs of individuals utilizing social stories.

The implementation of social stories in museums has proven to be beneficial for visitors with ASC. These stories provide comprehensive information about the museum environment, including any adjustments that have been made to ensure visitor comfort. Moreover, they offer a breakdown of individual steps, addressing potential intellectual or social barriers that visitors may encounter (Garzotto et al., 2018a). In contrast to sensory maps that primarily focus on providing sensory information about the environment, social stories adopt a narrative approach that encompasses a broader range of information.

Examples of museums that have integrated social stories into their accessibility resources include the San Diego Natural History Museum's Spectrum Project and the Brandywine Museum of Art. The Spectrum Project at the San Diego Natural History Museum offers social stories specifically designed for individuals with autism, which can be accessed on their website (https://www.sdnhm.org/visit/accessibility/social-stories/) (Theriault & Jones, 2018). Similarly, the Brandywine Museum of Art provides a social story on their website that familiarizes visitors with the museum experience (https://www.brandywine.org/museum/accessibility/social-story). These examples highlight the adoption of storytelling strategies and therapeutic interventions to support the needs of individuals with ASC, promoting their understanding of social situations and enhancing their overall museum visit experience.

Social stories, also referred to as social narratives, serve as descriptive tools that address challenging situations for individuals with autism by clearly identifying social behaviors and cues (Watermeyer, 2012). These narratives are designed to inform and prepare individuals with socialization challenges for potentially difficult situations. Museums and educational institutions have recognized the value of social narratives in fostering inclusivity and accessibility for diverse visitors (Kidd, 2011; Sandell, 1998).

Prominent cultural institutions like the Eugene Science Center, the Chicago Children's Museum, the Boston Children's Museum, and The Metropolitan Museum of Art in New York have incorporated social narratives into their accessibility resources (Alexander et al., 2017; Schwartzman & Knowles, 2022). These narratives are embedded on their websites and can be downloaded and printed as PDFs, making them easily accessible to visitors (e.g., https://bostonchildrensmuseum.org/visit/accessibility/). By utilizing storytelling strategies as therapeutic and educational interventions, these institutions aim to provide support to the target population (Ioannides, 2016). The social narratives are presented in a concise format, incorporating visual aids and text to guide individuals and provide reassurance about what to expect in specific social events, exchanges, or activities (McCoy et al., 2014).

These resources serve as valuable materials for promoting the development of autonomy and social skills among individuals with ASC. They assist in familiarizing visitors with routines, understanding rules, and establishing expectations, ultimately enhancing their overall museum experience (Kisiel, 2003). By equipping individuals with knowledge and strategies to navigate social situations, social narratives play a vital role in facilitating a sense of comfort and inclusion for the population (Dawson, 2014).

Regrettably, the current format of social stories predominantly relies on print media, which limits their accessibility and fails to fully leverage the potential of digital and virtual interventions (Cordón-García et al., 2013). To truly address the daily needs of individuals beyond the museum context, it is essential to explore new options that align with modern technological advancements. In response to this challenge, innovative approaches are emerging, such as the utilization of new, immersive technologies (Tsiviltidou & Vavoula, 2023).

One notable development in this realm is the application of Wearable Immersive Virtual Reality (WIVR) technology, which has led to the creation of an immersive social story known as the Wearable Immersive Social Story (WISS) (Garzotto et al., 2018b). By incorporating AR and VR into social narratives, the WISS takes advantage of 360° videos that include interactive elements. Through visual cues comprising audio, images, and geometric shapes, these immersive experiences become more engaging and entertaining, allowing individuals to gain a comprehensive understanding of the social expectations associated with visiting specific institutions (Sami et al., 2023).

As digital media continues to expand its presence within museums, incorporating multimedia elements such as images, videos, and audio, the broader adoption of VR presents an opportunity to provide wider support for individuals with ASC (Rahaman et al., 2023). However, it is important to note that immersive and wearable social stories, including those employing AR and VR, are primarily utilized within therapeutic and educational interventions for individuals with autism. Their applications extend beyond museum contexts and encompass various scenarios, such as teaching students essential skills like road safety (Josman et al., 2008).

While the potential of AR and VR technologies in the realm of social stories is promising, further research and development are necessary to ensure their integration into museum environments (Geroimenko, 2020). By embracing the possibilities offered by these immersive and interactive digital tools, museums can create more inclusive and engaging experiences for individuals with ASC, ultimately enhancing their overall access to cultural heritage. Moreover, as technological advancements continue to progress, the opportunities for leveraging AR and VR in social narratives will likely expand, opening new avenues for supporting neurodiverse individuals in diverse contexts.

2.4 Community Storytelling

Community engagement plays a crucial role in cultural heritage, and its significance cannot be overstated, especially when it comes to community storytelling in museums and heritage sites. It is increasingly recognized that cultural heritage is a collective endeavor, involving both institutions and the communities they serve. Museums and heritage sites strive to foster strong connections with these communities to ensure that diverse

Table 2.6 Examples of community storytelling in museums

Museum	Community storytelling example
The Smithsonian National Museum of American History	The Smithsonian National Museum of American History invites community members to share their personal stories and experiences related to American history. These stories are collected and showcased through exhibitions, oral histories, and digital platforms, highlighting the diverse perspectives and voices of the community.
The Canadian Museum for Human Rights	The Canadian Museum for Human Rights actively engages with local communities to gather and present their stories of human rights struggles and triumphs. Through community partnerships, the museum hosts storytelling events, workshops, and exhibitions that allow community members to share their lived experiences and create a collective narrative.
The Museum of the City of New York	The Museum of the City of New York conducts community storytelling projects that document the stories and histories of different neighborhoods in the city. These projects involve collaboration with local residents, organizations, and schools to collect and share personal narratives that reflect the rich cultural heritage of each community.
The National Museum of African American History and Culture	The National Museum of African American History and Culture actively engages with the African American community to collect and preserve their stories. Through oral history initiatives, community dialogues, and digital platforms, the museum amplifies the voices and experiences of African Americans, fostering a sense of community storytelling and connection.
The Museum of London	The Museum of London hosts community-led exhibitions and projects that highlight the stories and experiences of Londoners from diverse backgrounds. By partnering with local community groups and organizations, the museum provides a platform for community members to share their narratives and contribute to the museum's collective storytelling.

voices are heard, respected, and celebrated, resulting in a more inclusive and authentic representation of cultural heritage (Flinn, 2011).

Facilitating community storytelling is a powerful method for engaging with local communities and encouraging their active participation in shaping the narratives and experiences within museums and heritage sites (Table 2.6). These projects provide a platform for individuals to share their personal stories, experiences, and memories, contributing to a collective understanding of history and culture (Sylaiou & Dafiotis, 2020). By amplifying these voices, museums and heritage sites create valuable opportunities for diverse perspectives to be heard, recognized, and integrated into the broader cultural heritage narrative (Zhao et al., 2023). This approach fosters a sense of ownership, pride, and belonging within communities while enriching the cultural heritage landscape with a more comprehensive and inclusive representation of shared history.

One notable illustration of community storytelling is the Indian Memory Project, an endeavor that invites individuals from all over India to contribute their family photographs and narratives, capturing personal histories and experiences within the Indian subcontinent (https://www.indianmemoryproject.com/). The project encompasses a wide range of stories, encompassing themes such as migration, cultural traditions, and significant historical events. Through this participatory approach, the project strives to create a multifaceted and inclusive representation of Indian history and culture by empowering people to share their own narratives (Yadav, 2020).

In a similar vein, the Crossing Borders, Bridging Generations Oral History project by the Center for Brooklyn History focuses specifically on collecting and sharing stories of immigration and the diverse experiences of communities in Brooklyn (https://oralhistory.brooklynhistory.org/collections/crossing-borders-bridging-generations-oral-history-collection/). Through various methods such as oral history interviews, public programs, and exhibitions, the project documents the narratives of individuals and families who have migrated to the borough. By delving into themes of identity, belonging, and cultural exchange, the initiative sheds light on the profound impact of personal stories in comprehending the intricate dynamics of migration (McClurken, 2016).

The Canadian Museum for Human Rights has also collected and shared oral stories, which centers around community storytelling related to the theme of human rights (Fig. 2.7) (https://humanrights.ca/). Collaborating with a wide range of groups, including Indigenous communities, LGBTQ+ communities, and newcomers, the museum aims to collect and present narratives that illuminate struggles, resilience, and triumphs in the pursuit of human rights. By amplifying the voices of individuals and communities, the project fosters empathy, understanding, and collective action toward social change (Dirk Moses, 2012).

The Smithsonian's Stories from Main Street initiative serves as another notable example, actively working to document and preserve the histories and experiences of diverse communities throughout the United States (https://museumonmainstreet.org/stories). Through partnerships with local organizations and individuals, the initiative collects oral histories,

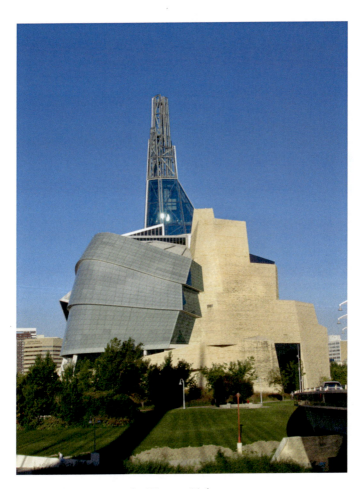

Fig. 2.7 Canadian Museum for Human Rights

photographs, and artifacts that reflect the lived experiences and cultural traditions of these communities. By involving community members as active participants and custodians of their own heritage, the Smithsonian cultivates a sense of ownership and pride within these communities while enriching the museum's understanding of the diverse cultural expressions across the nation (Ford, 2020).

Likewise, the Museum of Vancouver's *Our Stories Live Here* exhibition focuses on engaging with local communities and empowering them to share their narratives (https://museumofvancouver.ca/our-stories-live-here). Employing digital storytelling techniques, the project captures and presents the stories of individuals and communities in Vancouver using multimedia elements like videos, photographs, and personal accounts. Through these immersive experiences, the project creates a multidimensional depiction of Vancouver's cultural fabric, fostering a sense of belonging, connection, and shared history among local residents and stakeholders (Anderson, 2019).

Moreover, community storytelling projects not only contribute to a more inclusive cultural heritage, but they also have the potential to generate social impact and positive change within communities. By providing a platform for individuals to share their stories, museums and heritage sites create opportunities for dialogue, empathy, and understanding (Ghahramani et al., 2020). These examples demonstrate the power of collective narratives in promoting a sense of belonging, identity, and shared history within cultural heritage contexts. By actively involving communities in the process of storytelling, museums and heritage sites can break down barriers, challenge dominant narratives, and create spaces where diverse voices are heard and celebrated. Community storytelling not only enriches the cultural heritage experience but also strengthens the connection between institutions and the communities they serve (Yeh et al., 2021).

Institutions have access to valuable resources that can greatly enhance their storytelling efforts and create immersive experiences for visitors. One such resource is The Automatic Museum Guide, a revolutionary technology designed specifically for museums (https://locatify.com/automatic-museum-guide/). This innovative app empowers curators to create fully immersive multimedia experiences, enabling them to engage visitors through seamless navigation, guidance, and narration. With The Automatic Museum Guide, visitors can explore exhibits at their own pace, and as they move through the museum, audio and other content are triggered automatically, enhancing their understanding and enjoyment of the artworks and artifacts. This technology offers a new level of interactivity and engagement, allowing museums to captivate and educate their audiences in a dynamic and personalized way (Wacker et al., 2016).

If developing an app in-house, best practices would recommend the following considerations. Incorporating mindful practices and promoting well-being through app development can greatly enhance the museum experience. Drawing inspiration from initiatives like MoMA's Artful Practices for Well-Being, developers can consider creating apps that encourage mindful walks and exploration of museum gardens (Schall et al., 2018). These apps can provide prompts, activities, and reflections that help visitors cultivate a deeper connection with their surroundings and discover art inspiration in everyday experiences. By offering features such as guided mindful walks, prompts for observation and reflection, and access to relevant artworks in the museum's collection, visitors can engage in a more contemplative and enriching museum visit. This integration of mindfulness and art appreciation creates an opportunity for visitors to enhance their well-being and develop a greater appreciation for the beauty and inspiration found in their surroundings (Sheldon, 2020).

Community engagement and storytelling are essential components of a vibrant and inclusive cultural heritage landscape. By facilitating community storytelling projects, museums and heritage sites enable diverse voices to be heard, celebrated, and integrated into the broader cultural narrative. These initiatives foster a sense of belonging, identity, and shared history within communities, while challenging dominant narratives and contributing to social impact. By actively engaging with communities, museums can ensure that cultural heritage is a collective endeavor that reflects the diverse experiences and perspectives of the people it serves.

This chapter has delved into the power of storytelling in cultural heritage institutions. Through various forms of storytelling, such as personal narratives, social stories, and community engagement, museums and heritage sites can create meaningful connections with visitors and foster a deeper appreciation for cultural heritage. The significance of personal narratives in allowing individuals to share their unique perspectives, experiences, and memories has been highlighted. By incorporating personal narratives into exhibitions and programs, museums can humanize history, making it more relatable and engaging for visitors. Personal narratives provide a platform for underrepresented voices to be heard, contributing to a more inclusive and diverse cultural heritage narrative.

Moreover, the use of social stories has proven to be an effective tool in preparing individuals, especially those with autism or sensory sensitivities, for museum visits. By providing clear expectations, visual aids, and contextual information, social stories enable individuals to navigate social situations and unfamiliar environments with confidence and ease.

The chapter has also emphasized the importance of community engagement in cultural heritage institutions. By involving communities in the storytelling process, museums and heritage sites can ensure that their narratives are authentic, representative, and relevant. Community storytelling projects enable individuals to contribute their own stories, experiences, and knowledge, enriching the collective understanding of cultural heritage.

Additionally, the chapter has explored the emerging technologies and digital platforms that enhance storytelling experiences. From immersive storymaps to virtual reality, these innovative tools offer new ways of engaging with cultural heritage and creating immersive and interactive narratives.

In all, storytelling is a fundamental aspect of cultural heritage institutions, connecting people to the past, fostering empathy, and shaping collective identities. By embracing personal narratives, social stories, community engagement, and technological advancements, museums and heritage sites can create inclusive and impactful storytelling experiences that resonate with diverse audiences. Through storytelling, cultural heritage becomes a living, dynamic, and accessible entity, inspiring curiosity, understanding, and a deeper appreciation for our shared human history.

References

Alexander, E. P., Alexander, M., & Decker, J. (2017). *Museums in motion: An introduction to the history and functions of museums.* Rowman & Littlefield.

Anderson, M. (2019). Towards cultural democracy: Museums and their communities. *Museum International, 71*(1–2), 140–149.

Anglin, A. H., Reid, S. W., & Short, J. C. (2023). More than one way to tell a story: A configurational approach to storytelling in crowdfunding. *Entrepreneurship Theory and Practice, 47*(2), 461–494.

Arts, K., Van der Wal, R., & Adams, W. M. (2015). Digital technology and the conservation of nature. *Ambio, 44,* 661–673.

Beck, T. J. (2020). From cybernetic networks to social narratives: Mapping value in mental health systems beyond individual psychopathology. *Journal of Theoretical and Philosophical Psychology, 40*(2), 85.

Black, G. (2005). *The engaging museum: Developing museums for visitor involvement.* Psychology Press.

Black, G. (2012). *Transforming museums in the twenty-first century.* Routledge.

Burdick, A., Drucker, J., Lunenfeld, P., Presner, T., & Schnapp, J. (2016). *Digital_humanities.* MIT Press.

Calabria, V. (2019). Self-reflexivity in oral history research: The role of positionality and emotions. In *Voices of illness: Negotiating meaning and identity* (pp. 271–292). Brill.

Cañas-Bajo, J. (2020). Emotional film experience. In *Emotions in technology design: From experience to ethics* (pp. 105–123). Springer Nature.

Cecilia, R. R. (2021). COVID-19 pandemic: Threat or opportunity for blind and partially sighted museum visitors? *Journal of Conservation and Museum Studies, 19*(1).

Charitonos, K., Blake, C., Scanlon, E., & Jones, A. (2012). Museum learning via social and mobile technologies: (How) can online interactions enhance the visitor experience? *British Journal of Educational Technology, 43*(5), 802–819.

Clouder, L., Karakus, M., Cinotti, A., Ferreyra, M. V., Fierros, G. A., & Rojo, P. (2020). Neurodiversity in higher education: A narrative synthesis. *Higher Education, 80*(4), 757–778.

Coenen, T., Mostmans, L., & Naessens, K. (2013). MuseUs: Case study of a pervasive cultural heritage serious game. *Journal on Computing and Cultural Heritage (JOCCH), 6*(2), 1–19.

Cordón-García, J. A., Alonso-Arévalo, J., Gómez-Díaz, R., & Linder, D. (2013). *Social reading: Platforms, applications, clouds and tags.* Elsevier.

Dawson, E. (2014). Equity in informal science education: Developing an access and equity framework for science museums and science centres. *Studies in Science Education, 50*(2), 209–247.

Dias, D. (2022). Thinker, learner, and practitioner: Using an insider's lens to explore critical, cultural, and global consciousness through multicultural literature. *Language and Literacy, 24*(1), 41–59.

Dionisio, M., & Nisi, V. (2021). Leveraging Transmedia storytelling to engage tourists in the understanding of the destination's local heritage. *Multimedia Tools and Applications, 80*(26–27), 34813–34841.

Dirk Moses, A. (2012). The Canadian Museum for Human Rights: The 'uniqueness of the Holocaust' and the question of genocide. *Journal of Genocide Research, 14*(2), 215–238.

Dohoney, R. (2020). The Chicago sound show at the smart museum of art, the University of Chicago. *Sound Studies, 6*(2), 271–274.

Eardley, A. F., Mineiro, C., Neves, J., & Ride, P. (2016). Redefining access: Embracing multimodality, memorability and shared experience in museums. *Curator: The Museum Journal, 59*(3), 263–286.

Echavarria, K. R., Samaroudi, M., Dibble, L., Silverton, E., & Dixon, S. (2022). Creative experiences for engaging communities with cultural heritage through place-based narratives. *ACM Journal on Computing and Cultural Heritage (JOCCH), 15*(2), 1–19.

El-Sayyad, N. (2019, April). Role of sensory maps in cultural planning to shape the future of deteriorated heritage sites. In *8th International Conference "ARCHCAIRO8:" Building the Future "Now"–Rights to Better Living, Architecture and Contexts* (pp. 8–10).

Fakfare, P., Cho, G., Hwang, H., & Manosuthi, N. (2021). Examining the sensory impressions, value perception, and behavioral responses of tourists: The case of floating markets in Thailand. *Journal of Travel & Tourism Marketing*, *38*(7), 666–681.

Filov, K. (2012). Oral history interview project witnesses, collaborators and perpetrators, project in Macedonia.

Fletcher, T. S., Wiskera, E. S., Wilbur, L. H., & Garcia, N. M. (2022). The sensory totes programme: Sensory-friendly autism program innovations designed to meet COVID-19 challenges. *World Federation of Occupational Therapists Bulletin*, *78*(1), 44–52.

Flinn, A. (2011). Archival activism: Independent and community-led archives, radical public history and the heritage professions. *InterActions: UCLA Journal of Education and Information Studies*, *7*(2).

Ford, E. (2020). Profession-based learning and collaborative community projects with the Smithsonian's Museum on Main Street Program. In *Leading professional development: Growing librarians for the digital age* (p. 101). Bloomsbury Academic.

Gao, B. W., Zhu, C., Song, H., & Dempsey, I. M. B. (2022). Interpreting the perceptions of authenticity in virtual reality tourism through postmodernist approach. *Information Technology & Tourism*, *24*(1), 31–55.

Garzotto, F., Gelsomini, M., Matarazzo, V., Messina, N., & Occhiuto, D. (2018a). Designing wearable immersive "social stories" for persons with neurodevelopmental disorder. In *Universal access in human-computer interaction. Methods, technologies, and users: 12th International Conference, UAHCI 2018, held as part of HCI International 2018, Las Vegas, NV, USA, July 15–20, 2018, Proceedings, Part I 12* (pp. 517–529). Springer International Publishing.

Garzotto, F., Matarazzo, V., Messina, N., Gelsomini, M., & Riva, C. (2018b, October). Improving museum accessibility through storytelling in wearable immersive virtual reality. In *2018 3rd Digital Heritage International Congress (DigitalHERITAGE) held jointly with 2018 24th International Conference on Virtual Systems & Multimedia (VSMM 2018)* (pp. 1–8). IEEE.

Geroimenko, V. (2020). *Augmented reality in education*. Springer.

Ghahramani, L., McArdle, K., & Fatorić, S. (2020). Minority community resilience and cultural heritage preservation: A case study of the gullah geechee community. *Sustainability*, *12*(6), 2266.

Giglitto, D. (2014). Using wiki software to enhance community empowerment by building digital archives for intangible cultural heritage. In *Euro Med 2014, intangible cultural heritage documentation* (pp. 267–277).

Goodson, L., & Ralph, S. (2020). Dyane Smokorowski: Expanding teachers' professional learning networks means greater options for students. *Educational Considerations*, *46*(1), 2.

Gretzel, U., & Koo, C. (2021). Smart tourism cities: A duality of place where technology supports the convergence of touristic and residential experiences. *Asia Pacific Journal of Tourism Research, 26*(4), 352–364.

Hadley, B. (2022). A 'Universal Design' for audiences with disabilities? In *Routledge companion to audiences and the performing arts* (pp. 177–189). Routledge.

Harrell, M. H., & Kotecki, E. (2015). The flipped museum: Leveraging technology to deepen learning. *Journal of Museum Education, 40*(2), 119–130.

Harter, L. M., Yamasaki, J., & Kerr, A. M. (2021). Narrative features, forms, and functions: Telling stories to foster well-being, humanize healthcare, and catalyze change 1. In *The Routledge handbook of health communication* (pp. 47–60). Routledge.

Henderson, J. (2019). Oceans without history? Marine cultural heritage and the sustainable development agenda. *Sustainability, 11*(18), 5080.

Hoffman, A., Gobel, S., Schneider, O., & Iurgel, I. (2008). Storytelling-based edutainment applications. In *Online and distance learning: Concepts, methodologies, tools, and applications* (pp. 1439–1460). IGI Global.

Holcombe-James, I. (2022). Digital access, skills, and dollars: Applying a framework to digital exclusion in cultural institutions. *Cultural Trends, 31*(3), 240–256.

Howard, G. S. (1991). Culture tales: A narrative approach to thinking, cross-cultural psychology, and psychotherapy. *American Psychologist, 46*(3), 187.

Hur, J. W., & Suh, S. (2012). Making learning active with interactive whiteboards, podcasts, and digital storytelling in ELL classrooms. *Computers in the Schools, 29*(4), 320–338.

Hymes, D. (2003). *Ethnography, linguistics, narrative inequality: Toward an understanding of voice.* Taylor & Francis.

Ioannides, E. (2016). Museums as therapeutic environments and the contribution of art therapy. *Museum International, 68*(3–4), 98–109.

Izzo, M. V., & Bauer, W. M. (2015). Universal design for learning: Enhancing achievement and employment of STEM students with disabilities. *Universal Access in the Information Society, 14*, 17–27.

Jordan, P., & Fiebig, A. (2020, October). New descriptors for capturing perceptions within historic soundscapes. In *INTER-NOISE and NOISE-CON Congress and Conference Proceedings* (Vol. 261, No. 3, pp. 3489–3496). Institute of Noise Control Engineering.

Josman, N., Ben-Chaim, H. M., Friedrich, S., & Weiss, P. L. (2008). Effectiveness of virtual reality for teaching street-crossing skills to children and adolescents with autism. *International Journal on Disability and Human Development, 7*(1), 49–56.

Katifori, A., Perry, S., Vayanou, M., Antoniou, A., Ioannidis, I. P., McKinney, S., et al. (2020). "Let them talk!" Exploring guided group interaction in digital storytelling experiences. *Journal on Computing and Cultural Heritage (JOCCH), 13*(3), 1–30.

Kelly, E., Manning, D. T. A., Boye, S., Rice, C., Owen, D., Stonefish, S., & Stonefish, M. (2021). Elements of a counter-exhibition: Excavating and countering a Canadian history and legacy of eugenics. *Journal of the History of the Behavioral Sciences, 57*(1), 12–33.

Kidd, J. (2011). Enacting engagement online: Framing social media use for the museum. *Information Technology & People, 24*(1), 64–77.

King, B., & Lord, B. (Eds.). (2015). *The manual of museum learning*. Rowman & Littlefield.

Kisiel, J. F. (2003). *Revealing teacher agendas: An examination of teacher motivations and strategies for conducting museum fieldtrips*. University of Southern California.

Korzun, D. G., Marchenkov, S. A., Vdovenko, A. S., & Petrina, O. B. (2016). A semantic approach to designing information services for smart museums. *International Journal of Embedded and Real-Time Communication Systems (IJERTCS), 7*(2), 15–34.

Krishnasamy, R., Selvadurai, V., & Vistisen, P. (2020, December). Designing context-aware mobile systems for self-guided exhibition sites. In *International Conference on ArtsIT, Interactivity and Game Creation* (pp. 21–44). Springer International Publishing.

Ladson-Billings, G. (2021). I'm here for the hard re-set: Post pandemic pedagogy to preserve our culture. *Equity & Excellence in Education, 54*(1), 68–78.

Langran, E., & DeWitt, J. (2020). *Navigating place-based learning*. Springer International Publishing.

Lanir, J., Kuflik, T., Dim, E., Wecker, A. J., & Stock, O. (2013). The influence of a location-aware mobile guide on museum visitors' behavior. *Interacting with Computers, 25*(6), 443–460.

Li, D., Ge, X., Ma, Q., Mehra, B., Liu, J., Han, T., & Liu, C. (2022). Evaluating three touch gestures for moving objects across folded screens. *Proceedings of the ACM on Interactive, Mobile, Wearable and Ubiquitous Technologies, 6*(3), 1–28.

Liu, Y., Ma, X., Shu, L., Yang, Q., Zhang, Y., Huo, Z., & Zhou, Z. (2020). Internet of things for noise mapping in smart cities: State of the art and future directions. *IEEE Network, 34*(4), 112–118.

Manik, H. F. G. G., Christanti, R., & Setiawan, W. (2022). Knowledge management and community-based enterprise: An initiative to preserve the shadow puppet traditional knowledge in Yogyakarta, Indonesia. *VINE Journal of Information and Knowledge Management Systems*.

Matsiola, M., Dimoulas, C., Kalliris, G., & Veglis, A. A. (2018). Augmenting user interaction experience through embedded multimodal media agents in social networks. In *Information retrieval and management: Concepts, methodologies, tools, and applications* (pp. 1972–1993). IGI Global.

Mazzocchi, F. (2022). Diving deeper into the concept of 'cultural heritage' and its relationship with epistemic diversity. *Social Epistemology, 36*(3), 393–406.

McClurken, J. (Ed.). (2016). Brooklyn waterfront history: Crossing borders, bridging generations and TeachArchives.org. *Journal of American History, 102*(4), 1280–1282.

McCoy, J., Treanor, M., Samuel, B., Reed, A. A., Mateas, M., & Wardrip-Fruin, N. (2014). Social story worlds with Comme il Faut. *IEEE Transactions on Computational Intelligence and AI in Games, 6*(2), 97–112.

Michalakis, K., & Caridakis, G. (2022). Context awareness in cultural heritage applications: A survey. *ACM Journal on Computing and Cultural Heritage (JOCCH), 15*(2), 1–31.

Montagud, M., Orero, P., & Matamala, A. (2020). Culture 4 all: Accessibility-enabled cultural experiences through immersive VR360 content. *Personal and Ubiquitous Computing, 24*(6), 887–905.

Mortara, M., Catalano, C. E., Bellotti, F., Fiucci, G., Houry-Panchetti, M., & Petridis, P. (2014). Learning cultural heritage by serious games. *Journal of Cultural Heritage, 15*(3), 318–325.

Ngarimu-Cameron, R. H. (2019). Weaving the two cultures of Aotearoa/New Zealand together: From the art of making traditional off-loom garments to a contemporary practice of on-loom weaving. *TEXTILE, 17*(2), 158–167.

Okanovic, V., Ivkovic-Kihic, I., Boskovic, D., Mijatovic, B., Prazina, I., Skaljo, E., & Rizvic, S. (2022). Interaction in extended reality applications for cultural heritage. *Applied Sciences, 12*(3), 1241.

Olaz, X., Garcia, R., Ortiz, A., Marichal, S., Villadangos, J., Ardaiz, O., & Marzo, A. (2022). An interdisciplinary design of an interactive cultural heritage visit for in-situ, mixed reality and affective experiences. *Multimodal Technologies and Interaction, 6*(7), 59.

Parker, C., Yoo, S., Jenek, W., & Lee, Y. (2021). Augmenting cities and architecture with immersive technologies: Conference workshop proceedings.

Pattison, M., & Stedmon, A. W. (2006). Inclusive design and human factors: Designing mobile phones for older users. *PsychNology Journal, 4*(3), 267–284.

Phoenix, A. (2022). Humanizing racialization: Social psychology in a time of unexpected transformational conjunctions. *British Journal of Social Psychology, 61*(1), 1–18.

Pilgrim, J., & Pilgrim, J. M. (2021). Immersive storytelling: Virtual reality as a cross-disciplinary digital storytelling tool. In *Connecting disciplinary literacy and digital storytelling in K-12 education* (pp. 192–215). IGI Global.

Podsukhina, E., Smith, M. K., & Pinke-Sziva, I. (2022). A critical evaluation of mobile guided tour apps: Motivators and inhibitors for tour guides and customers. *Tourism and Hospitality Research, 22*(4), 414–424.

Pozzi-Thanner, E. (2005). Storycorps. *The Oral History Review, 32*(2), 103–105.

Pujol, L., Roussou, M., Poulou, S., Balet, O., Vayanou, M., & Ioannidis, Y. (2012, March). Personalizing interactive digital storytelling in archaeological museums: The CHESS project. In *40th Annual Conference of Computer Applications and Quantitative Methods in Archaeology* (pp. 93–100). Amsterdam University Press.

Qiu, M., Jin, X., & Scott, N. (2021). Sensescapes and attention restoration in nature-based tourism: Evidence from China and Australia. *Tourism Management Perspectives, 39*, 100855.

Rahaman, H., Champion, E., & McMeekin, D. (2023). Outside Inn: Exploring the heritage of a historic hotel through 360-panoramas. *Heritage, 6*(5), 4380–4410.

Ricciardelli, D. (2006). *A social skills program evaluation: Will social stories combine with a traditional social skills curriculum increase pro-social behavior in autistic children?* Fairleigh Dickinson University.

Rodriguez, M., & Kross, E. (2023). Sensory emotion regulation. *Trends in Cognitive Sciences*.

Roe, J., & McCay, L. (2021). *Restorative cities: Urban design for mental health and wellbeing*. Bloomsbury Publishing.

Roza, Z., & Rustam, S. (2023). Digital storytelling to facilitate academic public speaking skills: Case study in culturally diverse multilingual classroom. *Journal of Computers in Education*, 1–28.

Sabiescu, A., & Charatzopoulou, K. (2015). Shaping a culture of lifelong learning for young audiences: A case study on the Samsung Digital Discovery Centre at the British museum. *RICHES EU project deliverable*.

Sami, H., Hammoud, A., Arafeh, M., Wazzeh, M., Arisdakessian, S., Chahoud, M., ... & Guizani, M. (2023). The metaverse: Survey, trends, novel pipeline ecosystem & future directions. *arXiv preprint arXiv:2304.09240*.

Sandell, R. (1998). Museums as agents of social inclusion. *Museum Management and Curatorship, 17*(4), 401–418.

Schall, A., Tesky, V. A., Adams, A. K., & Pantel, J. (2018). Art museum-based intervention to promote emotional well-being and improve quality of life in people with dementia: The ARTEMIS project. *Dementia, 17*(6), 728–743.

Schwartzman, R., & Knowles, C. (2022). Expanding accessibility: Sensory sensitive programming for museums. *Curator: The Museum Journal, 65*(1), 95–116.

Shankar, G. (2022). Authoring stories of freedom: Concept, process and product from the American Folklife Center's archive. *The Journal of Cinema and Media Studies, 62*(7).

Sheldon, P. J. (2020). Designing tourism experiences for inner transformation. *Annals of Tourism Research, 83*, 102935.

Shopes, L. (2019). "Insights and Oversights": Reflections on the documentary tradition and the theoretical turn in oral history. *The Oral History Review*.

Spitzer, M., Nanic, I., & Ebner, M. (2018). Distance learning and assistance using smart glasses. *Education Sciences, 8*(1), 21.

Swaminathan, R., & Mulvihill, T. M. (2022). Theoretical, methodological, and ethical issues in oral history projects. In *Oral history and qualitative methodologies* (pp. 18–37). Routledge.

Sylaiou, S., & Dafiotis, P. (2020). Storytelling in virtual museums: Engaging a multitude of voices. In *Visual computing for cultural heritage* (pp. 369–388). Springer.

Terrado, M., Calvo, L., & Christel, I. (2022). Towards more effective visualisations in climate services: Good practices and recommendations. *Climatic Change, 172*(1–2), 18.

Theriault, S., & Jones, B. R. (2018). Constructing knowledge together: Collaborating with and understanding young adults with autism. *Journal of Museum Education, 43*(4), 365–374.

Torija, A. J., & Clark, C. (2021). A psychoacoustic approach to building knowledge about human response to noise of unmanned aerial vehicles. *International Journal of Environmental Research and Public Health, 18*(2), 682.

Tsiviltidou, Z., & Vavoula, G. (2023). Digital stories with the online collection of the V&A for inquiry-based learning. *ACM Journal on Computing and Cultural Heritage, 16*(1), 1–23.

Verde, D., Romero, L., Faria, P. M., & Paiva, S. (2022, September). Architecture for museums location-based content delivery using augmented reality and Beacons. In *2022 IEEE International Smart Cities Conference (ISC2)* (pp. 1–6). IEEE.

Vrettakis, E., Katifori, A., Kyriakidi, M., Koukouli, M., Boile, M., Glenis, A., et al. (2023). Personalization in digital ecomuseums: The case of Pros-Eleusis. *Applied Sciences, 13*(6), 3903.

Wacker, P., Kreutz, K., Heller, F., & Borchers, J. (2016, May). Maps and location: Acceptance of modern interaction techniques for audio guides. In *Proceedings of the 2016 CHI Conference on Human Factors in Computing Systems* (pp. 1067–1071).

Walker, V. L., & Smith, C. G. (2015). Training paraprofessionals to support students with disabilities: A literature review. *Exceptionality, 23*(3), 170–191.

Watermeyer, R. (2012). A conceptualisation of the post-museum as pedagogical space. *Journal of Science Communication, 11*(1), A02.

Whitebeach, T. (2014). Three madi projects in Tasmania. *Oral History Australia Journal, 36*, 16–22.

Yadav, A. (2020). All photographs are personal: Indian Memory Project. *Photography and Culture, 13*(3–4), 433–443.

Yeh, J. H. Y., Lin, S. C., Lai, S. C., Huang, Y. H., Yi-fong, C., Lee, Y. T., & Berkes, F. (2021). Taiwanese indigenous cultural heritage and revitalization: Community practices and local development. *Sustainability, 13*(4), 1799.

Zallio, M., & Clarkson, P. J. (2022). The inclusion, diversity, equity and accessibility audit. A post-occupancy evaluation method to help design the buildings of tomorrow. *Building and Environment, 217*, 109058.

Zhao, Y., Pettijohn, B. J., Wang, A. Y., Keehn, D. P., Dai, A., Dang, J., & Murray, J. H. (2023). Exploring location-based AR narrative design for historic site. In *PRESENCE: Virtual and augmented reality* (pp. 1–45). MIT Press.

Zhong, Z., Coates, H., & Jinghuan, S. (Eds.). (2019). *Innovations in Asian higher education*. Routledge.

CHAPTER 3

Inclusivity & Environment

Creating inclusive and accessible environments within cultural heritage institutions is a central focus of this chapter. The main arguments revolve around the implementation of practical strategies and tools to achieve this goal. Sensory kits are highlighted as valuable resources that provide visitors with sensory sensitivities and the necessary tools to engage with heritage spaces effectively. Social stories are presented as a structured framework that aids individuals in understanding and navigating social situations within cultural heritage contexts. The integration of sensory maps is discussed, emphasizing their role in assisting visitors with planning and navigating heritage sites by providing sensory information about the environment. Additionally, the chapter explores the design and implementation of immersive storymaps, which combine narrative elements with interactive experiences to deepen visitors' connection to cultural heritage. Through the utilization of these innovative approaches, heritage professionals can create more inclusive and accessible environments, ultimately fostering a more engaging and meaningful experience for all visitors.

3.1 Sensory Kits

Sensory kits play a vital role in enhancing accessibility and inclusivity within cultural heritage institutions, particularly for visitors with sensory sensitivities or processing challenges. These kits are carefully designed collections of tools and materials that aim to support individuals in engaging with and navigating heritage spaces more effectively. By providing sensory input and accommodating specific needs, sensory kits create a more welcoming and inclusive environment for all visitors (Schwartzman & Knowles, 2022).

The design and implementation of sensory kits have evolved over the years to cater to the diverse needs of individuals with sensory sensitivities. Initially, sensory kits primarily included tactile and visual elements, such as textured objects, visual cues, and calming sensory items. These early iterations recognized the importance of engaging multiple senses to create a supportive environment for individuals who may experience sensory overload or have difficulty processing sensory stimuli (Braden, 2016).

However, as our understanding of sensory sensitivities has deepened, the development of sensory kits has become more nuanced and comprehensive. Modern sensory kits now encompass a wide range of sensory experiences, including auditory, olfactory, and proprioceptive elements. They may include noise-canceling headphones to reduce auditory input, scented materials to evoke specific environments or memories, and weighted or fidget items to provide a sense of grounding and regulation (Harpenau, 2020).

The use cases for sensory kits in museums and heritage contexts are diverse and adaptable to various visitor needs. For individuals on the autism spectrum, sensory kits can help create a predictable and controlled environment by offering familiar objects and sensory supports (Fletcher et al., 2022). Visitors with sensory sensitivities may find comfort and reassurance in the presence of sensory tools that promote self-regulation and reduce anxiety. Sensory kits can also benefit individuals with attention difficulties or cognitive impairments by providing tangible and engaging resources that enhance focus and comprehension (Camic & Chatterjee, 2013).

Table 3.1 outlines the contents of a sensory kit specifically designed for neurodiverse visitors, with each item serving a specific purpose to support their sensory needs. The inclusion of noise-canceling headphones aims to reduce auditory input, creating a quiet and calming environment for individuals who are sensitive to noise. The weighted lap pad or blanket provides deep pressure stimulation, offering a sense of grounding and relaxation. Fidget toys, such as sensory balls or textured cards, offer tactile and proprioceptive input, promoting focus and self-regulation.

Visual schedules or social stories are included to support predictability and provide a structured framework for the museum visit, helping

Table 3.1 Standard contents of a sensory kit for neurodiverse visitors

Item	Purpose
Noise-canceling headphones	Reduces auditory input and provides a quiet and calming environment
Weighted lap pad or blanket	Offers deep pressure stimulation for a sense of grounding and relaxation
Fidget toys	Provides tactile and proprioceptive input to promote focus and self-regulation
Visual schedule or social story	Supports predictability and provides a structured framework for the museum visit
Texture cards or sensory balls	Offers tactile stimulation and sensory exploration opportunities
Scented materials	Evokes specific environments or memories through pleasant scents
Stress balls or squeezy toys	Offers a physical outlet for stress and anxiety
Chewable or oral motor tools	Supports oral sensory needs and provides a safe alternative for chewing
Calming essential oil roll-on	Provides a soothing scent for relaxation and emotional support
Communication card or badge	Assists in communication and identification of specific needs or accommodations
Guidebook or brochure	Provides information about the museum or heritage site, including maps and exhibits

individuals understand what to expect and navigate the experience more effectively. Scented materials, such as essential oil roll-ons, can evoke specific environments or memories through pleasant scents, contributing to a multisensory experience. Stress balls or squeezy toys provide a physical outlet for stress and anxiety, allowing individuals to release tension and find comfort.

For individuals with oral sensory needs, chewable or oral motor tools offer a safe alternative for chewing, supporting their oral sensory needs and promoting self-regulation. A communication card or badge assists in communication and helps identify specific needs or accommodations, facilitating effective communication between visitors and museum staff (Fig. 3.1). Guidebooks or brochures provide valuable information about the museum or heritage site, including maps and exhibits, allowing individuals to navigate the space and access relevant information (Beaney, 2020).

Fig. 3.1 Verbal communication card, Columbia River Maritime Museum, Astoria

By including these items in a sensory kit, museums and heritage sites can create a supportive and inclusive environment that addresses the sensory needs of neurodiverse visitors. These items help reduce sensory overload, promote self-regulation, provide comfort, and enhance the overall museum experience for individuals with diverse neurological profiles (Fowler, 2008).

There are several institutions that can provide models for those looking to integrate sensory kits into their accessibility resources. For instance, the British Museum in London and London Natural History Museum provide examples and offer Sensory Backpacks designed for visitors with sensory sensitivities (Giaconi et al., 2021). These backpacks contain noise-canceling headphones, fidget toys, and visual aids to assist individuals in navigating the museum's galleries (https://www.britishmuseum.org/visit/accessibility). Similarly, the Museum of Science and Industry in Manchester, UK, provides Sensory Backpacks that include noise-canceling headphones, stress balls, and tactile objects to enhance the museum experience for visitors with sensory sensitivities (https://www.msimanchester.org.uk/accessibility).

In addition to museums, cultural heritage sites have also embraced the use of sensory kits to cater to the needs of neurodiverse visitors. The Tower of London offers sensory kits containing sensory toys, ear defenders, and a visual guide to support individuals with sensory sensitivities in exploring this historic site (https://www.hrp.org.uk/tower-of-london/visit/accessibility/#sensory-backpacks). The Guggenheim Museum in New York provides sensory kits through their Guggenheim For All Toolkit that are equipped with noise-canceling headphones, fidget toys, and sensory brushes to enhance the museum experience for visitors with sensory sensitivities (https://www.guggenheim.org/accessibility/guggenheim-for-all) (Salthouse, 2017).

These examples demonstrate the commitment of cultural heritage institutions to inclusivity and accessibility by providing sensory kits tailored to the specific needs of neurodiverse visitors. By offering these resources, museums and heritage sites create a more welcoming and accommodating environment, allowing individuals to engage with the exhibits and spaces in a way that suits their sensory preferences and promotes a positive and enriching experience (Nagib & Williams, 2017).

Furthermore, heritage sites have incorporated sensory kits to enhance visitor experiences in outdoor or historical environments. These kits may include tools, such as magnifying glasses, binoculars, or scent containers, to enrich sensory exploration of natural landscapes or archaeological sites. The Rocky Mountain National Park in the United States offers sensory backpacks containing items, such as field guides, activity booklets, and nature-themed sensory objects, to engage visitors with different sensory preferences and abilities (Frank, 2013).

Sensory kits are instrumental in creating accessible and inclusive environments within cultural heritage institutions. By addressing the specific sensory needs of visitors, these kits enable individuals with sensory sensitivities or processing challenges to engage more effectively with heritage spaces. The evolution of sensory kits, expanding beyond tactile and visual elements to encompass a broader range of sensory experiences, reflects a deeper understanding of diverse sensory sensitivities (Ceraso, 2014). The successful implementation of sensory kits in museums and heritage contexts demonstrates their potential to support visitors, promote inclusivity, and enhance the overall cultural heritage experience for all.

3.2 Wayfinding and Sensory Maps

Wayfinding plays a crucial role in creating inclusive and accessible environments for neurodiverse audiences. Individuals with neurodiverse conditions often face challenges related to spatial orientation, navigation, and sensory processing (Zallio & Clarkson, 2021). By incorporating augmented reality (AR), GPS technology, and sensory maps, museums and other cultural institutions can provide valuable support for neurodiverse visitors (Fig. 3.2) (Anderson, 2019). Through an investigation into best practices for wayfinding design based on research in the field, institutions and organizations can adopt strategies to serve a more diverse population (Table 3.2).

Wayfinding Technologies

Research on visual impairment can provide valuable insights and guidance for creating effective wayfinding materials for the neurodiverse population (Pionke, 2017). Visually impaired individuals face unique challenges in

Fig. 3.2 MTA launches app to assist blind and low-vision bus riders

Table 3.2 Best practices for wayfinding design

Principle	Description
Clear and consistent signage	Ensure signage is clear, visible, and easy to understand. Use consistent symbols, fonts, and colors throughout the facility to create a cohesive wayfinding system.
Intuitive path layout	Design paths and routes that are logical and intuitive. Use landmarks, visual cues, and architectural elements to guide visitors along the desired path.
User-centered navigation	Consider the needs and abilities of different users, including those with disabilities or sensory impairments. Provide alternative navigation options such as tactile maps or audible directions to accommodate diverse needs.
Effective information hierarchy	Prioritize information based on its relevance and importance. Use clear headings, labels, and hierarchies to guide visitors through the space and help them locate specific destinations or points of interest.
Adequate lighting	Ensure that the wayfinding system is well-lit to enhance visibility and legibility. Proper lighting helps visitors read signage and navigate the space more easily, especially in areas with low natural light or during nighttime hours.
Digital wayfinding solutions	Incorporate digital technologies, such as interactive kiosks, mobile apps, or touchscreen displays, to provide real-time information, dynamic maps, and personalized navigation assistance.
Regular maintenance	Regularly inspect and maintain the wayfinding system to ensure that signs are in good condition and information is up to date. Repair or replace any damaged or outdated signage to prevent confusion among visitors.

understanding the relationships between navigation items expressed visually. To successfully navigate, users need to develop a mental model of the underlying navigational space. For sighted users, visual cues such as grouping, labeling, text size, color, and formatting offer insights into the intended structure of the navigation space. However, visually impaired individuals rely on linear representations of navigational items and audio cues to form their mental model (Khan & Khusro, 2021).

Tactile and touch information play a crucial role in supporting spatial performance for visually impaired individuals through active touch. Active touch involves the engagement of receptors in the joints, along with the detection of changing patterns on the skin (Palivcová et al., 2020). Tactile information is primarily provided by the hands, palm, and fingers, allowing for the recognition of object form, texture, and location. Low-resolution scanning of the immediate surroundings and surface information through feet provide additional tactile feedback (Sankar et al., 2021). Auditory channels complement touch information by providing cues about events, the presence of objects or people, and estimates of distance within a space. The olfactory channel also contributes additional information related to specific contacts or people (Sekhavat et al., 2022).

Studies indicate that visually impaired individuals employ mainly two spatial strategies: route and map. The route strategy relies on linear recognition of spatial features, while the map strategy takes a holistic approach by encompassing multiple perspectives of the target space (Kuriakose et al., 2022; Real & Araujo, 2019; Simões et al., 2020; Zhao et al., 2020). Understanding these strategies can inform the design of wayfinding materials that align with the cognitive processes of neurodiverse individuals (Percival, 2023).

In the development of assistive technologies, examples such as the Oticon device stand out as one of the pioneering tactile-vision substitution devices. It utilizes a matrix of pins to detect patterns of light and dark as material is moved underneath (Wall & Brewster, 2006). The output is represented through vibrating pens on a tactile display, providing tactile feedback to the user (Kilian et al., 2022). Audio assistive technologies, such as text-to-speech and print text reading machines, also play a significant role in conveying information to individuals with visual impairments (Wallace et al., 2022).

Furthermore, wayfinding materials can be classified into two categories: passive aids and active aids (Huston & Hamburger, 2023). Passive aids provide users with information before their arrival in an environment, while active aids supply information in real-time (Xu et al., 2022). By considering the tactile, auditory, and olfactory channels, along with spatial strategies and assistive technologies, designers can create inclusive and effective wayfinding materials that cater to the diverse needs of the neurodiverse population (Wang & Jeon, 2023).

Exhibition design and wayfinding play a crucial role in creating inclusive and accessible environments for individuals with a variety of sensory processing conditions. For instance, ASC cognition is often characterized by a tendency to be visual thinkers rather than verbal thinkers (Grandin & Panek, 2014). This means that individuals often rely on visual processing to construct meaning, elaborate on information, and solidify memories. Therefore, exhibition design should incorporate visual elements that effectively communicate information and engage individuals with ASC (Broomfield et al., 2022).

Thus, one important consideration in exhibition design for individuals with ASC is the need for order, precise visual organization, and reliable predictability. These individuals thrive in environments that offer clear structure and consistency (Grandin & Panek, 2014). By providing visual cues, clear pathways, and well-defined zones, exhibition spaces can help individuals navigate and understand the layout of the environment. Predictable access modes, such as consistent signage and wayfinding systems, also help orient individuals independently within the exhibition space and understand the function connected to a specific place or activity (Seetharaman et al., 2021). Furthermore, the use of digital platforms and online communities can extend the predictability and familiarity beyond the physical visit, allowing individuals to continue engaging with the content and connecting with others in a digital space (Parini & Yus, 2023).

Another important aspect of exhibition design for individuals with ASC is the clarification of symbols, codes, or other socially inferred behavioral signs within the space. People with ASC may have difficulties interpreting implicit social cues and understanding unwritten rules (Grandin & Panek, 2014). By providing explicit and clear visual cues, such as universally recognized symbols and signage, exhibition spaces can help individuals navigate social expectations and interactions more easily. This not only fosters a sense of comfort and confidence within the exhibition environment but also promotes their understanding of the intended meaning and purpose of different areas or exhibits (Roach Anleu & Sarantoulias, 2022).

Of the ways to support wayfinding, AR and GPS have demonstrated their viability. AR, for instance, has proven quite useful by overlaying digital information onto the physical environment (Barakat et al., 2022). This can help individuals with neurodiverse conditions to better understand their surroundings, locate points of interest, and navigate through complex spaces. By using AR technology, visual cues and directions can be presented in a more engaging and intuitive manner, reducing confusion and anxiety (Lee, 2021). GPS technology is another powerful tool for wayfinding, especially in outdoor spaces. By leveraging GPS-enabled devices, museums can provide visitors with real-time navigation assistance, helping them to easily find their desired destinations within the museum grounds or in nearby areas (López Salas, 2021). GPS can also be integrated with interactive maps or apps to provide step-by-step directions and highlight accessible routes for individuals with specific needs (Paratore & Leporini, 2023).

Building on AR and GPS that address the challenges faced by individuals with disabilities in navigating inaccessible environments, additional innovative wayfinding technologies have emerged. Foresight Augmented Reality (FAR) utilizes modern technology, including smartphone apps and a combination of Bluetooth, GPS, and Ultra-Wideband (UWB) technology, to create inclusive and equitable spaces (Karimi & Iordanova, 2021). By deploying highly precise Bluetooth beacons, FAR goes beyond traditional GPS navigation by guiding individuals to specific locations within a facility. These beacons can be strategically placed throughout a venue, directing visitors to important facilities and enhancing their navigation experience (Kunhoth et al., 2020).

Indoor wayfinding can be particularly challenging, with many of us experiencing frustration when trying to locate specific offices or sections within a building. FAR addresses this issue by offering dynamic, digitally accessible directories that empower all visitors to find their desired destinations with ease and confidence (Bbosale et al., 2019). By leveraging this technology, individuals with disabilities can navigate indoor spaces independently, eliminating barriers to access and promoting a sense of autonomy.

Furthermore, wayfinding technology is not limited to indoor environments. Parks, walking trails, zoos, and other outdoor locations also need to ensure accessibility for all visitors (Bandukda et al., 2020). FAR is one such solution that provides a cost-effective way for installing their technology in outdoor spaces, giving a voice to these environments and creating enjoyable and safe experiences for individuals with disabilities (Padfield et al., 2023).

Researchers at Ajman University in the United Arab Emirates are also working on the development of smart glasses that integrate artificial intelligence (AI) capabilities (Arar et al., 2021). These smart glasses have the potential to read text, provide navigational information, and even identify faces. By connecting to a processing unit and operating without an internet connection, these smart glasses aim to enhance the independence and social inclusion of visually impaired individuals (Ridha & Shehieb, 2021). The facial recognition feature of the smart glasses allows users to identify familiar faces, as the device stores facial images in its cloud system. When encountering someone known to the user, the smart glasses can instantly recognize them in real-time, providing valuable information and facilitating meaningful interactions (Gacem et al., 2019).

Incorporating these advanced wayfinding technologies not only improves navigation for individuals with disabilities but also fosters a more inclusive and accessible environment for all visitors. By leveraging the power of augmented reality, Bluetooth beacons, and AI-enabled devices, museums and other cultural institutions can create spaces where everyone can navigate with confidence, independence, and a sense of belonging.

Sensory Maps
Sensory maps, also known as visual stories, play a valuable role in preparing visitors for their onsite experience at cultural heritage institutions. These maps provide descriptions and specific information about what visitors can expect in different situations, events, or activities within the museum environment. By highlighting sensory-friendly areas and features, such as quiet spaces (Fig. 3.3), low lighting, and tactile exhibits, sensory maps serve as helpful guides for individuals with autism or sensory processing disorders (SPD) (Gray, 1998).

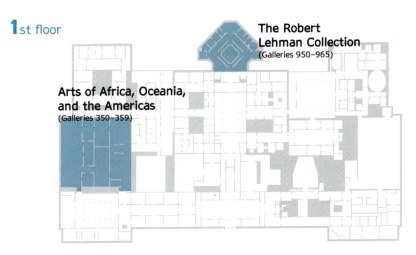

Fig. 3.3 Quiet and less-crowded spaces, sensory-friendly map of The Metropolitan Museum of Art for visitors on the autism pectrum, 2015

Sensory maps are particularly important for neurodiverse audiences who may have heightened sensitivities to sensory stimuli. These maps provide information about the sensory environment, including areas that may be noisy, crowded, or have bright lighting (Fig. 3.4) (Nolan et al., 2023). By including sensory maps, museums can empower neurodiverse visitors to make informed decisions about their visit, allowing them to choose routes and spaces that align with their sensory preferences and comfort levels (Table 3.3).

Research has shown that families with children on the autism spectrum often face challenges related to sensory processing and participation that are 40–90% greater compared to other populations (Mitchell et al., 2015). Even adults who are over-responsive to environmental stimuli describe their museum visits as disorganized, overwhelming, irritating, and distracting, leading them to cope by spending extended periods of time alone in order to regulate their emotional state (Kinnealey et al., 2011). These experiences can result in feelings of isolation and exhaustion.

To address these challenges, sensory maps provide visitors with crucial information about the museum environment in a visual and accessible format. These maps not only enhance predictability but also enable visitors to plan their visit in a way that aligns with their sensory needs and preferences (McLean, 2019). By knowing in advance which areas are more

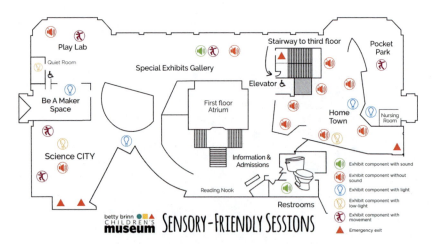

Fig. 3.4 Sensory-friendly sessions, a visit to the museum, Betty Brinn Children's Museum

Table 3.3 Elements for consideration in sensory maps

Element	Description
Visual information	Highlight areas with specific visual characteristics, such as bright lights, contrasting colors, or visual clutter. Indicate visually stimulating or calming areas based on their visual attributes.
Auditory information	Identify areas with varying levels of noise or sound characteristics, such as quiet zones, areas with ambient music, or spaces with potential loud noises.
Tactile information	Note areas with different tactile experiences, such as interactive exhibits, textured surfaces, or objects that can be touched. Indicate areas with tactile materials or hands-on activities.
Olfactory information	Highlight areas with distinctive smells or scents, such as fragrances, natural aromas, or areas with potential strong odors.
Taste information	Specify areas where tasting or sampling experiences are available, such as food and beverage stations or sensory-related exhibits involving taste.
Crowding information	Indicate areas that may be crowded or have a high density of visitors, helping individuals who prefer less crowded spaces plan their routes and avoid overwhelming environments.
Calm and quiet areas	Identify designated quiet or calm areas where visitors can retreat to relax or find respite from sensory stimuli. Provide information on the characteristics of these areas for easy identification.
Accessible facilities	Highlight the locations of accessible facilities, such as restrooms, elevators, ramps, or sensory-friendly rooms, to assist individuals with specific accessibility needs.
Wayfinding information	Include wayfinding elements, such as clear directions, landmarks, and symbols, to help individuals navigate the space and find their way between different sensory areas.
Additional instructions	Provide any additional instructions or considerations for visitors to enhance their sensory experience and ensure their understanding of the map and its symbols.

sensory-friendly or which exhibits have interactive and tactile components, visitors can navigate the museum space more comfortably and engage in experiences that are better suited to their sensory profiles (McLean, 2019).

Sensory maps may include symbols, icons, or colors to represent different sensory elements, such as noise levels, lighting conditions, and tactile experiences (Fig. 3.5). The maps can be presented as physical handouts, downloadable resources on the museum's website, or interactive digital tools that visitors can access through mobile devices or museum kiosks. They can also be tailored to different age groups or specific sensory sensitivities (Cho, 2021).

Fig. 3.5 Sensory symbols, a visit to the museum, Betty Brinn Children's Museum

As the name suggests, "sensory" includes all senses in supporting diverse populations. For instance, research has shown that color plays a crucial role in the sensory experiences of children, even those who are visually impaired. Surprisingly, studies have shown that visually impaired children exhibit an interest in knowing whether objects possess color and inquire about their descriptions (Bollini et al., 2023; Jabbar et al., 2021). This early curiosity demonstrates their innate understanding of the symbolic associations tied to colors. Furthermore, research has found that many legally blind children are capable of perceiving bright and contrasting colors, highlighting their sensitivity to visual stimuli. Color identification can also serve as a powerful social tool, fostering collaboration among children who share similar interests at a basic perceptual level (Pedersini et al., 2023).

To enhance the engagement and understanding of visually impaired children, audio cues can also be utilized in addition to considerations of color identification and associations. One example is the ludic audio cues, which provide auditory cues to help children establish connections between symbolic representations and their everyday experiences (Yoo et al., 2021). By associating specific sounds with colors or objects, these audio cues facilitate a deeper comprehension of color symbolism and foster a sense of inclusivity (Yoo, 2020).

Finally, the integration of tactile elements in exhibition design plays a crucial role in creating inclusive and accessible experiences for visitors, particularly those with visual impairments (Hou, 2023). One notable example of this approach can be seen in the British Museum's efforts, in collaboration with access consultant Barry Ginley, to provide tactile line drawings that enable visually impaired visitors to understand and engage with images (Shaligram, 2019). In the British Gallery, raised lines were strategically installed to outline the edges of structures and highlight significant details within the exhibited objects. Additionally, the design incorporated further raised lines that extended from the outer part of the panel to the letters of the alphabet, indicating important areas of the building. These lines served as tactile guides, directing users to access Braille information (Halder & Squires, 2023).

While the inclusion of tactile elements is a commendable step towards inclusivity, it is important to acknowledge the challenges that may arise in their implementation. In the case of the British Museum, it was noted that the substantial number of raised lines within the tactile line drawings could make it difficult for visitors to follow the images smoothly. Nonetheless, the effort made by institutions like the British Museum and the collaboration with access consultants like Barry Ginley highlight the commitment to providing inclusive experiences for all visitors. Tactile elements in exhibition design not only enhance accessibility but also offer an opportunity for individuals with visual impairments to engage with the exhibited objects and gain a deeper understanding of their form and details through touch (Holloway et al., 2019).

To further improve the effectiveness of tactile elements, ongoing research and collaboration with individuals from the visually impaired community can help inform design decisions. It is essential to ensure that tactile representations are clear, coherent, and easily comprehensible, allowing for a meaningful and inclusive engagement with the exhibited content (Adams, 2021). By incorporating tactile elements into exhibition design, museums and cultural institutions can foster a more inclusive environment where visitors of all abilities can actively participate and connect with the displayed objects. This approach recognizes the importance of sensory diversity and underscores the significance of tactile experiences as a means to enhance accessibility and enrich the cultural engagement of all visitors.

Moreover, tactile globes have also been found to increase engagement among children. These three-dimensional models allow children to explore and interact with geographical features through touch (Poonja et al., 2023). The tactile nature of the globe enables visually impaired children to gain a tactile understanding of the world, enhancing their spatial awareness and geographical knowledge. The tactile globe serves as both an educational tool and a source of fascination for children, promoting a multisensory approach to learning (Tilhou et al., 2020).

In a similar vein, the use of Braille for providing information to visually impaired visitors has declined in recent years, with audio guides becoming a more prevalent tool. However, it is essential to recognize that tactile experiences still hold value, particularly for neurodiverse audiences who process information in a tactile fashion (Leporini et al., 2020). Multimodal exhibition design that incorporates tactile elements benefits both low-vision or visually impaired visitors and the broader neurodiverse audience (Koseff, 2023).

The Missouri History Museum's file cabinet of tactile maps serves as an example of the importance of tactile engagement. To ensure accessibility, rail panels should be placed next to objects on flat surfaces, allowing visitors of all heights to comfortably read the information (Alexander et al., 2017). The placement of panels is crucial, as they should be located next to the object and not obstructed by circulatory routes. Grade 1 Braille, which provides information in alphabetical form, is often the first level of Braille learnt, while Grade 2 Braille contracts words for efficient reading (Ginley, 2013).

While the trend has shifted towards audio descriptions for visually impaired visitors, it is still important to consider the tactile quality for a comprehensive accessibility approach. The use of audio guides that can be downloaded to smartphones or accessed via museum websites is beneficial (Montagud et al., 2020). However, including directional information along with auditory descriptions can assist visitors when walking distances between objects. Internal guidance systems, similar to external GPS, can be helpful for wayfinding, but it is crucial to ensure they are user-friendly and not frustrating (Saha et al., 2019).

An example of this in practice comes from the V&A (Victoria and Albert Museum) and a collaboration with the Royal National Institute for Blind People to create tactile books with gallery plans, providing visitors with orientation and concise descriptions of tactile images (Loran, 2005). The V&A also initiated touch tours for the visually impaired in 1985, where visitors select their preferred subject and date of the talk, working with curators to select suitable objects for touch. Assistance from volunteer guides during the tour enhances the visitor's experience (Nightingale & Swallow, 2005).

In addition to touch tours and tactile books, the inclusion of photography, drawing, and painting workshops has proven beneficial for visually impaired visitors (Pye, 2016). Workshops led by artists such as Eric Richmond and Sally Booth provide opportunities for participants to engage with art through various mediums. These workshops allow participants to create their own artwork inspired by the museum's collections, fostering a deeper understanding and connection with the art (Ginley, 2013).

Tactile approaches play a crucial role in providing inclusive and engaging experiences for individuals with visual impairments (Huang & Lau, 2020). Recognizing the importance of tactile learning, the Swedish Library of Talking Books and Braille has developed web-based games specifically designed for young children with visual impairments (Eriksson & Gärdenfors, 2005). These tactile games utilize inputs and outputs through tactile boards or Braille displays, combined with audio feedback to create interactive experiences (Gärdenfors, 2003). The TiM project, funded by the European Commission, has also contributed to the development of tactile games (Archambault et al., 2007). One such game is an accessible version of *Reader Rabbit Toddler*, where children can explore tactile buttons on a tactile board and control the game through this tactile interface (Archambault & Buaud, 2003). Another example is *Find It*, a simple audio and tactile matching game. The game generator tool allows educators and teachers to design scenarios and associate them with tactile sheets, providing customizable and interactive experiences for learners (Archambault et al., 2007).

In addition to tactile games, the use of Swell-Touch Paper has been instrumental in creating tactile graphics for individuals with visual impairments. Swell paper, also known as capsule paper, microcapsule paper, or flexi paper, is a specialized medium used in Tactile Graphics machines (Mukhiddinov & Kim, 2021). When processed with heat, the paper swells along specified black or dark lines and diagrams, creating raised tactile representations. This enables individuals with visual impairments to explore and comprehend graphical information through touch (Grice et al., 2015). Swell paper has been widely utilized in educational settings to produce tactile diagrams, maps, and illustrations, allowing individuals to access visual content in a tactile format (Fusco & Morash, 2015).

The integration of tactile approaches, such as tactile games and Swell-Touch Paper, offers valuable opportunities for individuals with visual impairments to engage with and understand visual concepts (Melfi et al., 2020). By providing tactile feedback and access to graphical information, these approaches enhance learning experiences, foster sensory exploration, and promote inclusive education. The development and utilization of tactile resources and technologies highlight the commitment of educational institutions, libraries, and organizations to support individuals with visual impairments in their educational and recreational pursuits (Fernández-López et al., 2013).

While Braille and physical tactile usage has decreased in favor of audio guides, the tactile dimension remains significant for inclusive exhibition design. Tactile elements, touch tours, tactile books, and art workshops contribute to a more inclusive and engaging museum experience for both visually impaired individuals and the broader neurodiverse audience (Cavazos Quero et al., 2021). By providing diverse sensory experiences, museums can ensure that all visitors, regardless of their abilities, can actively participate in and appreciate the rich cultural heritage offered within their walls (Wu & Wall, 2017).

By acknowledging the significance of color in the experiences of visually impaired children and providing tactile and auditory supports, educators and caregivers can create inclusive environments that foster curiosity, collaboration, and a deeper understanding of the world (Cho, 2021). These inclusive practices, combined with sensory maps, not only enhance the learning experiences of visually impaired children but also promote a sense of equality and shared experiences among all children, regardless of their visual abilities.

By providing visitors with sensory maps, cultural heritage institutions demonstrate their commitment to inclusivity and accessibility. These maps empower individuals with autism or sensory sensitivities to make informed decisions about their museum visit, reducing anxiety and enhancing their overall experience (Eardley et al., 2016). Moreover, sensory maps contribute to a more welcoming and accommodating environment that recognizes and respects the diverse sensory needs of all visitors.

Visitors with sensory processing disorders (SPD) can be categorized into two main groups: sensory avoiders and sensory seekers (Fletcher et al., 2018). Sensory avoiders are individuals with SPD who have heightened sensitivity to certain stimuli, such as loud noises or specific textures. They may actively avoid or feel discomfort with certain types of sensory input. On the other hand, sensory seekers are individuals with SPD who have lower sensitivity to certain stimuli and actively seek out more intense or varied sensory experiences. This group may have a greater need for movement and touch, leading to a tendency to become easily bored in environments with limited sensory input (Ben-Avi et al., 2012).

Both sensory avoiders and sensory seekers face challenges in processing sensory information and may exhibit behaviors that either seek or avoid sensory stimuli. These behaviors can include compulsive movements, bumping into others, difficulty maintaining spatial awareness, covering ears to block out noise, and struggles with multitasking when presented with multiple sensory inputs (Reynolds & Lane, 2008). These difficulties can make it challenging for individuals to navigate and engage with museum environments.

To address the needs of both sensory avoiders and sensory seekers, sensory maps play a crucial role. These maps consider the specific sensory profiles of these individuals and plot routes within the museum environment that take into account factors such as congestion levels, areas with loud noises, and potential tactile exhibitions (Schwartzman & Knowles, 2022). By identifying and highlighting these sensory elements, the maps enable visitors to plan their visit in a way that minimizes overwhelming stimuli or provides opportunities for more intense sensory experiences, depending on their individual sensory needs.

For sensory avoiders, the maps can guide them towards quieter areas, provide information about noise levels, and highlight exhibits with gentle or predictable sensory input. This allows them to navigate the museum with reduced anxiety and discomfort. For sensory seekers, the maps can direct them to areas with more dynamic sensory experiences, such as interactive exhibits or tactile elements (Engel-Yeger et al., 2013). By meeting their sensory needs, these maps help prevent boredom and support their engagement with the museum environment.

In essence, sensory maps serve as valuable tools for addressing the sensory challenges faced by individuals with SPD. They assist visitors in interpreting and processing sensory information more effectively, enabling a more comfortable and engaging museum experience. By catering to the unique needs of both sensory avoiders and sensory seekers, cultural heritage institutions demonstrate their commitment to inclusivity and accessibility, ensuring that all visitors can fully participate and benefit from the rich offerings of the museum environment.

Understanding the different sensory processing subcategories and groups affected is crucial for museum administrations to better serve these populations. Sensory processing encompasses various sensory domains, including auditory, gustatory, tactile, proprioception, vestibular, visual, and olfactory (Ben-Sasson et al., 2009). Within the realm of sensory processing disorder (SPD), there are generally three subtypes: hypersensitivity, hyposensitivity, and general sensory overload (Table 3.4).

Hypersensitivity, or over-responsivity, refers to individuals who are overly sensitive to certain sensory inputs. They may have strong aversions to specific stimuli, such as loud noises or certain textures, and tend to avoid or react negatively to them (Panagiotidi et al., 2018). On the other hand, hyposensitivity, or under-responsivity, describes individuals who are less sensitive to certain sensory inputs. They may actively seek out intense or varied sensory experiences and have a greater need for movement and touch (Howe & Stagg, 2016). Finally, general sensory overload encompasses individuals who have difficulty processing and interpreting sensory information accurately overall. They may struggle with tasks such as paying attention, staying organized, or completing daily activities. Symptoms of both hypersensitivity and hyposensitivity may be present in individuals with general sensory overload (Miller et al., 2009).

Addressing the needs of these subtypes requires careful consideration of stimuli or the lack thereof. Individuals with hypersensitivity require sensitivity to and avoidance of highly stimulating areas within a museum. On the other hand, individuals with hyposensitivity seek out tactile, auditory, and other stimuli to meet their sensory needs. Those with general sensory overload may exhibit symptoms of both hypersensitivity and

Table 3.4 Sensory processing subtypes

Sensory processing subtype	Description
Hypersensitivity	Individuals are overly sensitive to certain sensory inputs. They have aversions to specific stimuli and may react strongly or avoid them.
Hyposensitivity	Individuals are less sensitive to certain sensory inputs. They seek out intense or varied sensory experiences and have a greater need for movement and touch.
General sensory overload	Individuals have difficulty processing and interpreting sensory information accurately. They may struggle with tasks such as attention, organization, and daily activities.

hyposensitivity, highlighting the complex nature of sensory processing difficulties (Crane et al., 2009; Harricharan et al., 2017). The threshold for the number and intensity of stimuli that the nervous system can process varies among diverse populations, emphasizing the importance of modulating these stimuli before, during, and after museum visits (Murray et al., 2009).

Considering that the processing of stimuli and information is influenced by the environment, there is a growing call to redefine disability as a result of environmental factors rather than an inherent characteristic of the individual (Rappolt-Schlichtmann & Daley, 2013). This reframing encourages cultural heritage institutions to actively adapt their environments and resources to be more inclusive and supportive of individuals with diverse sensory processing needs.

In supporting visitors with sensory sensitivities, the availability of sensory maps in various formats can greatly enhance their experience. Sensory maps can be provided in printed form, digitally through websites or apps, or even downloaded onto mobile devices (Ghosh et al., 2011). By providing sensory maps in advance, visitors can familiarize themselves with the layout of the museum, plan their visit, and reduce anxiety associated with new and unfamiliar environments (Chang, 2015). This resource not only benefits the neurodiverse individual but also their entire family or support network who may be visiting with them.

Sensory maps highlight areas within the museum that may be crowded or overwhelming, as well as provide information on high-traffic times and potential changes in lighting. For example, the Sensory Friendly Map of the Metropolitan Museum of Art (Fig. 3.6) offers a detailed visual guide that assists visitors in navigating the museum while identifying areas that may be challenging for individuals with sensory sensitivities (https://www.metmuseum.org/-/media/files/events/programs/progs-for-visitors-with-disabilities/sensory-friendly-map.pdf) (Harper, 2022). Similarly, the British Museum has developed a comprehensive sensory map that goes beyond physical layout and includes additional details such as information on areas with strong odors, staff uniforms, entrances and exits, and special events that may affect visitor experience (https://www.britishmuseum.org/sites/default/files/2019-11/British-Museum-Sensory-Map-PDF-Download.pdf) (Crang & Tolia-Kelly, 2010). By incorporating detailed sensory maps, cultural heritage institutions can effectively address the specific needs of individuals with sensory sensitivities, creating an inclusive and accommodating environment. These maps

Spaces with natural light

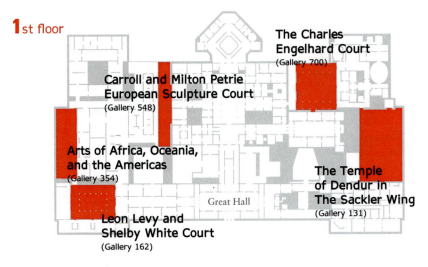

Fig. 3.6 Spaces with natural light, sensory-friendly map of The Metropolitan Museum of Art for visitors on the autism spectrum, 2015

go beyond traditional floor plans and provide crucial information about the museum environment that may impact visitors with sensory processing challenges (Diamond et al., 2016).

One important aspect that sensory maps address is crowded areas, which can be overwhelming and anxiety-inducing for individuals who are hypersensitive to sensory stimuli (Powell, 2010). By highlighting these areas, visitors can plan their visit accordingly, choosing quieter times or alternative routes to avoid crowded spaces. This advance information creates a more predictable and manageable experience for individuals with hypersensitivity. Additionally, sensory maps can include information on specific sensory triggers that may affect certain individuals. For example, highlighting areas or exhibits with strong odors accommodates individuals with olfactory sensitivities (Krishna, 2012). This level of detail demonstrates museums' commitment to creating an inclusive environment that considers the unique needs of each visitor. These maps also consider variations in lighting throughout the museum. Sudden changes in brightness or flickering lights can be challenging for individuals with sensory sensitivities. By indicating areas where lighting changes occur, sensory maps allow visitors to prepare themselves and potentially adjust their visit to minimize discomfort or sensory overload (Lupton & Lipps, 2018).

Sensory maps can also provide information on staff uniforms, enhancing communication and facilitating interactions between visitors and staff members. Including visuals or descriptions of staff uniforms improves accessibility for individuals who rely on visual cues or may have difficulty recognizing or approaching museum staff for assistance (Hutson & Hutson, 2023). Furthermore, sensory maps offer details about entrances, exits, and accessible facilities within the museum. Clear markings and directions ensure that visitors can easily navigate the space and find essential amenities, promoting independence and confidence (Pressman & Schulz, 2021).

These maps can also be combined with other resources for diverse visitors. The Museum of English Rural Life (MERL) is a shining example of how museums can prioritize accessibility and provide support for neurodivergent visitors (Roach Anleu & Sarantoulias, 2022). One of the key initiatives at MERL is the provision of sensory maps and materials on their website, which aim to assist visitors in preparing for their museum experience. The map is a valuable resource that covers various sensory aspects, including sound, light, and touch. By consulting the sensory map, visitors can anticipate and plan for potential sensory stimuli within the museum. For those who may be sensitive to certain sounds, the museum encourages the use of personal ear defenders (Olorunda et al., 2022).

In addition to the sensory map, MERL offers a Social Story that specifically addresses the safety changes implemented due to Covid-19. This guide takes visitors through the galleries, highlighting the route and the signage, ensuring that individuals are well-prepared for the visit and aware of any modifications made for safety purposes. By providing these visual aids and detailed explanations, MERL aims to alleviate any anxieties or uncertainties that visitors may have (Smith, 2012). Furthermore, the institution offers the MERL Explorer Sensory Backpacks, which are available to borrow during a visit. These backpacks contain various sensory resources and activities designed to enhance the museum experience for neurodivergent individuals. Visitors can access the backpacks from the activity trolley, and it is kindly requested that they are returned to a staff member after use.

Another remarkable feature offered by MERL is the inclusion of a 360-degree street view on their website. This feature allows individuals to have a progressive visual experience and explore the museum in advance at their own pace. By offering this virtual tour, MERL provides visitors with the opportunity to familiarize themselves with the museum's layout and exhibits before their visit. This can be particularly beneficial for neurodivergent individuals who may benefit from familiarizing themselves with a new environment beforehand (Carlsson, 2019).

These initiatives, including the sensory maps, social stories, sensory backpacks, and virtual street view, exemplify how MERL is dedicated to making the museum experience inclusive and accessible for all. By providing these resources and support, MERL creates a safe and welcoming environment that enables neurodivergent individuals to explore and engage with the museum's collections in a way that suits their unique needs and preferences.

Overall, sensory maps serve as valuable resources that empower individuals with sensory sensitivities to navigate and enjoy cultural heritage institutions. By providing comprehensive and informative sensory maps, museums create a welcoming and inclusive environment that promotes equal access and engagement for all visitors. These maps allow visitors to plan their visit according to their own comfort levels, enabling a more enjoyable and stress-free museum experience for everyone involved.

3.3 Immersive Storymaps

In recent years, the use of immersive storymaps has gained significant attention in heritage contexts as a powerful tool for enhancing visitor engagement and understanding of cultural heritage (Garr & Morgan, 2022; Howland et al., 2020; Neville, 2015). Immersive storymaps go beyond traditional storytelling methods by combining narrative elements with interactive, multimedia experiences, offering visitors a dynamic and immersive way to explore and connect with heritage spaces and stories (Zhao, 2023).

The design and implementation of immersive storymaps require careful consideration of narrative structure, visual design, and technological integration. The narrative elements of the storymap are carefully crafted to guide visitors through a curated storytelling experience, weaving together historical facts, personal stories, and cultural context to create a compelling and meaningful narrative journey (Berendsen et al., 2018). Through the use of multimedia elements such as images, videos, audio recordings, and interactive features, immersive storymaps provide visitors with a multisensory experience that brings heritage sites and stories to life (Table 3.5) (Stephens & Richards, 2020).

Recognizing the needs of visitors who arrive at a museum with limited prior knowledge is essential for creating inclusive and immersive experiences. One exemplary case that exemplifies this approach is the Acropolis Museum Chess app, discussed by Joseph (2023). This innovative app utilizes the power of storytelling and technology to engage visitors and enhance their understanding of the museum's exhibits and takes visitors on a captivating journey by integrating different personas into guided tours. Each persona represents a unique perspective and historical context, enabling visitors to connect with the rich history and significance of the museum's artifacts and collections (Pujol et al., 2013). By immersing visitors in a narrative-driven experience, the app brings the exhibits to life, transforming the museum visit into an engaging and educational adventure.

Table 3.5 Examples of immersive storymaps

Storymap	Description
The Lost City Adventure	An immersive storymap that takes visitors on a journey through a fictional lost city, combining interactive storytelling with augmented reality elements. Visitors can explore different locations, solve puzzles, and uncover the mysteries of the city while following the narrative.
Journey to Ancient Egypt	This storymap provides an immersive experience of ancient Egypt, allowing visitors to virtually travel back in time and explore significant landmarks, such as the pyramids, temples, and tombs. Through interactive maps, 3D models, and multimedia content, visitors can learn about the history, culture, and architecture of ancient Egypt.
Through the Eyes of Explorers	This immersive storymap takes visitors on a virtual expedition, following the footsteps of famous explorers. Visitors can explore different locations around the world, learn about the challenges and discoveries made by the explorers, and engage with multimedia content, including photographs, videos, and historical documents.
The Magical Forest Adventure	A whimsical and interactive storymap designed for children, inviting them to embark on a magical journey through an enchanted forest. The storymap features animated characters, interactive games, and hidden surprises, allowing children to engage with the narrative and explore the wonders of the forest in a fun and immersive way.
The Evolution of a City	This immersive storymap explores the transformation of a city over time, showcasing historical landmarks, architectural developments, and urban growth. Through interactive maps, 360-degree images, and multimedia content, visitors can delve into the city's past and witness its evolution through engaging narratives and visual representations.

One of the notable features of the app is the use of scanned statues to create 3D models that are historically accurate. These models provide a realistic representation of the statues, capturing intricate details and nuances that are often lost in traditional displays. By leveraging cutting-edge technology, the Acropolis Museum Chess app allows visitors to explore these virtual 3D models and gain a deeper understanding of the artworks and their historical significance (Vayanou et al., 2014). In addition to the accurate 3D models, the app incorporates virtual overlays that add a layer of colorized visual information to the exhibits. These overlays provide contextual details, historical facts, and additional visual elements that enhance the visitors' understanding and engagement. By superimposing the virtual overlays onto the physical exhibits, the app seamlessly blends the past and the present, offering visitors a unique and immersive experience (Pujol et al., 2012).

The combination of different personas, accurate 3D models, and virtual overlays in the Acropolis Museum Chess app creates a captivating storymap that guides visitors through the museum's exhibits. This immersive approach not only educates and informs visitors but also sparks their curiosity and fosters a deeper appreciation for the cultural heritage preserved within the museum's walls (Keil et al., 2013). By employing interactive storytelling and advanced technologies, museums can bridge the gap between visitors with limited prior knowledge and the exhibits they encounter. The Acropolis Museum Chess app serves as an exemplary case study, demonstrating how immersive storymaps can enrich the museum experience and provide visitors with a deeper understanding of the historical and cultural significance of the artifacts on display (Hassan & Ramkissoon, 2017).

Another compelling example of the application of immersive storymaps in heritage contexts is the project *Mapping Indigenous LA* by the University of California, Los Angeles. This immersive storymap invites visitors to explore the rich history and contemporary experiences of Indigenous communities in the Los Angeles area (https://mila.ss.ucla.edu/). Through interactive maps, archival photographs, oral histories, and personal narratives, visitors can delve into the diverse cultural heritage of the Indigenous peoples who have called this region home for thousands of years (Senier, 2018).

The storymap provides a dynamic and engaging platform for visitors to learn about the Indigenous history, traditions, and contributions that often go unnoticed or underrepresented in mainstream narratives. It allows visitors to navigate through different neighborhoods, highlighting significant sites, landmarks, and cultural institutions associated with Indigenous communities. By immersing visitors in the stories and experiences of Indigenous peoples, the storymap fosters a deeper understanding and appreciation for their enduring presence and resilience in the face of historical and ongoing challenges. It offers a unique opportunity to explore the complexities of Indigenous cultural heritage, identity, and community engagement in the urban landscape (Senier, 2018).

Through the interactive elements of the storymap, such as audio recordings, videos, and clickable points of interest, visitors can engage with the narratives in a multisensory and participatory manner. This immersive storytelling experience not only educates visitors about Indigenous history but also prompts them to reflect on the significance of Indigenous perspectives and contributions in shaping the cultural fabric of Los Angeles (Goeman, 2008).

Another notable example is the *Journey through Hallowed Ground* storymap developed by the National Park Service. This immersive storymap takes visitors on a virtual tour of the historic sites and landscapes along the Journey through Hallowed Ground National Heritage Area, spanning from Gettysburg, Pennsylvania, to Monticello, Virginia (https://www.nps.gov/places/journey-through-hallowed-ground.htm). Through interactive maps, historical photographs, and personal stories, visitors can explore the rich history and significance of this region, including its connection to the American Civil War (Fig. 3.7) (Demski-Hamelin, 2018). The immersive nature of the storymap creates a sense of presence and connection with the past, allowing visitors to engage with the heritage landscape in a profound way. By virtually experiencing the sites and stories along this historic route, visitors can deepen their understanding of the events and people that shaped this important part of American history (Cappucci, 2019).

Furthermore, immersive storymaps are also utilized to promote environmental conservation. The *Great Barrier Reef* storymap by the Great Barrier Reef Marine Park Authority offers a virtual exploration of the iconic Great Barrier Reef in Australia (Fig. 3.8) (https://storymaps.arcgis.com/stories/96d90b1b147c427db6c5168b1ae961e9). Through interactive maps, stunning underwater imagery, and educational content, visitors can learn about the reef's biodiversity, conservation efforts, and the challenges it faces (Authority, 2019). This immersive storymap raises awareness about the importance of environmental conservation and

Fig. 3.7 Journey Through Hallowed Ground Byway, Catoctin Furnace

fosters a deeper understanding of the reef's ecological significance. By immersing visitors in the beauty and fragility of the Great Barrier Reef, the storymap inspires a sense of responsibility and encourages action to protect this natural wonder.

These examples demonstrate the power of immersive storymaps in connecting visitors to heritage sites, historical events, cultural traditions, and environmental conservation efforts. By leveraging interactive maps, multimedia elements, and engaging narratives, immersive storymaps create compelling and educational experiences that foster a deeper connection between visitors and the stories and spaces they encounter in cultural heritage institutions.

The use of immersive storymaps in heritage contexts offers numerous benefits for both visitors and cultural heritage institutions. For visitors, immersive storymaps provide a more engaging and interactive experience that goes beyond traditional text-based exhibits (Kleinman et al., 2020). They offer a deeper level of exploration, allowing visitors to navigate

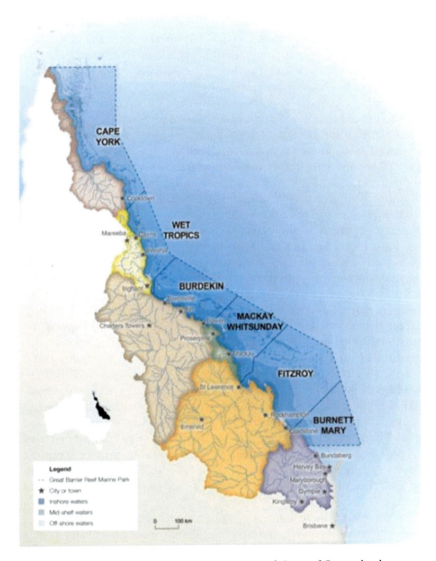

Fig. 3.8 Catchments along the Great Barrier Reef, State of Queensland

through different layers of information, choose their own paths, and delve into specific aspects of cultural heritage that interest them the most. This level of personalization and interactivity fosters a sense of ownership and empowerment among visitors, as they actively participate in the discovery and interpretation of heritage stories.

For cultural heritage institutions, immersive storymaps offer opportunities to expand their reach and impact beyond physical spaces. They provide a platform for sharing stories and engaging with audiences who may not have the opportunity to visit the heritage site in person (Fassoulas et al., 2022). Immersive storymaps can be accessed remotely through digital platforms, reaching a wider audience and extending the institution's educational and interpretive offerings (Jackson, 2023).

The strategies and tools discussed in this chapter offer valuable insights into creating inclusive and accessible environments within cultural heritage institutions. Sensory kits, with their carefully selected contents like noise-canceling headphones, weighted lap pads, and fidget toys, provide essential support for neurodiverse visitors, fostering a more comfortable and engaging experience. Similarly, sensory maps serve as invaluable resources that go beyond traditional floor plans, providing detailed information about crowded areas, lighting changes, and sensory triggers. By incorporating sensory maps, cultural heritage institutions empower visitors to plan their visits according to their specific needs, resulting in a more predictable and manageable experience.

Additionally, the integration of immersive storymaps and their associated elements (Table 3.6) combines narrative elements with interactive multimedia experiences, deepening the connection between visitors and cultural heritage. Through projects like *Journey through Hallowed Ground* and *Mapping Indigenous LA*, immersive storymaps allow visitors to explore history, culture, and environmental significance in a dynamic and engaging way, fostering a deeper understanding and appreciation for cultural heritage.

By embracing these innovative approaches, cultural heritage institutions can create inclusive and accommodating spaces that cater to the diverse needs of their visitors. These strategies not only enhance accessibility but also promote a more meaningful and engaging experience for all individuals. By actively incorporating sensory kits, sensory maps, and immersive storymaps, institutions contribute to a more vibrant and inclusive cultural heritage landscape. Ultimately, the implementation of these strategies and tools exemplifies the commitment of cultural heritage

Table 3.6 Elements of immersive storymaps

Element	Description
Interactive design	Immersive storymaps incorporate interactive elements, such as clickable hotspots, navigation tools, quizzes, and games, to engage users.
Multimedia content	Storymaps integrate various types of multimedia content, such as images, videos, audio clips, and 3D models, to enhance the storytelling.
Spatial navigation	Utilizing maps or 3D environments, immersive storymaps allow users to navigate through different locations and explore the narrative space.
Personalization	Immersive storymaps can offer personalized experiences by adapting content based on user preferences, choices, or input.
Augmented reality	Some immersive storymaps leverage augmented reality technology to overlay virtual elements onto the real world, enhancing the immersion.
Storytelling arc	Immersive storymaps follow a well-defined narrative structure with a clear beginning, middle, and end to guide users through the story.
Gamification	Gamification elements, such as challenges, rewards, and achievements, are incorporated to increase engagement and promote interactivity.
Seamless transitions	Smooth transitions between different scenes or locations create a seamless and immersive experience for users as they explore the storymap.
User feedback	Immersive storymaps can incorporate interactive elements that allow users to provide feedback, leave comments, or rate their experience.
Accessibility features	Consideration of accessibility features, such as text alternatives, captions, and adjustable font sizes, to ensure inclusivity for all users.

institutions to provide enriching experiences for diverse audiences, ensuring that cultural heritage remains accessible and relevant to all individuals, regardless of their unique needs and backgrounds.

References

Adams, E. (2021). New light on 'the viewer': Sensing the Parthenon galleries in the British Museum. In *Disability Studies and the Classical Body* (pp. 130–159). Routledge.

Alexander, E. P., Alexander, M., & Decker, J. (2017). *Museums in motion: An introduction to the history and functions of museums*. Rowman & Littlefield.

Anderson, A. (2019). *Virtual reality, augmented reality and artificial intelligence in special education: A practical guide to supporting students with learning differences.* Routledge.

Arar, M., Jung, C., Awad, J., & Chohan, A. H. (2021). Analysis of smart home technology acceptance and preference for elderly in Dubai, UAE. *Designs, 5*(4), 70.

Archambault, D., & Buaud, A. (2003). Independent living for persons with disabilities 179 and elderly people. In M. Mokhtari (Ed.), *Independent living for persons with disabilities and elderly people: ICOST'2003 1st International Conference on Smart Homes and Health Telematics* (Vol. 12, p. 179). IOS Press.

Archambault, D., Ossmann, R., Gaudy, T., & Miesenberger, K. (2007). Computer games and visually impaired people. *Upgrade, 8*(2), 43–53.

Authority, G. B. R. M. P. (2019). *Great barrier reef outlook report 2019.* Great Barrier Reef Marine Park Authority.

Bandukda, M., Holloway, C., Singh, A., & Berthouze, N. (2020, October). PLACES: A framework for supporting blind and partially sighted people in outdoor leisure activities. In *Proceedings of the 22nd International ACM SIGACCESS Conference on Computers and Accessibility* (pp. 1–13).

Barakat, B., Hall, L., & Keates, S. (2022, June). Integrating machine learning with augmented reality for accessible assistive technologies. In *Universal access in human-computer interaction. User and context diversity: 16th International Conference, UAHCI 2022, held as part of the 24th HCI International Conference, HCII 2022, Virtual Event, June 26–July 1, 2022, Proceedings, Part II* (pp. 175–186). Springer International Publishing.

Bbosale, A., Benny, G., Jaison, R., Kbot, A., & Pati, S. (2019, January). Indoor navigation system using BLE beacons. In *2019 International Conference on Nascent Technologies in Engineering (ICNTE)* (pp. 1–6). IEEE.

Beaney, J. (2020). *Autism through a sensory lens: Sensory assessment and strategies.* Routledge.

Ben-Avi, N., Almagor, M., & Engel-Yeger, B. (2012). Sensory processing difficulties and interpersonal relationships in adults: An exploratory study. *Psychology, 3*(01), 70.

Ben-Sasson, A., Hen, L., Fluss, R., Cermak, S. A., Engel-Yeger, B., & Gal, E. (2009). A meta-analysis of sensory modulation symptoms in individuals with autism spectrum disorders. *Journal of Autism and Developmental Disorders, 39,* 1–11.

Berendsen, M. E., Hamerlinck, J. D., & Webster, G. R. (2018). Digital story mapping to advance educational atlas design and enable student engagement. *ISPRS International Journal of Geo-Information, 7*(3), 125.

Bollini, A., Cocchi, E., Salvagno, V., & Gori, M. (2023). The causal role of vision in the development of spatial coordinates: Evidence from visually impaired children. *Journal of Experimental Psychology: Human Perception and Performance.*

Braden, C. (2016). Welcoming all visitors: Museums, accessibility, and visitors with disabilities. *University of Michigan Working Papers in Museum Studies*, p. i.

Broomfield, K., Harrop, D., Jones, G. L., Sage, K., & Judge, S. (2022). A qualitative evidence synthesis of the experiences and perspectives of communicating using augmentative and alternative communication (AAC). *Disability and Rehabilitation. Assistive Technology*, 1–15.

Camic, P. M., & Chatterjee, H. J. (2013). Museums and art galleries as partners for public health interventions. *Perspectives in Public Health, 133*(1), 66–71.

Cappucci, K. C. (2019). Marietta Pennsylvania Historic District & the Susquehanna National Heritage Area designation ArcGIS StoryMap.

Carlsson, M. K. (2019). *Seeing systems and the beholding eye: Computer-aided visions of the Postwar British landscape* (Doctoral dissertation, Massachusetts Institute of Technology).

Cavazos Quero, L., Iranzo Bartolomé, J., & Cho, J. (2021). Accessible visual artworks for blind and visually impaired people: Comparing a multimodal approach with tactile graphics. *Electronics, 10*(3), 297.

Ceraso, S. (2014). (Re)educating the senses: Multimodal listening, bodily learning, and the composition of sonic experiences. *College English, 77*(2), 102–123.

Chang, H. H. (2015). Which one helps tourists most? Perspectives of international tourists using different navigation aids. *Tourism Geographies, 17*(3), 350–369.

Cho, J. D. (2021). A study of multi-sensory experience and color recognition in visual arts appreciation of people with visual impairment. *Electronics, 10*(4), 470.

Crane, L., Goddard, L., & Pring, L. (2009). Sensory processing in adults with autism spectrum disorders. *Autism, 13*(3), 215–228.

Crang, M., & Tolia-Kelly, D. P. (2010). Nation, race, and affect: Senses and sensibilities at national heritage sites. *Environment and Planning A, 42*(10), 2315–2331.

Demski-Hamelin, D. (2018). Curating heritage in the digital age: An exploration of how America's national heritage areas are using technology to share their stories.

Diamond, J., Horn, M., & Uttal, D. H. (2016). *Practical evaluation guide: Tools for museums and other informal educational settings*. Rowman & Littlefield.

Eardley, A. F., Mineiro, C., Neves, J., & Ride, P. (2016). Redefining access: Embracing multimodality, memorability and shared experience in museums. *Curator: The Museum Journal, 59*(3), 263–286.

Engel-Yeger, B., Palgy-Levin, D., & Lev-Wiesel, R. (2013). The sensory profile of people with post-traumatic stress symptoms. *Occupational Therapy in Mental Health, 29*(3), 266–278.

Eriksson, Y., & Gärdenfors, D. (2005). Computer games for children with visual impairments. *International Journal on Disability and Human Development, 4*(3), 161–168.

Fassoulas, C., Nikolakakis, E., & Staridas, S. (2022). Digital tools to serve geotourism and sustainable development at Psiloritis UNESCO Global Geopark in COVID times and beyond. *Geosciences, 12*(2), 78.

Fernández-López, Á., Rodríguez-Fórtiz, M. J., Rodríguez-Almendros, M. L., & Martínez-Segura, M. J. (2013). Mobile learning technology based on iOS devices to support students with special education needs. *Computers & Education, 61,* 77–90.

Fletcher, T. S., Blake, A. B., & Shelffo, K. E. (2018). Can sensory gallery guides for children with sensory processing challenges improve their museum experience? *Journal of Museum Education, 43*(1), 66–77.

Fletcher, T. S., Wiskera, E. S., Wilbur, L. H., & Garcia, N. M. (2022). The sensory totes programme: Sensory-friendly autism program innovations designed to meet COVID-19 challenges. *World Federation of Occupational Therapists Bulletin, 78*(1), 44–52.

Fowler, S. (2008). *Multisensory rooms and environments: Controlled sensory experiences for people with profound and multiple disabilities.* Jessica Kingsley Publishers.

Frank, J. J. (2013). *Making Rocky Mountain National Park: The environmental history of an American treasure.* University Press of Kansas.

Fusco, G., & Morash, V. S. (2015, October). The tactile graphics helper: Providing audio clarification for tactile graphics using machine vision. In *Proceedings of the 17th International ACM SIGACCESS Conference on Computers & Accessibility* (pp. 97–106).

Gacem, M. A., Alghlayini, S., Shehieb, W., Saeed, M., Ghazal, A., & Mir, M. (2019, December). Smart assistive glasses for Alzheimer's patients. In *2019 IEEE International Symposium on Signal Processing and Information Technology (ISSPIT)* (pp. 1–5). IEEE.

Gärdenfors, D. (2003). Designing sound-based computer games. *Digital Creativity, 14*(2), 111–114.

Garr, M., & Morgan, M. (2022). Student-centered immersive StoryMaps to build language and cultural proficiency.

Ghosh, S., Larson, S. D., Hefzi, H., Marnoy, Z., Cutforth, T., Dokka, K., & Baldwin, K. K. (2011). Sensory maps in the olfactory cortex defined by long-range viral tracing of single neurons. *Nature, 472*(7342), 217–220.

Giaconi, C., Ascenzi, A., Del Bianco, N., D'Angelo, I., & Capellini, S. A. (2021). Virtual and augmented reality for the cultural accessibility of people with autism spectrum disorders: A pilot study. *International Journal of the Inclusive Museum, 14*(1).

Ginley, B. (2013). Museums: A whole new world for visually impaired people. *Disability Studies Quarterly, 33*(3).

Goeman, M. (2008). (Re)mapping Indigenous presence on the land in Native women's literature. *American Quarterly, 60*(2), 295–302.

Grandin, T., & Panek, R. (2014). *The autistic brain: Helping different kinds of minds succeed* (p. 256). Mariner Books.

Gray, C. A. (1998). Social stories and comic strip conversations with students with Asperger syndrome and high-functioning autism. In *Asperger syndrome or high-functioning autism?* (pp. 167–198).

Grice, N., Christian, C., Nota, A., & Greenfield, P. (2015). 3D printing technology: A unique way of making hubble space telescope images accessible to non-visual learners. *Journal of Blindness Innovation & Research, 5*(1).

Halder, S., & Squires, G. (Eds.). (2023). *Inclusion and diversity: Communities and practices across the world*. Taylor & Francis.

Harpenau, P. (2020). An organization-level occupational therapy consultation approach: Increasing art museum access for visitors with autism spectrum and sensory processing disorders.

Harper, S. (2022). Field trip for one: Self-directed learning with the# MetKids website# MetKids, the Metropolitan Museum of Art (2015). *International Journal of Education Through Art, 18*(2), 279–281.

Harricharan, S., Nicholson, A. A., Densmore, M., Théberge, J., McKinnon, M. C., Neufeld, R. W., & Lanius, R. A. (2017). Sensory overload and imbalance: Resting-state vestibular connectivity in PTSD and its dissociative subtype. *Neuropsychologia, 106*, 169–178.

Hassan, A., & Ramkissoon, H. (2017). 10 augmented reality application to museum visitor experiences. *Visitor Management in Tourism Destinations, 117*.

Holloway, L., Marriott, K., Butler, M., & Borning, A. (2019, May). Making sense of art: Access for gallery visitors with vision impairments. In *Proceedings of the 2019 CHI Conference on Human Factors in Computing Systems* (pp. 1–12).

Hou, S. (2023). Making art accessible to all: Co-creating multi-sensory art with visually impaired people.

Howe, F. E., & Stagg, S. D. (2016). How sensory experiences affect adolescents with an autistic spectrum condition within the classroom. *Journal of Autism and Developmental Disorders, 46*, 1656–1668.

Howland, M. D., Liss, B., Levy, T. E., & Najjar, M. (2020). Integrating digital datasets into public engagement through ArcGIS StoryMaps. *Advances in Archaeological Practice, 8*(4), 351–360.

Huang, L., & Lau, N. (2020). Enhancing the smart tourism experience for people with visual impairments by gamified application approach through needs analysis in Hong Kong. *Sustainability, 12*(15), 6213.

Huston, V., & Hamburger, K. (2023). Navigation aid use and human wayfinding: How to engage people in active spatial learning. *KI-Künstliche Intelligenz*, 1–8.

Hutson, J., & Hutson, P. (2023). Museums and the metaverse: Emerging technologies to promote inclusivity and engagement.

Jabbar, M. S., Lee, C. H., & Cho, J. D. (2021). ColorWatch: Color perceptual spatial tactile interface for people with visual impairments. *Electronics*, *10*(5), 596.

Jackson, M. (2023). Digital storytelling and user experience in online exhibition development.

Joseph, B. (2023). *Making dinosaurs dance.* American Alliance of Museums.

Karimi, S., & Iordanova, I. (2021). Integration of BIM and GIS for construction automation, a systematic literature review (SLR) combining bibliometric and qualitative analysis. *Archives of Computational Methods in Engineering*, 1–22.

Keil, J., Pujol, L., Roussou, M., Engelke, T., Schmitt, M., Bockholt, U., & Eleftheratou, S. (2013, October). A digital look at physical museum exhibits: Designing personalized stories with handheld augmented reality in museums. In *2013 Digital Heritage International Congress (DigitalHeritage)* (Vol. 2, pp. 685–688). IEEE.

Khan, A., & Khusro, S. (2021). An insight into smartphone-based assistive solutions for visually impaired and blind people: Issues, challenges and opportunities. *Universal Access in the Information Society*, *20*, 265–298.

Kilian, J., Neugebauer, A., Scherffig, L., & Wahl, S. (2022). The unfolding space glove: A wearable spatio-visual to haptic sensory substitution device for blind people. *Sensors*, *22*(5), 1859.

Kinnealey, M., Koenig, K. P., & Smith, S. (2011). Relationships between sensory modulation and social supports and health-related quality of life. *The American Journal of Occupational Therapy*, *65*(3), 320–327.

Kleinman, E., Caro, K., & Zhu, J. (2020). From immersion to metagaming: Understanding rewind mechanics in interactive storytelling. *Entertainment Computing*, *33*, 100322.

Koseff, S. (2023). *Tactile interpretations of historical embroidered patches: Methods and best practices* (Doctoral dissertation, New York University Tandon School of Engineering).

Krishna, A. (2012). An integrative review of sensory marketing: Engaging the senses to affect perception, judgment and behavior. *Journal of Consumer Psychology*, *22*(3), 332–351.

Kunhoth, J., Karkar, A., Al-Maadeed, S., & Al-Ali, A. (2020). Indoor positioning and wayfinding systems: A survey. *Human-centric Computing and Information Sciences*, *10*(1), 1–41.

Kuriakose, B., Shrestha, R., & Sandnes, F. E. (2022). Tools and technologies for blind and visually impaired navigation support: A review. *IETE Technical Review*, *39*(1), 3–18.

Lee, I. J. (2021). Kinect-for-windows with augmented reality in an interactive roleplay system for children with an autism spectrum disorder. *Interactive Learning Environments*, *29*(4), 688–704.

Leporini, B., Rossetti, V., Furfari, F., Pelagatti, S., & Quarta, A. (2020). Design guidelines for an interactive 3D model as a supporting tool for exploring a cultural site by visually impaired and sighted people. *ACM Transactions on Accessible Computing (TACCESS), 13*(3), 1–39.

López Salas, E. (2021). A collection of narrative practices on cultural heritage with innovative technologies and creative strategies. *Open Research Europe, 1*, 130.

Loran, M. (2005). Use of websites to increase access and develop audiences in museums: Experiences in British national museums. *Digithum, 7*, 23–28.

Lupton, E., & Lipps, A. (Eds.). (2018). *The senses: Design beyond vision*. Chronicle Books.

McLean, K. (2019). *Sensory maps*. Elsevier.

Melfi, G., Müller, K., Schwarz, T., Jaworek, G., & Stiefelhagen, R. (2020, April). Understanding what you feel: A mobile audio-tactile system for graphics used at schools with students with visual impairment. In *Proceedings of the 2020 CHI Conference on Human Factors in Computing Systems* (pp. 1–12).

Miller, L. J., Nielsen, D. M., Schoen, S. A., & Brett-Green, B. A. (2009). Perspectives on sensory processing disorder: A call for translational research. *Frontiers in Integrative Neuroscience, 22*.

Mitchell, A. W., Moore, E. M., Roberts, E. J., Hachtel, K. W., & Brown, M. S. (2015). Sensory processing disorder in children ages birth–3 years born prematurely: A systematic review. *The American Journal of Occupational Therapy, 69*(1).

Montagud, M., Orero, P., & Matamala, A. (2020). Culture 4 all: Accessibility-enabled cultural experiences through immersive VR360 content. *Personal and Ubiquitous Computing, 24*(6), 887–905.

Mukhiddinov, M., & Kim, S. Y. (2021). A systematic literature review on the automatic creation of tactile graphics for the blind and visually impaired. *Processes, 9*(10), 1726.

Murray, M., Baker, P. H., Murray-Slutsky, C., & Paris, B. (2009). Strategies for supporting the sensory-based learner. *Preventing School Failure: Alternative Education for Children and Youth, 53*(4), 245–252.

Nagib, W., & Williams, A. (2017). Toward an autism-friendly home environment. *Housing Studies, 32*(2), 140–167.

Neville, D. O. (2015). The story in the mind: The effect of 3D gameplay on the structuring of written L2 narratives. *ReCALL, 27*(1), 21–37.

Nightingale, E., & Swallow, D. (2005). The arts of the Sikh kingdoms: Collaborating with a community. In *Museums and Source Communities* (pp. 66–82). Routledge.

Nolan, C., Doyle, J. K., Lewis, K., & Treanor, D. (2023). Disabled students' perception of the sensory aspects of the learning and social environments within one Higher Education Institution. *British Journal of Occupational Therapy, 86*(5), 367–375.

Olorunda, E., McCrindle, R., & Heath, P. (2022, June). Promoting reminiscence and social interaction through a multisensory toolkit–A non-pharmacological intervention for people living with dementia. In *HCI International 2022 Posters: 24th International Conference on Human-Computer Interaction, HCII 2022, Virtual Event, June 26–July 1, 2022, Proceedings, Part IV* (pp. 430–437). Springer International Publishing.

Padfield, N., Agius Anastasi, A., Camilleri, T., Fabri, S., Bugeja, M., & Camilleri, K. (2023). BCI-controlled wheelchairs: End-users' perceptions, needs, and expectations, an interview-based study. *Disability and Rehabilitation: Assistive Technology*, 1–13.

Palivcová, D., Macík, M., & Míkovec, Z. (2020, April). Interactive tactile map as a tool for building spatial knowledge of visually impaired older adults. In *Extended Abstracts of the 2020 CHI Conference on Human Factors in Computing Systems* (pp. 1–9).

Panagiotidi, M., Overton, P. G., & Stafford, T. (2018). The relationship between ADHD traits and sensory sensitivity in the general population. *Comprehensive Psychiatry, 80*, 179–185.

Paratore, M. T., & Leporini, B. (2023). Exploiting the haptic and audio channels to improve orientation and mobility apps for the visually impaired. *Universal Access in the Information Society*, 1–11.

Parini, A., & Yus, F. (2023). The discursive construction of place through the online-offline interface. From physical locations to wikispaces. *The Discursive Construction of Place in the Digital Age*, 9–32.

Pedersini, C. A., Miller, N. P., Gandhi, T. K., Gilad-Gutnick, S., Mahajan, V., Sinha, P., & Rokers, B. (2023). White matter plasticity following cataract surgery in congenitally blind patients. *Proceedings of the National Academy of Sciences, 120*(19), e2207025120.

Percival, J. (2023). *Autism friendly business: Neurodiverse customers.* CRC Press.

Pionke, J. J. (2017). Toward holistic accessibility: Narratives from functionally diverse patrons. *Reference and User Services Quarterly, 57*(1), 48–56.

Poonja, H. A., Shirazi, M. A., Khan, M. J., & Javed, K. (2023). Engagement detection and enhancement for STEM education through computer vision, augmented reality, and haptics. *Image and Vision Computing, 104720*.

Powell, K. (2010). Making sense of place: Mapping as a multisensory research method. *Qualitative Inquiry, 16*(7), 539–555.

Pressman, H., & Schulz, D. (2021). *The art of access: A practical guide for museum accessibility.* Rowman & Littlefield Publishers.

Pujol, L., Katifori, A., Vayanou, M., Roussou, M., Karvounis, M., Kyriakidi, M., ... & Ioannidis, Y. (2013). From personalization to adaptivity—Creating immersive visits through interactive digital storytelling at the Acropolis Museum. In *Workshop Proceedings of the 9th International Conference on Intelligent Environments* (pp. 541–554). IOS Press.

Pujol, L., Roussou, M., Poulou, S., Balet, O., Vayanou, M., & Ioannidis, Y. (2012, March). Personalizing interactive digital storytelling in archaeological museums: The CHESS project. In *40th Annual Conference of Computer Applications and Quantitative Methods in Archaeology* (pp. 93–100). Amsterdam University Press.

Pye, E. (Ed.). (2016). *The power of touch: Handling objects in museum and heritage context*. Routledge.

Rappolt-Schlichtmann, G., & Daley, S. G. (2013). Providing access to engagement in learning: The potential of universal design for learning in museum design. *Curator: The Museum Journal, 56*(3), 307–321.

Real, S., & Araujo, A. (2019). Navigation systems for the blind and visually impaired: Past work, challenges, and open problems. *Sensors, 19*(15), 3404.

Reynolds, S., & Lane, S. J. (2008). Diagnostic validity of sensory over-responsivity: A review of the literature and case reports. *Journal of Autism and Developmental Disorders, 38*, 516–529.

Ridha, A. M., & Shehieb, W. (2021, September). Assistive technology for hearing-impaired and deaf students utilizing augmented reality. In *2021 IEEE Canadian Conference on Electrical and Computer Engineering (CCECE)* (pp. 1–5). IEEE.

Roach Anleu, S., & Sarantoulias, G. (2022). Complex data and simple instructions: Social regulation during the Covid-19 pandemic. *Journal of Sociology*.

Saha, M., Fiannaca, A. J., Kneisel, M., Cutrell, E., & Morris, M. R. (2019, October). Closing the gap: Designing for the last-few-meters wayfinding problem for people with visual impairments. In *Proceedings of the 21st International ACM SIGACCESS Conference on Computers and Accessibility* (pp. 222–235).

Salthouse, C. (2017). *Gateway to inclusion: Understanding the structure of early open autism events in museums* (Doctoral dissertation).

Sankar, S., Balamurugan, D., Brown, A., Ding, K., Xu, X., Low, J. H., et al. (2021). Texture discrimination with a soft biomimetic finger using a flexible neuromorphic tactile sensor array that provides sensory feedback. *Soft Robotics, 8*(5), 577–587.

Schwartzman, R., & Knowles, C. (2022). Expanding accessibility: Sensory sensitive programming for museums. *Curator: The Museum Journal, 65*(1), 95–116.

Seetharaman, K., Shepley, M. M., & Cheairs, C. (2021). The saliency of geographical landmarks for community navigation: A photovoice study with persons living with dementia. *Dementia, 20*(4), 1191–1212.

Sekhavat, Y. A., Azadehfar, M. R., Zarei, H., & Roohi, S. (2022). Sonification and interaction design in computer games for visually impaired individuals. *Multimedia Tools and Applications, 81*(6), 7847–7871.

Senier, S. (2018). Where a bird's-eye view shows more concrete: Mapping indigenous LA for tribal visibility and reclamation. *American Quarterly, 70*(4), 941–948.

Shaligram, S. (2019). *Accessibility in museums: Where are we and where are we headed* (Doctoral dissertation, Massachusetts Institute of Technology).

Simões, W. C., Machado, G. S., Sales, A. M., de Lucena, M. M., Jazdi, N., & de Lucena, V. F., Jr. (2020). A review of technologies and techniques for indoor navigation systems for the visually impaired. *Sensors, 20*(14), 3935.

Smith, R. (2012). Searching for "Community": Making English rural history collections relevant today. *Curator: The Museum Journal, 55*(1), 51–63.

Stephens, S. H., & Richards, D. P. (2020). Story mapping and sea level rise: Listening to global risks at street level. *Communication Design Quarterly Review, 8*(1), 5–18.

Tilhou, R., Taylor, V., & Crompton, H. (2020). 3D virtual reality in K-12 education: A thematic systematic review. *Emerging Technologies and Pedagogies in the Curriculum*, 169–184.

Vayanou, M., Karvounis, M., Katifori, A., Kyriakidi, M., Roussou, M., & Ioannidis, Y. E. (2014, July). The CHESS project: Adaptive personalized storytelling experiences in museums. In *UMAP Workshops*.

Wall, S. A., & Brewster, S. (2006). Sensory substitution using tactile pin arrays: Human factors, technology and applications. *Signal Processing, 86*(12), 3674–3695.

Wallace, S. E., Hux, K., Knollman-Porter, K., Brown, J. A., Parisi, E., & Cain, R. (2022). Reading behaviors and text-to-speech technology perceptions of people with aphasia. *Assistive Technology, 34*(5), 599–610.

Wang, M., & Jeon, M. (2023). Assistive technology for adults on the autism spectrum: A systematic survey. *International Journal of Human Computer Interaction*, 1–20.

Wu, M. Y., & Wall, G. (2017). Visiting heritage museums with children: Chinese parents' motivations. *Journal of Heritage Tourism, 12*(1), 36–51.

Xu, Y., Qin, T., Wu, Y., Yu, C., & Dong, W. (2022). How do voice-assisted digital maps influence human wayfinding in pedestrian navigation? *Cartography and Geographic Information Science, 49*(3), 271–287.

Yoo, M. (2020). Understanding everyday experiences of reminiscence for people living with blindness: Practices, tensions and probing new design possibilities.

Yoo, M., Odom, W., & Berger, A. (2021, May). Understanding everyday experiences of reminiscence for people with blindness: Practices, tensions and probing new design possibilities. In *Proceedings of the 2021 CHI Conference on Human Factors in Computing Systems* (pp. 1–15).

Zallio, M., & Clarkson, P. J. (2021). Inclusion, diversity, equity and accessibility in the built environment: A study of architectural design practice. *Building and Environment, 206*, 108352.

Zhao, X. (2023). *A virtual reality application: Creating an alternative immersive experience for Dunhuang Mogao Cave visitors* (Doctoral dissertation, Duke University).

Zhao, Y., Kupferstein, E., Rojnirun, H., Findlater, L., & Azenkot, S. (2020, April). The effectiveness of visual and audio wayfinding guidance on smartglasses for people with low vision. In *Proceedings of the 2020 CHI conference on human factors in computing systems* (pp. 1–14).

CHAPTER 4

Gamification

This chapter delves into the realm of gamification and its applications within cultural heritage institutions. It highlights the potential of game-based learning, treasure hunts, and gamified digital storytelling in creating immersive, engaging, and memorable experiences for diverse audiences in museums and heritage sites. The discussion begins with an overview of game-based learning, exploring its principles, cognitive benefits, and effectiveness in fostering a deeper understanding and appreciation of cultural heritage. Case studies of game-based learning projects are presented. The chapter then examines treasure hunts as a means of engaging audiences with heritage, discussing their design and implementation to create interactive and exciting experiences. Case studies of treasure hunt projects in heritage sites showcase their transformative potential. Lastly, the chapter explores how gamification can enhance digital storytelling in heritage contexts, covering the design and implementation of gamified digital storytelling and demonstrating the benefits through examples of projects. Emphasizing the power of gamification, the chapter highlights its role in enriching the visitor experience and fostering a deeper connection with cultural heritage. Through these techniques, cultural heritage institutions can create engaging and interactive experiences that captivate and educate diverse audiences.

© The Author(s), under exclusive license to Springer Nature Switzerland AG 2024
J. Hutson, P. Hutson, *Inclusive Smart Museums*,
https://doi.org/10.1007/978-3-031-43615-4_4

4.1 Gamification and Game-Based Learning

The integration of game-based learning within cultural heritage institutions has instigated a transformative shift in visitor engagement strategies (Foster & Shah, 2015). Predicated on the principles of active involvement, immersion, and interactive learning, these strategies aim to bolster visitor engagement and make these institutions more inclusive for neurodiverse populations (Levitis et al., 2021). The systematic inclusion of gamification techniques within heritage settings not only enriches the visitor experience but also seeks to bring about cognitively beneficial outcomes, such as enhanced retention, problem-solving abilities, and critical thinking skills (Pellas et al., 2019).

Gamification of learning and game-based learning, while sharing commonalities in the aim of fostering learning outcomes, differ fundamentally in their design and application (Table 4.1). For instance, gamification of learning, as defined by Deterding et al. (2011), refers to the application of game design elements in non-game contexts. It does not necessitate the design of an entire game but rather employs specific game mechanisms, such as badges, points, leaderboards, and levels, to enhance user engagement and learning. An example offered by Shernoff et al. (2014) involved a classroom environment where a system of points and badges was utilized to motivate and reward student engagement and learning. This case illustrates how gamification elements can be infused into traditional learning contexts to stimulate motivation and engagement.

In contrast, game-based learning, as elucidated by Prensky (2003), involves using actual games—digital or physical—with an inherent educational purpose to promote learning. Unlike gamification, which borrows game elements, game-based learning implies the existence of a fully realized game intended for learning outcomes. An instance is highlighted by Squire (2006), where the historical strategy game *Civilization III* was integrated into a high school history class to enable students to grapple with complex historical phenomena and develop problem-solving skills. This particular application underscores how game-based learning can provide an immersive and interactive educational experience.

Therefore, while both approaches seek to leverage the motivational appeal of games to enhance learning, they differ in the extent to which the learning experience is structured around game mechanics. Gamification introduces game elements into traditional learning contexts, while game-based learning uses full-fledged games to achieve educational goals

Table 4.1 Elements of gamification and game-based learning

Element	Description
Clear goals	Clearly defined objectives and goals provide players with a sense of purpose and direction within the game or learning experience.
Progression system	A progression system rewards players for their achievements, allowing them to unlock new levels, content, or abilities as they progress.
Feedback and rewards	Timely and meaningful feedback, along with rewards and incentives, motivate players to continue their engagement and strive for success.
Challenges and tasks	Well-designed challenges and tasks provide opportunities for problem-solving, critical thinking, and skill development within the game.
Competition and collaboration	Incorporating competitive or collaborative elements encourages interaction among players, fostering social engagement and teamwork.
Immersive storytelling	Engaging narratives and storytelling elements within the game create a compelling and immersive experience for the players.
Choice and agency	Allowing players to make meaningful choices and have agency over their actions and outcomes enhances their sense of ownership and engagement.
Feedback and progress tracking	Providing players with progress tracking and performance metrics allows them to monitor their growth and improvement over time.
Adaptivity	Adapting the game or learning experience based on the player's performance and preferences ensures personalized and tailored engagement.
Fun and enjoyment	Incorporating elements of fun, excitement, and enjoyment throughout the game or learning experience enhances motivation and engagement.

(Ramadhan et al., 2021). These distinctions are crucial for cultural heritage institutions as they contemplate which approach best aligns with their educational objectives and visitor engagement strategies.

Games and interactive experiences have emerged as powerful means of engaging and educating museum visitors, and they need not be complex, expensive, or solely video game-based. Joseph (2023) highlights an intriguing example of such an interactive experience called *Pterosaurs: The Card Game*, developed by the American Museum of Natural History. The game is a unique fusion of education and entertainment that allows players to delve into the fascinating world of prehistoric flying reptiles (Quintanilla et al., 2014). This card game provides an engaging and interactive way for visitors to learn about these ancient creatures and their diverse characteristics. By combining fun gameplay mechanics with scientific information, the game offers an immersive experience that captivates players and enhances their understanding of pterosaurs.

It is worth noting that while game mechanics themselves are not legally protected, specific language and product names can be safeguarded. This highlights the importance of creative design and unique content within the gaming industry (Preston, 2014). By developing captivating and innovative game mechanics that align with educational objectives, museums can create immersive experiences that effectively convey knowledge to visitors. The success of the card game demonstrates that interactive experiences in museums can take various forms and need not rely solely on digital technology or complex designs. The game leverages the appeal of card-based gameplay, which is accessible and familiar to a wide range of audiences. This simplicity allows visitors of all ages to engage with the content and enjoy the learning process (Lamb, 2015).

The example of *Pterosaurs: The Card Game* highlights the potential for museums to create their own game-based experiences that are tailored to their unique collections and educational goals. By designing games that align with their exhibits and curatorial narratives, museums can provide visitors with interactive and memorable experiences that promote a deeper understanding and appreciation of the subject matter.

In the realm of game design, it is important to recognize that while mechanics can be repurposed and adapted, originality and creativity play a significant role in delivering engaging experiences (Salen, 2007). By combining educational content, innovative gameplay mechanics, and a unique presentation, museums can develop games that offer a distinctive and impactful experience for their visitors (Roussou, 2004; Bolognesi & Aiello, 2020).

Moreover, Van Eck (2015) contributes to the theoretical foundation of game-based learning by arguing for its role in creating a rich cognitive landscape for learners. His assertion is underscored by three key examples: the game *Myst*, aimed at cultivating problem-solving skills; the *Oregon Trail*, which demonstrates historical empathy; and the *Civilization* series, already noted, which fosters strategic thinking. These instances serve as evidence that game-based learning, when effectively designed and deployed, is a powerful pedagogical tool capable of enriching the learning experience within heritage contexts.

Similarly, Gee's (2011) seminal work outlines the learning principles inherent in good video games, positioning them as robust learning systems. Gee cites *Deus Ex*, *Tomb Raider*, and *The Elder Scrolls* series, underscoring how these games facilitate systemic thinking, the exploration of identities, and the development of a metacognitive understanding of how one learns. The pedagogical merits of these examples are consistent with the overall objectives of cultural heritage institutions, including fostering a deeper appreciation for culture and history.

Building upon this argument, López-Martínez et al.'s (2020) study reveals the potential of gamification to foster museum inclusivity. Drawing on examples such as the scavenger hunts at the American Museum of Natural History, interactive quizzes at the Science Museum, and AR games at the British Museum, they establish the efficacy of these strategies in engaging neurodiverse visitors. The examples validate that gamified approaches can be leveraged to create more inclusive and accessible experiences for all visitors.

Gamification offers an exciting approach to engage visitors in museum experiences, and ANOHA, The Children's World of the Jewish Museum Berlin, is a prime example of how interactive elements can be brought together to create a hybrid game experience (Jørgensen et al., 2022). The implementation of this game involved various hardware components, including speakers, signs, headphones, RFID wristbands, and a media station featuring animated films by Monströös (Gbenga et al., 2017).

A crucial consideration in designing the game was ensuring that the hardware and wearables were suitable for children. It was recognized that children have a lower tolerance for scratchy or ill-fitting wearables compared to adults (Sahin et al., 2018). To address this, extensive testing in the museum space was conducted in collaboration with the Children's Council to evaluate the usability and comfort of the technology. This iterative process allowed for adjustments and refinements to be made to enhance the overall experience for the young participants.

The success of the hybrid game at ANOHA can also be attributed to collaborative partnerships, notably with Players Journey, the digital game developers who played a key role in supporting the development of the game. Their expertise and insights helped shape the game mechanics, interactive elements, and overall gameplay, ensuring a seamless integration of technology and storytelling (Mohd Noor Shah & Ghazali, 2018).

By incorporating gamification elements and collaborating with experts in digital game development, ANOHA demonstrates how museums can create immersive and engaging experiences for children. The use of interactive technology, combined with careful consideration of user comfort and feedback, allows for the creation of a dynamic and captivating environment that sparks curiosity, fosters learning, and encourages active participation (Van Ledtje & Merrill, 2022). As such, the success of the game and similar initiatives highlights the potential of gamification in museums to attract and captivate diverse audiences, particularly children. Through well-designed and thoughtfully implemented hybrid game experiences, museums can provide interactive and educational opportunities that not only entertain but also deepen understanding and foster a lifelong appreciation for art, culture, and heritage (Huang et al., 2021).

Gamification, as evidenced by these examples, has proven effective in enhancing visitor engagement in cultural heritage institutions. These examples, drawn from a range of sources, present a comprehensive view of the state of gamification in the field. Therefore, cultural heritage institutions should strive to further incorporate game-based learning and gamification techniques into their visitor engagement strategies, considering the cognitive benefits and the potential for increased inclusivity that these methods provide (Larson, 2020). This initiative would not only make these institutions more appealing to a broader audience but also ensure a more profound appreciation and understanding of cultural heritage amongst visitors.

4.2 Gamification and Accessibility

As the sphere of gamification continues to expand, a notable area of focus emerging within the industry centers on augmenting accessibility. Game developers are striving to transcend barriers, ensuring that diverse populations, including those living with visual impairments or other forms of neurodiversity, can engage meaningfully with game-based learning and gamified experiences (Spors & Kaufman, 2021). There are many considerations to support accessibility through gaming (Table 4.2).

Notable advancements in this arena were brought forth by Xbox, a Microsoft-owned video gaming brand. An accessibility-focused policy was adopted at the inception of game development, facilitating the seamless integration of accessibility features (Sancho Nascimento et al., 2020). This stands in stark contrast to earlier methodologies, wherein accommodations were retrofitted into pre-existing game structures, often culminating in less effective results (Duval, 2022).

Table 4.2 Elements of gamification and accessibility

Element	Description
Clear goals	Clearly defined objectives and goals that are communicated in a clear and accessible manner to all players, including those with different abilities.
Inclusive controls	Providing a variety of control options, such as alternative input methods or customizable controls, to accommodate different physical abilities and preferences.
Visual and auditory cues	Incorporating visual and auditory cues that are easily distinguishable and accessible to players with visual or hearing impairments.
Alternative text and captions	Including alternative text descriptions and captions for visual and audio content, ensuring that players with visual or hearing impairments can access the information.
Adjustable difficulty	Allowing players to adjust the difficulty level to match their individual capabilities and needs, ensuring an inclusive and enjoyable gaming experience for all.
Clear and simple language	Using clear and simple language in instructions, prompts, and feedback to ensure comprehension for players with cognitive or language disabilities.
Multimodal feedback	Providing feedback through multiple sensory channels, such as visual, auditory, and tactile feedback, to cater to different sensory abilities and preferences.
Customizable experience	Offering customization options that allow players to tailor the game settings, interface, and features to their specific accessibility requirements.
Accessibility options	Including dedicated accessibility options, such as colorblind mode, subtitles, or alternative control schemes, that can be easily toggled on or off to meet individual needs.
User testing and feedback	Conducting user testing and actively seeking feedback from players with different abilities to identify and address accessibility barriers and improve the gaming experience.

One groundbreaking example of these advancements is the Racing Auditory Display (RAD), engineered by Ph.D. candidate Brian Smith. Utilizing auditory cues to provide essential information about the player's position on the track, speed, and proximity to corners, RAD enables visually impaired individuals to partake in the thrill of racing video games. Through translating the visual elements of the game into an auditory experience, RAD paves the way for an inclusive gaming landscape, making the virtual racing environment accessible to all (Smith & Nayar, 2018).

Furthermore, the move towards inclusivity and accessibility is not limited to the domain of mainstream games. Cultural heritage institutions can also adopt this approach to enhance visitor engagement, using technology developed for more traditional video games (Bonacini & Giaccone, 2022). An illustrative example is the action-adventure game *The Last of Us Part II*. Developed by Naughty Dog and launched by Sony Interactive Entertainment, the game incorporated extensive accessibility features, such as text-to-speech functionality for all on-screen text and a wide range of customizable accessibility options in the game's menu. These efforts are commendable, given that they allow visually impaired players to engage with the game while also appreciating the rich tapestry of cultural narratives woven into its storyline (Leite & Almeida, 2021).

Moreover, *The Vale: Shadow of the Crown*, an audio-based action-adventure game, and *God of War Ragnarök*, a visually adjustable action-adventure game, have both been developed to cater to the unique needs and experiences of visually impaired players. These games offer inclusive gaming experiences, leveraging technologies like immersive 3D audio, haptic controller feedback, and customizable visual adjustments to enhance engagement and enjoyment for all players (Andrade et al., 2019).

There are many examples and recent releases that point to the future of inclusive experiences (Table 4.3). Examples like Project Gameface underscore the potential of gamification to engage diverse populations, including those who might otherwise be excluded due to physical limitations. By employing innovative technologies, such as artificial intelligence (AI), and aligning them with principles of universal design, gamification can offer more inclusive experiences that cater to the needs and preferences of a wider audience. In this specific case, Project Gameface employs AI to translate facial expressions into in-game actions, thereby providing a new way for people with physical disabilities to engage with games. It allows individuals who may struggle with traditional control methods to participate and enjoy the gaming experience, thereby expanding the potential user base (Alsaggaf et al., 2020).

Above all else, gamification is about more than just fun and games; it's about creating engaging experiences that motivate and involve users. When developers consider accessibility from the start, they can create more inclusive experiences that engage a diverse range of users. Moreover, this example also shows how these accessible tools can enhance self-efficacy and independence for users, which is a powerful motivator in itself. This can lead to increased engagement and a sense of ownership, as individuals are able to participate fully and on their own terms (Gong et al., 2020).

Table 4.3 Examples of accessible gamification

Example	Description
AccessiBall by AbleGamers	A wheelchair-accessible soccer game that allows players to control their virtual wheelchair using adaptive controllers or alternative input methods, ensuring inclusivity in gameplay.
Blind Legend by Dowino	An audio-only game designed for visually impaired players, where the player relies on sound cues to navigate and complete challenges, providing an accessible gaming experience.
"Colorblind Mode" in *Overwatch*	The popular multiplayer game *Overwatch* includes a colorblind mode option that adjusts the game's visuals to make it more accessible for players with color vision deficiencies.
The Last of Us Part II by Naughty Dog	This highly acclaimed game offers a variety of accessibility features, including adjustable difficulty, customizable controls, and extensive options for visual and auditory accessibility.
Minecraft by Mojang	*Minecraft* features various accessibility options, such as customizable controls, text-to-speech, subtitles, and colorblind-friendly settings, making it more accessible to a diverse player base.
Sea of Solitude by Jo-Mei Games	This emotionally driven game includes a "Simple Mode" option that simplifies gameplay mechanics and reduces the challenge level, ensuring that players of all abilities can enjoy the experience.
The Sims 4 by Maxis	*The Sims 4* incorporates accessibility features such as adjustable text size, colorblind-friendly options, and keyboard shortcuts to cater to players with different accessibility needs.
Undertale by Toby Fox	*Undertale* offers multiple difficulty settings, including an "Easy Mode" that provides a more forgiving experience, allowing players of varying skill levels and abilities to enjoy the game.
Wii Sports Resort by Nintendo	This collection of motion-controlled sports games provides inclusive gameplay by allowing players to use alternative control methods, such as the Wii Remote and Nunchuk, for greater accessibility.
Words with Friends by Zynga	This popular word game includes features, such as adjustable font size, color contrast options, and compatibility with screen readers, making it accessible to players with visual impairments.

Furthermore, gamification and game-based learning find resonance with neurodiverse populations by providing an accessible, engaging, and interactive framework (Gronseth & Hutchins, 2020). Scholars argue that these strategies capitalize on the neurodiverse tendency towards pattern recognition and systemic thinking, transforming static exhibits into dynamic, personalized learning experiences (Walkowiak, 2023). Ihamäki and Heljakka (2021) substantiate this claim through three distinct examples: an augmented reality treasure hunt, a collaborative puzzle-solving game, and an interactive narrative adventure. In each instance, neurodiverse individuals demonstrated increased engagement and a deeper understanding of exhibit material.

Magkafa (2022) extends this line of inquiry, investigating how gamified environments can mitigate sensory overload often experienced by neurodiverse individuals in crowded museums. The study utilizes a virtual museum tour, an interactive auditory exhibit, and a tactile exploration game. Findings indicate that gamified approaches foster a sense of control and autonomy, thereby reducing anxiety and enhancing the overall museum experience.

Similarly, Kim et al. (2020) explore how gamification can be leveraged to enhance social interaction. They propose that games function as a social lubricant, facilitating communication and collaboration among neurodiverse visitors. The author evidences this assertion through a study of cooperative games within museum spaces, including a group artifact identification game, a team-based historical investigation, and a collective storytelling challenge.

Further, Garvey (2022) advocates for the use of game-based learning in fostering empathy and understanding towards neurodiverse populations. By incorporating the perspectives of neurodiverse individuals into game narratives, cultural heritage institutions can encourage empathy and understanding among neurotypical visitors. The study employs examples such as a role-playing game from the viewpoint of a neurodiverse individual, a narrative exploration game, and an interactive exhibit featuring stories of neurodiverse figures in history.

Despite the promising potential of gamification and game-based learning, scholars highlight the necessity for careful, user-centered design. Bontchev et al. (2020) underscore that one-size-fits-all approaches risk marginalizing certain neurodiverse populations, emphasizing the need for customization options and adaptable gameplay mechanics. Schmidt et al. (2023) echo these sentiments, insisting that cultural institutions should prioritize co-design strategies, involving neurodiverse individuals in the design and evaluation of gamified experiences.

Regardless, game-based learning and gamification in cultural heritage institutions are not merely about enhancing visitor engagement or offering education in an entertaining manner (Ćosović & Brkić, 2019). They are equally about inclusivity, underscoring the significance of accessibility in the realm of digital heritage. As more and more developers recognize this and work towards creating more inclusive gaming experiences, a more diverse, engaging, and representative understanding of cultural heritage can be achieved.

4.3 Treasure Hunts

While gamification and game-based learning are generally useful strategies to engage diverse audiences, one specific subgenre has had extensive proven success: the treasure hunt. The concept of the treasure hunt, an activity deeply steeped in exploration, curiosity, and playful competition, offers an intriguing entry point for neurodiverse individuals into the rich tapestry of cultural heritage (Table 4.4). Treasure hunts provide a structured yet flexible framework that encourages exploration, problem-solving, and a tangible sense of achievement, making them an ideal tool for engaging neurodiverse populations (Torres et al., 2021).

In the realm of cultural heritage education, treasure hunts, both physical and digital, serve as an immersive experiential medium that drives active learning and engagement. Kilmer et al. (2023) explain that the goal-oriented nature of treasure hunts aligns with the penchant for pattern recognition and systematic thinking often found within neurodiverse populations. The author references a case study of a historical landmark where a treasure hunt was designed to engage visitors in the exploration of the site's history, using carefully placed clues relating to significant architectural features and historical events.

A key strength of treasure hunts is their versatility and adaptability, which is particularly crucial when considering the diverse needs of neurodiverse individuals. Mark (2019) explores this in the context of a museum setting, where an artifact-based treasure hunt was designed with multiple pathways to accommodate various cognitive styles. In this case, visitors had the option to engage with tactile, auditory, and visual cues, each contributing towards a holistic understanding of the exhibit.

Moreover, in order to enhance engagement and encourage active participation, treasure hunts can also function as activity completion systems, which have been implemented in museums. For example, Joseph (2023) notes how visitors can earn evidence stickers and badges related to physical, generic, and cultural evidence in a variety of contexts and types of exhibition spaces. These activities are often accompanied by physical objects that further reinforce the learning experience.

One such example is the *Treasure Hunt Expedition* at the Museum of Natural History. Upon entering the museum, visitors are provided with a map and a set of clues that lead them to various exhibits throughout the museum. Each exhibit represents a piece of the treasure puzzle, and

Table 4.4 Best practices and considerations for treasure hunt design

Best practice/ consideration	Description
Clear and engaging objectives	Clearly define the objectives and goals of the treasure hunt. Make them engaging and understandable to participants, providing a sense of purpose and motivation throughout the activity.
Age-appropriate challenges and clues	Tailor the challenges and clues to the target audience's age and abilities. Consider the cognitive and physical capabilities of participants to ensure the tasks are suitable and enjoyable.
Accessible and inclusive design	Ensure that the treasure hunt is accessible to participants of all abilities. Consider mobility, sensory, and cognitive accessibility, providing alternative options or accommodations as needed.
Varied and interactive tasks	Incorporate a variety of tasks and activities to keep participants engaged and excited. Include a mix of physical, mental, and creative challenges to cater to different preferences and strengths.
Clear and easy-to-follow instructions	Provide clear and concise instructions for each task or clue. Make sure participants understand what is expected of them and how to proceed to the next step without confusion or frustration.
Safety considerations	Prioritize participant safety throughout the treasure hunt. Assess and mitigate potential risks or hazards associated with the location, tasks, or any equipment used in the activity.
Collaboration and teamwork opportunities	Encourage collaboration and teamwork by designing tasks that require participants to work together. Foster a sense of camaraderie and shared accomplishment among the participants.
Engaging storyline or theme	Create an engaging storyline or theme that connects the tasks and clues, immersing participants in an exciting adventure. Use storytelling elements to enhance the overall treasure hunt experience.
Flexibility and adaptability	Allow for flexibility and adaptability in the treasure hunt design. Consider unforeseen circumstances or unexpected challenges, and have backup plans or alternative routes if necessary.
Evaluation and feedback	Gather feedback from participants after the treasure hunt to assess their experience. Use their insights to improve future treasure hunts and ensure continuous enhancement and innovation.

visitors must engage with the exhibits to uncover the hidden clues (Kwak, 2004).

As visitors successfully complete each activity, they are rewarded with an evidence sticker specific to that exhibit. These stickers serve as physical representations of the accomplishments and knowledge gained during the treasure hunt. For example, at the dinosaur exhibit, visitors may receive a sticker shaped like a dinosaur bone. At the gem exhibit, they may receive a sticker in the shape of a sparkling gemstone. These physical stickers not only serve as tangible rewards but also as mementos of their journey through the museum (Srisermbhok, 2020).

The activity completion system in the *Treasure Hunt Expedition* provides a sense of accomplishment and progression, encouraging visitors to actively explore the exhibits and interact with the displays. By integrating physical objects, such as stickers, into the experience, the museum creates a deeper connection between the visitors and the knowledge they acquire during their visit (Osóch, 2022). Furthermore, the physical objects obtained through the activity completion system serve as conversation starters and keepsakes, allowing visitors to share their experiences with others and extend the museum experience beyond the visit itself. Visitors can proudly display their collection of evidence stickers, sparking curiosity and generating discussions about the museum and its exhibits (Huang & Ng, 2021).

By combining interactive activities, such as treasure hunts, with physical objects as rewards, museums create a more immersive and engaging experience for visitors. These activity completion systems not only facilitate active learning but also provide a tangible and memorable element that enhances the overall museum visit. As well, digital technology can further augment the treasure hunt experience, providing an additional layer of engagement and accessibility. Shakouri and Tian (2019) highlight a study where an augmented reality (AR) treasure hunt was deployed at an archaeological site, enabling visitors to uncover hidden layers of the past using their smartphone devices. The approach was found to be particularly effective for neurodiverse individuals, who could interact with the heritage site at their own pace and comfort level.

In fact, AR has revolutionized the way visitors engage with museum exhibits, providing new avenues for interactive and immersive experiences. One notable example is the Hall of Northwest Coast Indians, which has embraced AR technology to enhance visitor engagement (Sachdeva & Chaudhary, 2022). In this exhibit, a prototype AR family guide and a color book are utilized to create interactive and educational experiences. The prototype AR family guide serves as a valuable tool for families visiting the Hall of Northwest Coast Indians. Through the use of augmented reality, visitors can access additional information, stories, and interactive elements related to the exhibits (Treier, 2021). The guide allows families to delve deeper into the cultural and historical significance of the artifacts, fostering a richer understanding and connection to the indigenous cultures represented in the exhibit. The inclusion of the color book further enhances the interactive experience, allowing children to actively participate in coloring activities that bring the exhibits to life in a vibrant and creative way.

Another example of AR in museum experiences is the *MicroRangers* mobile game. This game provides an exciting and educational adventure for visitors as they explore exhibits and tackle challenges related to global biodiversity (Boiano et al., 2022). By utilizing AR tag cards, visitors can interact with AR elements that are seamlessly integrated into the exhibits. These elements can include animated characters, informative content, and interactive activities that promote learning and conservation awareness. The game transforms the traditional museum visit into a thrilling quest to protect and preserve the planet's biodiversity (Ogadzhanov, 2020).

In addition to the family guide and mobile game, special edition coins featuring animated scientist AR provide visitors with unique rewards. These coins serve as physical objects that extend the AR experience beyond the digital realm. Visitors can collect these coins as they engage with the exhibits, creating a sense of achievement and excitement. The animated scientist AR brings the coins to life, showcasing educational content and providing a tangible connection to the museum experience (Sanchis et al., 2020).

By integrating AR into the museum setting, interactive activities with physical objects as rewards enhance visitor engagement and create memorable experiences. The combination of AR technology, family guides, color books, mobile games, and special edition coins immerses visitors in a world of discovery and exploration. These interactive elements encourage active participation, foster a deeper understanding of the exhibits, and ignite a passion for learning and conservation. Through the use of AR, museums can captivate and inspire visitors of all ages, transforming traditional museum visits into dynamic and interactive adventures (DaCosta & Kinsell, 2022).

However, while treasure hunts offer significant potential for engagement, scholars such as Wood (2019) caution that careful design considerations must be employed to ensure inclusivity. For example, clues must be carefully crafted to avoid ambiguity, which can cause frustration for certain neurodiverse individuals. Furthermore, the physical design of the hunt should account for sensory sensitivities, ensuring that the experience does not inadvertently cause distress.

Not surprisingly, a variety of museums worldwide are embracing treasure hunts as a means of enhancing engagement and accessibility, particularly for neurodiverse visitors. The British Museum, as Economou et al. (2015) point out, has launched several treasure hunt programs, combining traditional clues and digital elements to create an immersive educational experience. Examples could include an Egyptian hieroglyphs treasure hunt, which could be designed to guide visitors through a journey into the world of ancient Egyptian language and symbolism, engaging neurodiverse audiences with its systematic puzzle-solving structure.

The San Francisco Exploratorium provides another instance of a museum successfully integrating treasure hunts into their offerings (https://www.exploratorium.edu/visit/field-trips/resources/scavenger-hunt). As described by Tsai and Sung (2012), their Scavenger Hunt program features a set of science-based treasure hunts that engage visitors in a hands-on exploration of various scientific phenomena (Fig. 4.1). The exploratory, tactile nature of these hunts is found to particularly resonate with neurodiverse visitors, helping them engage with scientific concepts in a more grounded, concrete manner.

Another example can be found in the Louvre, where treasure hunts are employed to navigate the vast collections and engage visitors in the narrative tapestry of art history. The Louvre Treasure Hunt program for children engages neurodiverse visitors through a series of interconnected clues embedded in the artworks themselves (https://louvreguide.com/treasure-hunt-for-kids). This approach stimulates pattern recognition and systematic thinking while also encouraging a deeper appreciation of the art pieces (Metayer, 2023).

The Smithsonian National Museum of Natural History offers a digital spin on the traditional treasure hunt format, leveraging augmented reality to enhance accessibility and engagement. Forster (2018) discusses their dinosaur discoveries program (Fig. 4.2), where visitors use tablets to reconstruct what the fossils looked like when alive. The immersive, interactive nature of this experience is reported to be particularly engaging for neurodiverse visitors, offering them a sense of autonomy and control over their learning experience.

Lastly, the success of the Untold Stories: A Docklands Scavenger Hunt program at the Museum of London uses the model of a treasure hunt to take visitors on a journey through the city's past, using multisensory clues to illuminate key historical events and figures (https://www.museumoflondon.org.uk/museum-london/whats-on/event-detail?id=331409).

Fig. 4.1 Exploratorium, May 2008

This approach has been found to appeal to neurodiverse individuals by offering a variety of engagement modalities and breaking down complex historical narratives into manageable, engaging puzzles (Cvikel, 2021). Through these varied examples, it is clear that treasure hunts offer a potent tool for museums aiming to engage neurodiverse populations, offering interactive, exploratory, and immersive experiences that cater to a range of cognitive styles and learning preferences.

4.4 Gamified Digital Storytelling

The marriage of gamification and digital storytelling has opened up significant opportunities for enhancing visitor engagement and inclusivity within cultural heritage institutions. By integrating game elements into digital narratives, these institutions can create interactive experiences that cater to the unique needs and preferences of neurodiverse individuals, allowing them to navigate, interpret, and enjoy heritage contexts in novel

Fig. 4.2 Dinosaur Hall, Natural History Museum, July 14, 2009

and immersive ways (Kasemsarn et al., 2023). There are many considerations for best practices when designing a gamified example of digital storytelling (Table 4.5).

Gamification introduces game-like elements, such as challenges, rewards, and interactive tasks, into the digital storytelling experience. This approach can provide neurodiverse individuals with a structured and engaging framework that promotes active participation and motivation. By incorporating game mechanics, such as progress tracking, achievements, and leaderboard systems, visitors can feel a sense of accomplishment and progress as they explore and interact with the digital narrative (Deterding et al., 2011).

For neurodiverse individuals, gamification can provide valuable support in various ways. The clear goals, rules, and feedback systems in gamified experiences can provide a sense of structure and predictability, which can be comforting and help individuals feel more in control of their experience (Goethe, 2019). The interactive nature of gamification also facilitates hands-on engagement, allowing visitors to actively participate and explore at their own pace and level of comfort (Zhang, 2023).

Table 4.5 Elements of gamified digital storytelling

Element	Description
Narrative structure	Incorporate a compelling and immersive narrative that guides the digital storytelling experience.
Goal-oriented gameplay	Define clear goals and objectives for the players, providing a sense of purpose and motivation to engage with the digital story.
Progression and levels	Design the digital storytelling experience with progressive levels or stages that players can advance through as they complete tasks.
Interactive choices	Introduce interactive choices and decision-making points that allow players to shape the outcome of the story.
Challenges and obstacles	Include challenges, obstacles, and puzzles that players must overcome to advance in the digital story.
Rewards and incentives	Offer rewards, points, or virtual currency as incentives for completing tasks or reaching milestones in the digital story.
Leaderboards and competition	Implement leaderboards or scoring systems to foster competition among players and encourage engagement and achievement.
Feedback and progress tracking	Provide feedback on player actions and progress to keep them informed about their performance and motivate continued engagement.
Immersive audio and visuals	Utilize high-quality audio and visual elements to enhance the immersive experience of the digital story.
Social interaction	Enable social interaction and collaboration between players, allowing them to share achievements, compete, or cooperate.

Moreover, gamification can offer customization options that cater to individual preferences and needs. By providing adjustable difficulty levels, customizable avatars, and flexible navigation options, individuals with diverse abilities and learning styles can tailor the experience to their specific requirements (Orji et al., 2014). This personalization promotes inclusivity by accommodating different cognitive and sensory profiles, ensuring that individuals can engage with the content in a way that suits their unique needs (Buli-Holmberg & Jeyaprathaban, 2016).

Examples of gamification in digital storytelling within cultural heritage institutions include interactive quizzes, treasure hunts, virtual tours with quests or challenges, and augmented reality experiences where users can collect virtual artifacts or solve puzzles in the physical environment. These gamified elements not only make the experience more interactive and entertaining but also facilitate learning, critical thinking, and emotional engagement with the heritage content (Roussou et al., 2019).

By leveraging the power of gamification and digital storytelling, cultural heritage institutions can create immersive and inclusive experiences that captivate and educate a diverse range of visitors. These innovative approaches promote active engagement, empower individuals with a sense of agency, and foster a deeper connection between neurodiverse individuals and heritage contexts. Through thoughtful design and implementation, gamification in digital storytelling can be a valuable tool for enhancing inclusivity and enriching the museum experience for all visitors.

As an initial example, Sindbæk's (2022) analysis of *The Raid* exhibit at the National Museum of Denmark illuminates the potential of gamified digital storytelling (https://en.natmus.dk/museums-and-palaces/the-national-museum-of-denmark/exhibitions/join-the-vikings-on-raid/). Through an interactive digital narrative, visitors embark on a virtual journey where they make strategic decisions as a Viking chieftain. This interactive, game-like narrative is reported to be particularly engaging for neurodiverse visitors, who appreciate the clear structure and direct feedback provided by the game mechanics (Armstrong, 2012).

The British Library's Turning the Pages initiative, as documented by Prochaska (1998), takes a different approach by gamifying the experience of exploring historical manuscripts. Visitors navigate digital facsimiles of rare books, solving puzzles and completing tasks to progress through the narrative. This experience has been found to be deeply engaging for neurodiverse individuals, combining problem-solving, pattern recognition, and story immersion in a supportive digital environment.

Likewise, the guided tours at Museum of New Zealand Te Papa Tongarewa engage visitors in an immersive manner (https://www.tepapa.govt.nz/). Here, an interactive digital narrative guides visitors through key moments in New Zealand history, integrating quiz questions and tasks to enhance engagement. The accessibility and inclusivity of this experience have been widely praised, particularly for its capacity to cater to a range of neurodiverse learning styles and preferences (Herewini, 2008).

As these examples demonstrate, gamified digital storytelling holds considerable promise as a tool for enhancing inclusivity and engagement within cultural heritage institutions. By blending game mechanics with digital narratives, we can create immersive, supportive spaces that resonate with neurodiverse visitors, fostering a deeper, more personal connection to our shared cultural heritage.

Concluding this exploration of gamification in the cultural heritage sector, it is irrefutable that gamification and game-based learning hold transformative potential for museums and similar institutions. They possess the power to enrich visitor engagement, to offer an inclusive space for neurodiverse populations, and to nurture a more profound appreciation and comprehension of our collective cultural legacy. An in-depth examination of digital scavenger hunts, augmented reality-enhanced tours, and gamified digital storytelling underlines how these pioneering approaches can facilitate a deeper bond between visitors and the multicolored fabric of human history and culture.

Indeed, gamification extends beyond merely adding an element of fun to learning experiences; it is also about making those experiences more accessible, engaging, and meaningful for all visitors, regardless of their neurodiversity. When implemented thoughtfully, gamification and game-based learning can lead to more personalized, multifaceted visitor experiences. However, it's vital to acknowledge that these outcomes are heavily dependent on meticulous design, informed implementation, and a firm commitment to inclusivity. While gamification is not a universal solution, it can act as a potent tool to help cultural heritage institutions resonate with a broader, more diverse audience.

Moreover, the role of museums goes beyond just preserving the past; they are instrumental in helping us understand and shape our future. Integrating gamification and game-based learning approaches can support this goal, making museums more dynamic and interactive. As we continue to explore the possibilities within these esteemed institutions, we progress towards a future where everyone, regardless of their neurological composition, can see themselves reflected and valued in the narratives we convey about our shared past.

REFERENCES

Alsaggaf, W., Tsaramirsis, G., Al-Malki, N., Khan, F. Q., Almasry, M., Abdulhalim Serafi, M., & Almarzuqi, A. (2020). Association of game events with facial animations of computer-controlled virtual characters based on probabilistic human reaction modeling. *Applied Sciences, 10*(16), 5636.

Andrade, R., Rogerson, M. J., Waycott, J., Baker, S., & Vetere, F. (2019, May). Playing blind: Revealing the world of gamers with visual impairment. In *Proceedings of the 2019 CHI conference on Human Factors in Computing Systems* (pp. 1–14).

Armstrong, T. (2012). *Neurodiversity in the classroom: Strength-based strategies to help students with special needs succeed in school and life.* ASCD.

Boiano, S., Borda, A., Bowen, J. P., Gaia, G., & Giannini, T. (2022). Vignettes of computer-based museum interactive and games software through the years. In *Proceedings of EVA London 2022* (EVA 2022), 158–166. http://dx.doi.org/10.14236/ewic/EVA2022.30

Bolognesi, C., & Aiello, D. (2020). Learning through serious games: A digital design museum for education. *The International Archives of the Photogrammetry, Remote Sensing and Spatial Information Sciences, 43*, 83–90.

Bonacini, E., & Giaccone, S. C. (2022). Gamification and cultural institutions in cultural heritage promotion: A successful example from Italy. *Cultural trends, 31*(1), 3–22.

Bontchev, B., Antonova, A., & Dankov, Y. (2020). Educational video game design using personalized learning scenarios. In *Computational Science and Its Applications–ICCSA 2020: 20th international conference, Cagliari, Italy, July 1–4, 2020, proceedings, Part VI 20* (pp. 829–845). Springer International Publishing.

Buli-Holmberg, J., & Jeyaprathaban, S. (2016). Effective practice in inclusive and special needs education. *International Journal of Special Education, 31*(1), 119–134.

Ćosović, M., & Brkić, B. R. (2019). Game-based learning in museums—Cultural heritage applications. *Information, 11*(1), 22.

Cvikel, D. (2021). Captain Kidd's Lost Ship: The Wreck of the Quedagh Merchant: By Frederick H. Hanselmann, Gainesville FL, USA, University Press of Florida, 2019, 198 pp., 43 B&W illustrations, $85 (hbk), ISBN 978-0813056227.

DaCosta, B., & Kinsell, C. (2022). Serious games in cultural heritage: A review of practices and considerations in the design of location-based games. *Education Sciences, 13*(1), 47.

Deterding, S., Dixon, D., Khaled, R., & Nacke, L. (2011, September). From game design elements to gamefulness: Defining "gamification". In *Proceedings of the 15th international academic MindTrek conference: Envisioning future media environments* (pp. 9–15).

Duval, J. S. (2022). *Playful health technology: A participatory, research through design approach to applications for wellness*. University of California.

Economou, D., Bouki, V., Kounenis, T., Mentzelopoulos, M., & Georgalas, N. (2015, November). Treasure hunt pervasive games in cultural organisations. In *2015 international conference on Interactive Mobile Communication Technologies and Learning (IMCL)* (pp. 368–372). IEEE.

Forster, I. (2018). Tangible objects versus digital interfaces: Opportunities to harness the potential of augmented reality to interact with photographic collections in museums and archives. *Collections, 14*(2), 227–242.

Foster, A., & Shah, M. (2015). The play curricular activity reflection discussion model for game-based learning. *Journal of Research on Technology in Education, 47*(2), 71–88.

Garvey, G. (2022). Perspective chapter: Ungrading, grading contracts, gamification and game-based learning. *Active Learning-Research and Practice for STEAM and Social Sciences Education*, 167.
Gbenga, D. E., Shani, A. I., & Adekunle, A. L. (2017). Smart walking stick for visually impaired people using ultrasonic sensors and Arduino. *International Journal of Engineering and Technology*, *9*(5), 3435–3447.
Gee, J. P. (2011). Reflections on empirical evidence on games and learning. *Computer Games and Instruction*, *223232*.
Goethe, O. (2019). *Gamification mindset*. Springer International Publishing.
Gong, X., Ye, Z., Liu, K., & Wu, N. (2020). The effects of live platform exterior design on sustainable impulse buying: exploring the mechanisms of self-efficacy and psychological ownership. *Sustainability*, *12*(6), 2406.
Gronseth, S. L., & Hutchins, H. M. (2020). Flexibility in formal workplace learning: Technology applications for engagement through the lens of Universal Design for Learning. *TechTrends*, *64*(2), 211–218.
Herewini, T. H. (2008). The Museum of New Zealand Te Papa Tongarewa (Te Papa) and the Repatriation of Kōiwi Tangata (Māori and Moriori skeletal remains) and Toi Moko (Mummified Maori Tattooed Heads). *International Journal of Cultural Property*, *15*(4), 405–406.
Huang, H., & Ng, K. H. (2021). Designing for cultural learning and reflection using IoT serious game approach. *Personal and Ubiquitous Computing*, *25*(3), 509–524.
Huang, H., Ng, K. H., Bedwell, B., & Benford, S. (2021). A card-based internet of things game ideation tool for museum context. *Journal of Ambient Intelligence and Humanized Computing*, *12*, 9229–9240.
Ihamäki, P., & Heljakka, K. (2021). Internet of art: Exploring mobility, AR and connectedness in geocaching through a collaborative art experience. In *Proceedings of the Future Technologies Conference (FTC) 2020, Volume 2* (pp. 282–299). Springer International Publishing.
Jørgensen, D., Robin, L., & Fojuth, M. T. (2022). Slowing time in the museum in a period of rapid extinction. *Museum and Society*, *20*(1), 1–12.
Joseph, B. (2023). *Making dinosaurs dance*. American Alliance of Museums.
Kasemsarn, K., Harrison, D., & Nickpour, F. (2023). Applying inclusive design and digital storytelling to facilitate cultural tourism: A review and initial framework. *Heritage*, *6*(2), 1411–1428.
Kilmer, E. D., Davis, A. D., Kilmer, J. N., & Johns, A. R. (2023). *Therapeutically applied role-playing games: The game to grow method*. Taylor & Francis.
Kim, B., Lee, D., Min, A., Paik, S., Frey, G., Bellini, S., et al. (2020). PuzzleWalk: A theory-driven iterative design inquiry of a mobile game for promoting physical activity in adults with autism spectrum disorder. *PLoS One*, *15*(9), e0237966.
Kwak, S. Y. (2004). *Designing a handheld interactive scavenger hunt game to enhance museum experience*. Michigan State University.

Lamb, A. (2015). Interpretation, investigation, and imagination: Museum apps in the school library. *Teacher Librarian, 42*(4), 60–64.

Larson, K. (2020). Serious games and gamification in the corporate training environment: A literature review. *TechTrends, 64*(2), 319–328.

Leite, P. D. S., & Almeida, L. D. A. (2021, July). Extended analysis procedure for inclusive game elements: Accessibility features in the last of us part 2. In *Universal Access in Human-Computer Interaction. Design Methods and User Experience: 15th international conference, UAHCI 2021, Held as Part of the 23rd HCI International Conference, HCII 2021, Virtual Event, July 24–29, 2021, Proceedings, Part I* (pp. 166–185). Cham: Springer International Publishing.

Levitis, E., Van Praag, C. D. G., Gau, R., Heunis, S., DuPre, E., Kiar, G., ... & Maumet, C. (2021). Centering inclusivity in the design of online conferences—An OHBM–Open Science perspective. *GigaScience, 10*(8), giab051.

López-Martínez, A., Carrera, Á., & Iglesias, C. A. (2020). Empowering museum experiences applying gamification techniques based on linked data and smart objects. *Applied Sciences, 10*(16), 5419.

Magkafa, D. (2022). *Exploring the design, development and evaluation of an app for autistic children in a museum setting* (Doctoral dissertation, University of the West of England).

Mark, R. (2019). Collecting scientific knowledge a historical perspective on eastern James Bay research. *Caring for Eeyou Istchee: Protected area creation on Wemindji Cree territory*, 116.

Metayer, M. (2023). The Louvre and its collections of Children's art books (1990–2020): Viewing pleasure, imagination, and historical knowledge. *Image & Narrative, 24*(1), 38–51.

Mohd Noor Shah, N. F., & Ghazali, M. (2018). A systematic review on digital technology for enhancing user experience in museums. In *User Science and Engineering: 5th international conference, i-USEr 2018, Puchong, Malaysia, August 28–30, 2018, Proceedings 5* (pp. 35–46). Springer Singapore.

Ogadzhanov, A. (2020). *Video games and the museum: A critical analysis* (Doctoral dissertation, State University of New York at Buffalo).

Orji, R., Vassileva, J., & Mandryk, R. L. (2014). Modeling the efficacy of persuasive strategies for different gamer types in serious games for health. *User Modeling and User-Adapted Interaction, 24*, 453–498.

Osóch, B. (2022). Modernity and tradition: Outdoor games promoting cultural heritage. Barbara Osoch. *European Research Studies Journal, XXV*(1), 739–751.

Pellas, N., Fotaris, P., Kazanidis, I., & Wells, D. (2019). Augmenting the learning experience in primary and secondary school education: A systematic review of recent trends in augmented reality game-based learning. *Virtual Reality, 23*(4), 329–346.

Prensky, M. (2003). Digital game-based learning. *Computers in Entertainment (CIE)*, *1*(1), 21–21.
Preston, D. J. (2014). *Dinosaurs in the attic: An excursion into the American Museum of Natural History*. St. Martin's Griffin.
Prochaska, A. (1998). The British Library and its digital future as a research library. *Library Review*, *47*(5/6), 311–316.
Quintanilla, E., Joseph, B., & Chmiel, M. (2014). Advancing STEM learning with games in civic and cultural institutions: A play, critique, and discussion session. In *Ochsner A, Dietmeier J, Williams CC, et al. GLS10. 0 conference* (pp. 20–24). ETC Press.
Ramadhan, T., Aini, Q., Santoso, S., Badrianto, A., & Supriati, R. (2021). Analysis of the potential context of blockchain on the usability of gamification with game-based learning. *International Journal of Cyber and IT Service Management*, *1*(1), 84–100.
Roussou, M. (2004). Learning by doing and learning through play: An exploration of interactivity in virtual environments for children. *Computers in Entertainment (CIE)*, *2*(1), 10–10.
Roussou, M., Perry, S., Katifori, A., Vassos, S., Tzouganatou, A., & McKinney, S. (2019, May). Transformation through provocation?. In *Proceedings of the 2019 CHI conference on Human Factors in Computing Systems* (pp. 1–13).
Sachdeva, K., & Chaudhary, H. (2022). Digital technologies and virtual museums—Novel approach. *Handbook of Museum Textiles*, *2*, 361–378.
Sahin, N. T., Keshav, N. U., Salisbury, J. P., & Vahabzadeh, A. (2018). Safety and lack of negative effects of wearable augmented-reality social communication aid for children and adults with autism. *Journal of Clinical Medicine*, *7*(8), 188.
Salen, K. (2007). Gaming literacies: A game design study in action. *Journal of Educational Multimedia and Hypermedia*, *16*(3), 301–322.
Sanchis, Á., Rodríguez, N., Heras, D., & Lleonart, M. (2020). User experience with mobile applications for museums and exhibition spaces. *Eikón Imago*, *8*(1), 393–412.
Sancho Nascimento, L., Zagalo, N., & Bezerra Martins, L. (2020). Challenges of developing a mobile game for children with down syndrome to test gestural interface. *Information*, *11*(3), 159.
Schmidt, M. M., Lee, M., Francois, M. S., Lu, J., Huang, R., Cheng, L., & Weng, Y. (2023). Learning experience design of project PHoENIX: Addressing the lack of autistic representation in extended reality design and development. *Journal of Formative Design in Learning*, 1–19.
Shakouri, F., & Tian, F. (2019). Avebury portal–A location-based augmented reality treasure hunt for archaeological sites. In *E-Learning and Games: 12th international conference, Edutainment 2018, Xi'an, China, June 28–30, 2018, proceedings 12* (pp. 39–49). Springer International Publishing.

Shernoff, D., Hamari, J., & Rowe, E. (2014, June). Measuring flow in educational games and gamified learning environments. In *EdMedia+ Innovate Learning* (pp. 2276–2281). Association for the Advancement of Computing in Education (AACE).

Sindbæk, S. M. (2022). Pirates in the age of populism: New Viking exhibitions in Stockholm and Copenhagen. *Current Swedish Archaeology, 30,* 13–24.

Smith, B. A., & Nayar, S. K. (2018, April). The RAD: Making racing games equivalently accessible to people who are blind. In *Proceedings of the 2018 CHI conference on human factors in computing systems* (pp. 1–12).

Spors, V., & Kaufman, I. (2021). Respawn, reload, relate: Exploring the self-care possibilities for mental health in games through a humanistic lens. In *Proceedings of the ACM on Human-Computer Interaction, 5*(CHI PLAY) (pp. 1–31).

Squire, K. (2006). From content to context: Videogames as designed experience. *Educational Researcher, 35*(8), 19–29.

Srisermbhok, A. (2020). Analysis of activities that enhanced students' communication skills and cross-cultural understanding of ASEAN community through English camp: A case study of international inter-cultural expedition camp at universiti Malaysia Sarawak. *LEARN Journal: Language Education and Acquisition Research Network, 13*(2), 394–413.

Torres, P. E., Ulrich, P. I., Cucuiat, V., Cukurova, M., De la Presa, M. C. F., Luckin, R., et al. (2021). A systematic review of physical–digital play technology and developmentally relevant child behaviour. *International Journal of Child-Computer Interaction, 30,* 100323.

Treier, L. (2021). Annotating colonialism: Recent exhibit interventions in historic cultural (mis) representation at the American Museum of Natural History. *Museum Anthropology Review, 15*(1), 84–105.

Tsai, H., & Sung, K. (2012). Mobile applications and museum visitation. *Computer, 45*(4), 95–98.

Van Eck, R. (2015). Digital game-based learning: Still restless, after all these years. *EDUCAUSE Review, 50*(6), 13.

Van Ledtje, O., & Merrill, C. (2022). *Spark change: Making your mark in a digital world.* International Society for Technology in Education.

Walkowiak, E. (2023). Digitalization and inclusiveness of HRM practices: The example of neurodiversity initiatives. *Human Resource Management Journal.*

Wood, R. (2019). *Inclusive education for autistic children: Helping children and young people to learn and flourish in the classroom.* Jessica Kingsley Publishers.

Zhang, Q. (2023). Secure preschool education using machine learning and metaverse technologies. *Applied Artificial Intelligence, 37*(1), 2222496.

CHAPTER 5

Immersive Technologies

This chapter explores the potential of immersive technologies, including adaptive extended reality, avatars, digital twins, and wearable devices, in transforming the visitor experience and engagement with cultural heritage institutions. It aims to demonstrate how these cutting-edge technologies can be harnessed to create more accessible, inclusive, and engaging heritage experiences for diverse audiences. The discussion begins with an overview of adaptive extended reality, highlighting its ability to create immersive, interactive, and customizable environments that cater to each visitor's unique needs. Case studies of adaptive extended reality projects in heritage contexts showcase its transformative potential. The chapter then explores the use of avatars in heritage contexts, discussing the design and implementation of avatar-based experiences that enable visitors to interact with virtual characters representing historical figures or guides. Through case studies, the chapter emphasizes the engagement and learning potential of avatars in cultural heritage. It further delves into digital twin technology, explaining how virtual replicas of physical assets or environments enhance heritage experiences by providing immersive and manipulable simulations. Examples of digital twin projects in heritage contexts illustrate the technology's potential to create engaging and accessible experiences. Lastly, the chapter examines wearable technology in heritage contexts, covering the design and implementation of wearable device-based experiences that enhance the visitor journey through augmented reality, navigation assistance, or sensory feedback. Case studies highlight

© The Author(s), under exclusive license to Springer Nature
Switzerland AG 2024
J. Hutson, P. Hutson, *Inclusive Smart Museums*,
https://doi.org/10.1007/978-3-031-43615-4_5

the immersive, accessible, and engaging nature of wearable device-based heritage projects. By leveraging these immersive technologies, cultural heritage institutions can create transformative experiences that captivate and engage diverse audiences.

5.1 Adaptive Extended Reality

Adaptive extended reality (XR) technology, encompassing virtual reality (VR), augmented reality (AR), and mixed reality (MR) experiences, holds great promise for enhancing engaging and interactive experiences in cultural heritage contexts. By immersing visitors in dynamic and customizable environments, XR offers new avenues for exploration, interaction, and storytelling (Partarakis et al., 2020). This section explores the potential of XR to transform cultural heritage experiences, providing visitors with unprecedented opportunities to engage with historical sites, artifacts, and narratives in immersive and embodied ways. Through a synthesis of current scholarship and examples from various fields, this chapter showcases the transformative power of XR in fostering deeper connections with cultural heritage and encouraging active participation in knowledge construction and narrative building.

According to Bertrand et al. (2021), XR technology offers unprecedented opportunities for digital reconstructions and embodiment in cultural heritage. They argue that such immersive experiences enable users to engage with virtual reconstructions of historical sites, artifacts, and cultural practices, providing a sense of presence and immersion. There are, in fact, many benefits to adopting adaptive extended reality in the museum setting (Table 5.1). By virtually exploring ancient cities and architectural landmarks, users can experience the past in a more embodied and experiential manner (Pagano et al., 2020). Furthermore, XR allows users to step into the shoes of historical figures, gaining a deeper understanding of their lives and experiences (Wiehl, 2021).

Immersive videos, such as 360-degree videos, have emerged as a powerful tool for enhancing museum exhibits and providing visitors with a truly immersive and educational experience (Rahim et al., 2021). One notable example of this is the implementation of 360-degree videos at the Shed Aquarium in Chicago as part of their Park Voyagers program (Patin et al., 2018). By incorporating 360-degree videos into their exhibits, the aquarium allows visitors to dive into captivating underwater environments and witness marine life in a way that feels incredibly real and immersive.

Table 5.1 Benefits of adaptive extended reality in museums

Benefit	Description
Enhanced immersive experience	Adaptive extended reality (XR) technologies, such as virtual reality (VR) and augmented reality (AR), provide immersive and interactive experiences.
Accessibility and inclusivity	XR technologies can cater to diverse needs and abilities, offering accessible experiences for individuals with disabilities or sensory impairments.
Personalized learning	Adaptive XR can tailor the content and learning experiences based on individual preferences, enabling personalized and engaging educational journeys.
Multisensory engagement	XR immerses users in multisensory experiences, stimulating multiple senses and enhancing the overall engagement and impact of the museum visit.
Preservation and cultural heritage	XR allows museums to digitally preserve and showcase artifacts, artworks, and historical sites, ensuring their accessibility and long-term preservation.
Interactive and hands-on learning	XR technologies enable interactive and hands-on learning, encouraging active exploration and deepening visitors' understanding of the museum's content.
Innovative storytelling	XR offers new storytelling possibilities, allowing museums to create dynamic and interactive narratives that captivate and engage visitors.
Visitor empowerment	XR empowers visitors to actively participate in the museum experience, making them co-creators of their learning journey and fostering a sense of ownership.
Research and data collection	XR technologies can be used to collect data and insights on visitor behavior and preferences, aiding museums in improving their exhibitions and offerings.
Cultural exchange and collaboration	XR enables virtual collaborations and cultural exchanges, connecting museums and visitors globally and fostering cross-cultural dialogue and understanding.

These videos transport visitors to different underwater habitats, providing them with a unique perspective and fostering a deeper understanding and appreciation for the marine ecosystem (Braverman, 2020; Garibay, 2004).

Another fascinating application of immersive videos is seen in Galactic Golf, an interactive mixed reality experience that takes visitors on a playful journey through the concept of mass and gravity (Bornmann, 2022). This experience combines elements of virtual reality and augmented reality to create a truly engaging and educational encounter. Participants can step into the shoes of an astronaut and embark on a round of mixed reality

Martian golf, where they encounter various challenges and learn about the fundamental principles of mass and gravity in a fun and interactive way. By integrating immersive videos and interactive elements, museums can effectively communicate complex scientific concepts and spark curiosity and interest in visitors of all ages (Rose, 2021; Wills, 2019).

The incorporation of immersive videos into museum exhibits opens up a world of possibilities for creating dynamic and interactive experiences. These videos provide visitors with a sense of presence and transport them to different environments, whether it's exploring underwater ecosystems or venturing into outer space (Pan, 2021). The immersive nature of these videos stimulates curiosity, fosters a deeper connection to the subject matter, and encourages active engagement and learning. By harnessing the potential of immersive videos, museums can create memorable and impactful experiences that captivate and educate their visitors (Andersen et al., 2023).

Cultural heritage institutions have embraced various immersive experiences to engage visitors and create captivating interactions with art and history. Many examples should be noted to further illustrate use cases (Table 5.2). One notable example is the Pérez Art Museum Miami (PAMM), which has been a pioneer in integrating AR into its exhibits (Birbragher, 2022). In order to improve engagement, PAMM launched the first art exhibit using Apple's ARKit, allowing visitors to digitally view and interact with artworks that don't physically exist in the gallery space. This innovative use of AR enhances the visitor experience by adding virtual objects and expanding the dimensions of artistic interpretation (Prandi et al., 2021).

Another application of AR can be seen at the Pioneers Festival in Vienna, where Gustav Klimt's renowned artwork *The Tree of Life* is brought to life in a new dimension (Morowitz, 2022). By leveraging Apple's ARKit, visitors can use their smartphones' cameras and image recognition technology to experience the artwork in an immersive and interactive way. This approach offers a unique and immersive way to engage with cultural content, providing visitors with a fresh perspective and deeper understanding of the artwork.

Another notable example is the recent launch of the History Bites app by a British charity Black Learning Achievement and Mental Health (BLAM) dedicated to education and improving mental health (https://podcasts.apple.com/us/podcast/black-history-bites/id1515225350). This innovative app aims to shine a spotlight on the historic contributions

Table 5.2 Examples of adaptive extended reality in museums

Museum	Adaptive extended reality experience
British Museum, UK	Virtual reality (VR) experience that allows visitors to explore ancient artifacts in a virtual gallery, providing a closer look and interactive information.
Louvre Museum, France	Augmented reality (AR) app that overlays digital information on real-world exhibits, providing additional context and interactive elements for visitors.
Smithsonian National Museum of Natural History, USA	Virtual reality (VR) tour that transports visitors to prehistoric times, allowing them to interact with dinosaurs and explore ancient environments.
Museum of Modern Art (MoMA), USA	Augmented reality (AR) experience that brings artworks to life, allowing visitors to see animations, additional information, and interactive elements.
National Museum of Singapore	Mixed reality (MR) installation that reconstructs historical events, enabling visitors to witness significant moments in Singapore's history.
Museum of Science and Industry (MSI), USA	Virtual reality (VR) exhibit that simulates space exploration, allowing visitors to experience what it's like to walk on the moon or explore distant planets.
Museum of London, UK	Augmented reality (AR) app that superimposes historical scenes onto the modern cityscape, providing a glimpse into the city's past and its transformation over time.
National Museum of Emerging Science and Innovation, Japan	Holographic projection display that showcases scientific concepts and phenomena in an engaging and interactive manner.
Queensland Museum, Australia	Augmented reality (AR) experience that allows visitors to interact with virtual animals and learn about their habitats and conservation efforts.
Rijksmuseum, Netherlands	Virtual reality (VR) experience that takes visitors on a virtual tour through the museum's collection, offering a unique perspective on renowned artworks.

of black individuals throughout history. By leveraging AR technology, History Bites brings virtual statues of these remarkable figures into real-life settings, allowing visitors to engage with their stories in a dynamic and immersive way. Through the app, users can explore the virtual statues placed within their physical surroundings, creating a powerful juxtaposition of the past and present. Each virtual statue is accompanied by informative plaques that provide in-depth details about the lives and achievements of these historical black figures. This not only pays tribute to their legacies but also educates visitors about their significant contributions to various fields, such as arts, sciences, activism, and more.

By incorporating AR into the museum experience, History Bites offers a unique and interactive way to learn about and celebrate the diversity of historical narratives. It enables visitors to engage with the stories of these important individuals in a visually captivating and informative manner. The use of AR technology in this context bridges the gap between the past and the present, fostering a deeper understanding and appreciation for the historic roles played by black people throughout history. Furthermore, the History Bites app demonstrates the potential of AR in transforming how museums communicate and engage with their audiences. By seamlessly integrating virtual elements into real-world environments, AR opens up new avenues for storytelling, promoting inclusivity, and expanding historical discourse. Visitors can interact with the virtual statues and access detailed information at their own pace, creating a personalized and immersive learning experience.

Finally, in addition to content delivery, AR can also be utilized as a navigational tool within museums (Sundar et al., 2015). By using the visitor's smartphone camera, AR can overlay real-time directions and guidance, simplifying navigation through complex museum spaces. Whether it's directing visitors to specific galleries, restrooms, or cafes, AR enhances the visitor experience by providing seamless and intuitive wayfinding assistance (de Leon, 2017).

In addition to AR, the emergence of metaverse native art galleries has opened up new possibilities for showcasing and experiencing art. Notably, Sotheby's, a renowned auction house, has launched a presence in the metaverse, allowing users to explore and engage with artworks in a virtual environment (Yilmaz et al., 2022). This shift towards virtual art spaces offers increased accessibility and new opportunities for artists to showcase their work to a global audience.

Furthermore, virtual platforms like Second Life have enabled cultural institutions like the US Holocaust Museum to create immersive exhibits (Morgan, 2013). The museum's exhibit titled *Witnessing History: Kristallnacht, the 1938 Pogroms* takes visitors on an interactive journey through a harrowing period of history. Through the use of sound, text, and video, the exhibit tells the stories of survivors and victims of the Holocaust, creating an emotional and atmospheric experience. While some elements in the exhibit may be controversial, they are included to authentically represent the historical context (Baumann & Guesnet, 2019).

The National Museum of Singapore presents an engaging example of immersive installations through their current exhibition, *Story of the Forest* (2023) (https://www.nhb.gov.sg/nationalmuseum/our-exhibitions/exhibition-list/story-of-the-forest). This unique installation centers around the captivating William Farquhar Collection of Natural History Drawings, featuring 69 images. Leveraging the power of mobile apps, these two-dimensional drawings have been transformed into vibrant and interactive three-dimensional animations, offering visitors a captivating experience (Al-Bahri, 2023). By downloading the accompanying app, visitors can utilize the camera on their smartphones or tablets to unlock a whole new dimension of exploration within the paintings. This innovative use of mobile technology allows for a dynamic and interactive encounter with the artwork, blurring the boundaries between the physical and digital realms. It exemplifies the versatility and creative possibilities of mobile apps in creating immersive installations within museum settings (Gonzaga, 2019).

In recent years, interactive projection mapping has emerged as a powerful tool for conveying intangible cultural heritage in museums. This innovative approach involves superimposing virtual content onto physical artifacts, creating a dynamic and immersive storytelling experience. By combining physical and digital elements, interactive projection mapping allows for a deeper understanding and appreciation of cultural artifacts and their historical context.

For instance, the Chios Mastic Museum on the island of Chios in Greece has utilized interactive projection mapping to bring the history and traditions of mastic cultivation to life (Nikolakopoulou et al., 2022). The installation includes a double set of three-dimensional (3D) printed tangible artifacts placed in proximity to scale models. When activated, these artifacts trigger projections that depict historic events or illustrate the various activities associated with mastic cultivation throughout the year. This integration of architectural and intangible cultural heritage aims to engage visitors through vivid audiovisual presentations that enhance their understanding and connection to the heritage of the region (Karuzaki et al., 2021).

Through interactive projection mapping, museums can bridge the gap between physical artifacts and intangible cultural elements, providing a multi-sensory and immersive experience for visitors (Papathanasiou-Zuhrt et al., 2019). By visually and aurally highlighting significant aspects of a place's heritage, projection mapping installations create a captivating and informative environment. They not only educate and entertain but also foster a deeper appreciation for the cultural value and significance of the artifacts and their associated traditions.

Furthermore, Joseph (2023) emphasizes the significance of interactive social tools that enable parents to effectively convey information to their children during museum visits. Recognizing the importance of engaging both children and their parents, museums have developed various tools to facilitate this interactive experience. One notable example is the Crime Scene Neanderthal Augmented Reality (AR) app, which is featured at the American Museum of Natural History's Sackler lab and the Hall of Human Origins (Marom & Hovers, 2017).

The Crime Scene Neanderthal AR app utilizes cutting-edge technology to create an immersive and educational experience. Through this app, visitors are able to virtually mark objects within the museum's exhibits. By utilizing a virtual tool, visitors can interact with the objects and make comparisons between the virtual marks and the real objects themselves. This interactive process allows for a deeper understanding of the exhibits, promoting active learning and critical thinking (Hallam, 2022). Furthermore, the app incorporates additional features that contribute to the educational experience. For instance, visitors can use the app to sequence DNA in order to identify different species. This innovative approach not only enhances scientific understanding but also provides a hands-on experience that sparks curiosity and exploration (Gorman, 2020).

Additionally, the Crime Scene Neanderthal AR app allows visitors to investigate the cause of death of ancient specimens and even assists in locating missing bones within skeleton displays throughout the museum. By virtually reconstructing the skeletons and examining the evidence, visitors can actively participate in solving scientific mysteries and gain insights into the field of anthropology. The interactive nature of the Crime Scene Neanderthal AR app encourages meaningful engagement between parents and children. Parents can utilize this tool to initiate discussions, explain scientific concepts, and promote collaborative learning. The app creates a dynamic learning environment where families can work together to uncover the secrets of the past and develop a deeper appreciation for the exhibits.

By integrating interactive social tools like the Crime Scene Neanderthal AR app, museums empower parents to play an active role in their children's learning experiences. These tools not only foster communication and engagement but also provide opportunities for hands-on exploration and discovery (Sultana & Hawken, 2023). As technology continues to advance, museums have the potential to create increasingly interactive and immersive experiences that cater to the diverse needs and interests of visitors, ensuring that learning becomes a collaborative and enjoyable endeavor for both children and their parents (Wang, 2023).

In terms of collaborative learning and engagement, Doukianou et al. (2020) emphasize the potential of XR in heritage contexts. They contend that XR enables visitors to actively participate in knowledge construction and narrative building. XR's interactive and customizable environments allow users to explore cultural heritage according to their interests and pace. Collaborative XR applications invite visitors to co-create virtual exhibitions, contribute to historical narratives, and foster social interaction and dialogue (Dwivedi et al., 2022). Remote collaboration and shared experiences across locations are also facilitated by XR (Maddali & Lazar, 2023).

The impact of immersive technologies in challenging traditional modes of representation is emphasized by Ziker et al. (2021). The authors assert that the technology opens up new possibilities for storytelling by breaking away from linear narratives and granting users agency in constructing their own narratives. This interactive and immersive approach offered by XR enables visitors to actively engage with cultural heritage, moving beyond passive consumption (Theodoropoulos & Antoniou, 2022). Moreover, XR presents opportunities for diverse and inclusive representations of heritage by incorporating multiple perspectives and voices (Barbara et al., 2022).

Virtual reality (VR) is a particularly powerful tool for creating immersive experiences. Museums have embraced VR programs to provide visitors with unique and engaging encounters. For instance, the Brooklyn Academy of Music's Teknopolis (Lucie, 2021) and Philadelphia's Franklin Museum VR program have successfully deployed VR technologies to transform unused spaces into virtual galleries. This innovative approach allows for the exploration of new narratives and interactive experiences.

The utilization of virtual reality (VR) headsets, such as the HTC Vive, has revolutionized the way museums can reconstruct and visualize scientific references and scans, offering visitors immersive and awe-inspiring experiences. One remarkable example of this is the production *Skeleton Crew*, where VR headsets were employed to recreate and showcase a reconstructed Tyrannosaurus Rex, effectively bringing the extinct creature to life for museum visitors (Skalska-Cimer & Kadłuczka, 2022).

Through the power of VR technology, visitors can step into a virtual world where they can explore and interact with digital representations of scientific specimens and artifacts that may otherwise be inaccessible or too delicate to handle. In the case of *Skeleton Crew*, the VR experience allows visitors to witness the T. rex in its full glory, observing its anatomy, movements, and behavior in a way that is both educational and captivating (Ings, 2019).

The use of VR headsets in this context enables a level of immersion and realism that goes beyond traditional displays and exhibits. Visitors can virtually walk around the dinosaur, examine its skeletal structure from different angles, and even witness its movements and interactions with its environment. The sense of presence and interactivity offered by VR enhances the engagement and understanding of complex scientific concepts, enabling visitors to have a deeper appreciation for the subject matter (Kalantari & Neo, 2020).

By leveraging VR technology, museums can overcome the limitations of physical space and preservation constraints, allowing for the creation of dynamic and interactive experiences that bring scientific knowledge to life. The use of VR headsets not only enhances the educational value of museum exhibits but also sparks curiosity and wonder in visitors of all ages. It provides an opportunity to bridge the gap between the past and the present, allowing people to experience the magnificence of prehistoric creatures like the T. rex in ways that were previously unimaginable.

Likewise, France saw the establishment of its first museum room dedicated to VR at the National Museum of Natural History in Paris (Gobira & de Oliveira Silva, 2019). In 2018, the museum introduced *The Cabinet De Réalité Virtuelle*, a groundbreaking exhibition space. Upon entering this room, visitors are instantly immersed in an extraordinary adventure known as "Journey into the Heart of Evolution." The exhibition incorporates five VR stations, ensuring an engaging and personalized experience for each visitor. To enhance the immersive atmosphere, the room is equipped with soundproofing and dynamic lighting. Through the power of VR, visitors can embark on an awe-inspiring exploration of the intricate connections and evolution of various species, delving deep into the captivating history of our planet like never before. The introduction of this dedicated VR room at the National Museum of Natural History demonstrates the museum's commitment to embracing innovative technologies and providing visitors with unique and transformative encounters with scientific knowledge and natural history (Muñoz & Martí, 2020).

With the power of virtual reality, visitors are transported to environments where they can observe and study a diverse array of creatures, witnessing their intricate details and proportions up close and in accurate scale (Apollonio et al., 2021). This VR exhibition offers a unique opportunity for visitors to engage with the natural world in a way that surpasses traditional displays, enabling them to experience the wonders of biodiversity and deepen their understanding of the intricate relationships that exist among various species.

Additionally, in a remarkable collaboration between the Natural History Museum and broadcaster Sky, an educational VR experience called *Hold the World* was also unveiled in 2018 (Wang, 2023). This groundbreaking interactive journey allows participants to come face-to-face with the legendary Sir David Attenborough. Transporting users to the iconic Natural History Museum in London, the experience offers a unique opportunity to engage with rare specimens from the museum's renowned collection. Through the immersive VR environment, participants can physically handle and manipulate these objects, resizing them to gain a deeper understanding of their features. Meanwhile, the esteemed Sir David Attenborough serves as a knowledgeable guide, sharing captivating insights about the animals' lifestyles, feeding habits, respiration, and more (Jones et al., 2019). The experience revolutionizes the educational experience by combining cutting-edge virtual reality technology with the wisdom and expertise of a beloved naturalist, providing an unforgettable and enriching encounter with the natural world.

Continuing the trend of merging technology with the world of museums, the Muséum national d'Histoire naturelle in Paris (Fig. 5.1) introduced an awe-inspiring Augmented Reality experience in June 2021 (Hayes, 2023). Through the use of Microsoft's Hololens, visitors were transported back in time with the project aptly named *REVIVRE* or "To Live Again." This novel initiative allowed participants to encounter and interact with digital representations of long-extinct animals that once roamed the Earth. As users donned the Hololens, they found themselves face to face with creatures that were previously confined to the pages of history books. The AR experience breathed life into these majestic beings, offering a sense of presence and intimacy that is otherwise impossible (Giariskanis et al. 2022). Through *REVIVRE*, the Muséum national d'Histoire naturelle offered a captivating glimpse into the past, fostering a deeper understanding and appreciation for the rich biodiversity that has shaped our planet's history.

Fig. 5.1 Night of Museums, Muséum national d'Histoire naturelle. (May 11, 2011)

Creating immersive experiences for museums has become more accessible than ever before, thanks to advancements in technology and the availability of user-friendly tools. Systems like Matterport, generative artificial intelligence (AI), and game engines provide museums with the means to easily create and showcase immersive content (Ratican et al., 2023). Additionally, technology such as ArtformAR offers augmented reality capabilities specifically designed for museums (http://artformar.com/). With ArtformAR, museums can annotate works in immersive reality, provide commentary on specific items in their collection that visitors can access through their smartphones, and even offer location-tracking features within the museum space. This next level of technology opens up new possibilities for engaging and interactive museum experiences. To explore the cutting-edge technology for museums, early access to ArtformAR can be obtained, enabling institutions to unlock the full potential of immersive storytelling and digital experiences.

By leveraging VR and AR technologies, museums can transcend the limitations of physical space and traditional exhibition formats (Sylaiou et al., 2018). These immersive experiences provide visitors with the opportunity to engage with cultural heritage in a dynamic and captivating manner. Through the thoughtful integration of XR technologies, museums can offer visitors rich and transformative encounters that enhance their understanding and appreciation of heritage (Gröppel-Wegener & Kidd, 2019). In all, XR technologies, including AR, MR, and VR, have revolutionized the way museums present and engage with cultural heritage. These technologies offer innovative storytelling approaches, allow for diverse and inclusive representations, and provide immersive experiences that break free from traditional modes of consumption. By embracing XR, museums can create transformative encounters that captivate and educate visitors, fostering a deeper connection to cultural heritage.

5.2 Avatars and Inclusivity

Extended reality (XR) technologies have opened up new possibilities for cultural heritage experiences, and avatars are a fascinating component of this immersive landscape. Avatars, virtual representations of individuals, historical figures, guides, or even fellow visitors, have emerged as a powerful tool in heritage contexts (Fig. 5.2) (Underberg & Zorn, 2013). This section explores the design and implementation of avatar-based heritage

Fig. 5.2 Charlette Proto, Second Life

experiences and investigates their potential in creating engaging, interactive, and customizable environments that foster a deeper connection with cultural heritage. Through an examination of various case studies and a synthesis of scholarly insights, this chapter aims to shed light on the transformative capabilities of avatars, offering dynamic and participatory encounters with heritage.

Avatars have emerged as powerful tools in the realm of digital storytelling, particularly in cultural heritage institutions. Bekele and Champion (2019) highlight the potential of avatars to bridge the gap between visitors and historical figures, offering a means of direct engagement and personalized interactions. Through the use of avatars, visitors can assume the role of a specific historical figure, immersing themselves in their lives and experiences.

This immersive and experiential approach to learning enhances visitors' understanding of history by allowing them to actively participate in historical narratives. By embodying an avatar that represents a particular historical figure, visitors can gain insights into their thoughts, emotions, and motivations. They can witness events through the avatar's perspective, interact with other characters, and make decisions that shape the outcome of the narrative. This interactive experience offers a deeper level of engagement and fosters a sense of empathy and connection with the past (Bekele & Champion, 2019).

Avatars enable visitors to step into the shoes of historical figures and experience history firsthand. This unique opportunity allows for a more personal and meaningful connection with the past, as visitors can navigate historical contexts, engage in dialogue, and explore the complexities of different time periods and cultural perspectives. By immersing themselves in these experiences, visitors can develop a deeper appreciation for the human stories that have shaped our world (Arnold-de-Simine & Arnold-de Simine, 2013).

The use of avatars in cultural heritage institutions opens up new avenues for storytelling and interpretation. It enables institutions to go beyond traditional displays and static exhibits, offering dynamic and interactive experiences that captivate and educate visitors. Avatars can bring historical figures to life in a way that transcends time and space, making history more accessible, relatable, and engaging for a wide range of audiences.

Avatars have emerged as interactive guides in the realm of cultural heritage, offering immersive storytelling experiences that enrich visitors' engagement with the past. Bozzelli et al. (2019) emphasize the pivotal role of avatars in bringing cultural heritage to life by serving as knowledgeable companions. These virtual guides provide visitors with contextual information, engage them in interactive narratives, and enhance their overall understanding of the heritage site.

As interactive companions, avatars offer personalized guidance to visitors, tailoring their explanations and interactions based on individual interests and preferences. This tailored approach allows visitors to ask questions, seek clarification, and delve deeper into specific aspects of the cultural heritage being presented. Avatars act as virtual interpreters, bridging the gap between visitors and the historical or cultural context they are exploring (Bozzelli et al., 2019).

The interactive nature of avatars fosters engagement and active participation from visitors. Through conversations and interactions with the avatar guide, visitors can actively shape their own experience and explore the heritage site from different perspectives. Avatars provide a dynamic and responsive interface, enabling visitors to delve into specific areas of interest, access additional information, or embark on guided tours tailored to their preferences (Viñals et al., 2021). This interactive engagement not only enhances visitors' understanding but also makes the experience more memorable and impactful.

Avatars as virtual guides have the potential to transform the traditional museum visit into an interactive and personalized journey. By leveraging technology, avatars can unlock new dimensions of cultural heritage, presenting information and narratives in a dynamic and engaging manner. Visitors can experience the past through the eyes of different historical figures or explore different interpretations and viewpoints. The immersive and interactive nature of avatars fosters a deeper connection with the cultural heritage, making the visit more meaningful and resonant.

Furthermore, avatars have the advantage of adaptability and scalability. They can cater to diverse visitor profiles and preferences, providing guidance and content that aligns with individual interests and accessibility needs. Avatars can support multiple languages, accommodate different learning styles, and adjust the level of detail or complexity to meet the visitor's requirements. This flexibility allows for a more inclusive and accessible experience, ensuring that a wider range of visitors can engage with and appreciate the cultural heritage being presented.

Avatars not only serve as guides but also have the potential to facilitate social interaction and collaboration among visitors within virtual spaces.

Foster et al. (2022) emphasize the significance of avatars in enabling shared experiences and collective exploration of cultural heritage. In virtual environments, avatars can represent other visitors, creating opportunities for social engagement and community building.

Virtual spaces equipped with avatars offer visitors the ability to connect and interact with each other in a virtual community. Through their avatars, visitors can engage in conversations, share insights, and exchange perspectives. This social interaction fosters a sense of community among visitors, creating a collaborative environment where collective knowledge creation and interpretation of cultural heritage can thrive (Foster et al., 2022).

By connecting with fellow visitors through avatars, individuals have the opportunity to contribute to the overall understanding and interpretation of cultural heritage. Through discussions and shared experiences, visitors can gain new insights, challenge preconceived notions, and develop a richer understanding of the heritage site. The collaborative approach facilitated by avatars promotes active participation and a sense of ownership among visitors, empowering them to actively contribute to the collective knowledge and interpretation of cultural heritage (Underberg & Zorn, 2013).

Avatars as social representations within virtual spaces provide a platform for visitors to engage in meaningful dialogue, build connections, and learn from one another. These interactions foster a sense of shared experience and camaraderie among visitors, transcending physical barriers and geographical limitations. Avatars enable visitors to come together, explore cultural heritage collectively, and contribute to a more comprehensive and diverse understanding of the site.

Furthermore, the social interaction facilitated by avatars can lead to the formation of communities of interest or practice, where individuals with shared interests or expertise can connect and collaborate. Through these communities, visitors can continue to engage with cultural heritage beyond the museum visit, exchanging knowledge, sharing resources, and deepening their understanding and appreciation of the site.

The use of avatars to facilitate social interaction and collaboration aligns with the evolving nature of museums and cultural institutions. It embraces the idea of co-creation and participatory experiences, recognizing the valuable contributions of visitors as active participants in the interpretation and preservation of cultural heritage. By leveraging avatars as social representations, museums can create dynamic and engaging virtual spaces that foster social connections, facilitate knowledge exchange, and cultivate a sense of belonging and community among visitors.

The research conducted by Chen and Kent (2020) highlights the transformative potential of avatars in facilitating cultural exchange and understanding within virtual museum projects. By representing individuals from diverse cultural backgrounds, avatars serve as intermediaries that bridge the gap between different cultures, promoting dialogue, empathy, and intercultural interactions.

In their study, Chen and Kent explored the use of avatars to facilitate cross-cultural experiences in a virtual museum setting. These avatars, representing individuals from different cultural backgrounds, played a pivotal role in creating a platform for visitors to engage in meaningful intercultural interactions. By interacting with avatars, visitors had the opportunity to gain insights into unfamiliar cultures, challenge stereotypes, and broaden their perspectives.

Avatars acted as cultural ambassadors, providing visitors with a unique opportunity to engage in dialogue and exchange ideas with individuals from diverse cultural perspectives. Through these interactions, visitors were able to ask questions, share experiences, and learn about different cultural practices, beliefs, and traditions. The avatars facilitated meaningful conversations and fostered a sense of empathy, helping visitors develop a deeper understanding and appreciation of cultural diversity.

By transcending physical and geographical boundaries, avatars enable visitors to overcome the limitations of traditional museum settings and engage in intercultural exchange within virtual heritage spaces. Through the immersive and interactive nature of the virtual environment, visitors can step into the shoes of different cultural avatars, experiencing cultural contexts and perspectives firsthand.

The use of avatars as intermediaries for cultural exchange promotes cultural understanding, breaks down barriers, and fosters mutual respect among visitors. It challenges preconceived notions and biases, allowing individuals to explore and appreciate the richness and complexity of different cultures. Avatars facilitate a safe and inclusive space for dialogue, encouraging visitors to ask questions, share personal experiences, and engage in meaningful cross-cultural interactions.

The example presented by Chen and Kent (2020) showcases the potential of avatars in facilitating intercultural exchange and understanding within virtual heritage spaces. The use of avatars as cultural intermediaries opens up new avenues for fostering dialogue, empathy, and appreciation for diverse cultures. It offers a transformative and immersive experience that goes beyond the physical constraints of traditional museum settings, providing visitors with a unique opportunity to explore, connect, and learn about different cultures in a virtual environment.

Another compelling application of avatars in cultural heritage can be seen in the work of Chung (2015). Such research focuses on utilizing avatars to reanimate historical artifacts and objects. By assigning avatars to inanimate objects, such as ancient sculptures or paintings, visitors were able to engage with these artifacts in a dynamic and interactive manner. Avatars brought the objects to life, offering historical context, storytelling, and interactive elements. This approach not only enhances visitors' understanding of the objects but also sparks curiosity and emotional connections. Avatars act as mediators, breathing life into artifacts and enabling visitors to engage with heritage in novel and captivating ways (Ryding & Fritsch, 2020).

Furthermore, the study conducted by Ott and Pozzi (2011). explored the use of avatars in the context of cultural heritage education for children. The researchers developed an avatar-based educational game that immersed children in historical settings and enabled them to interact with avatars representing historical figures. Through interactive storytelling and gamified elements, children were actively involved in learning about cultural heritage. The avatars acted as guides, providing information, challenges, and rewards, creating a playful and engaging learning experience. This example showcases how avatars can be leveraged to make cultural heritage education more accessible, interactive, and enjoyable for younger audiences (Ondrejka, 2008).

By incorporating avatars into heritage experiences, cultural institutions have the opportunity to create dynamic and interactive encounters that go beyond traditional modes of engagement (King et al., 2016). Avatars enable visitors to directly engage with historical figures, personalized narratives, and fellow visitors, fostering a deeper connection with cultural heritage (Ryding & Fritsch, 2020). With the readily available and free services such as with Ready Player Me (https://readyplayer.me/), creating an interoperable avatar is easier than ever for the museum-going public (Altundas & Karaarslan, 2023). Through the ability to assume different roles, receive contextual information, and collaborate with others in virtual spaces, avatars provide immersive and participatory learning experiences (Dawley & Dede, 2014). As technology continues to advance, avatars hold immense potential for transforming heritage engagement and shaping the future of immersive technologies in cultural heritage contexts.

5.3 Digital Twins

Digital twin technology, characterized by the creation of virtual replicas of physical assets or environments, has emerged as a powerful tool in various domains (Qi et al., 2021). In this section, we explore the application of digital twins in the context of cultural heritage, focusing on how they can enhance heritage experiences by providing visitors with immersive and interactive simulations. By examining case studies and scholarly research, we aim to showcase the potential of digital twins in creating engaging, realistic, and accessible experiences that facilitate a deeper understanding and appreciation of cultural heritage.

Digital twin technology has opened up new avenues for preserving, exploring, and interacting with cultural heritage. By replicating physical assets, such as historical buildings, archaeological sites, or museum artifacts, in a virtual environment, digital twins offer visitors the opportunity to engage with heritage in novel and dynamic ways (Menaguale, 2023). These realistic simulations enable visitors to virtually explore and manipulate heritage spaces and objects, providing an immersive and interactive experience that transcends the limitations of traditional exhibits (Styliani et al., 2009). The benefits for museums and cultural heritage sites are numerous (Table 5.3).

The commencement of digitizing cultural heritage sites can be traced back to around 2001, initially focusing on both existing and ancient locations. During this early stage, access to these digital resources was primarily limited to researchers within the field, but it was clear that there was potential for broader applications. The Foundation of the Hellenic World (FHW), a cultural heritage institution in Athens, played a pivotal role in advancing the field through their use of Cave Automatic Virtual Environment (CAVE) technology to develop early virtual environments (Fig. 5.3). One notable example of their pioneering work was the digital reconstruction of the ancient city of Miletus, which showcased the transformative capabilities of this technology (Tzortzaki, 2001). Recognizing the advantages of digital preservation, researchers such as Roussou (2001) began advocating for its adoption to enhance physical museum exhibitions. This movement was driven by the concept of "edutainment," which

Table 5.3 Benefits of digital twins in museums and cultural heritage

Benefit	Description
Preservation and conservation	Digital twins enable the creation of accurate virtual replicas of artifacts, artworks, or historical sites, ensuring their preservation and conservation for future generations.
Accessibility and inclusivity	Digital twins provide virtual access to museums and cultural heritage sites, making them accessible to individuals who may not be able to visit in person due to physical or geographical limitations.
Education and research	Digital twins serve as educational tools, offering immersive and interactive experiences that enhance learning and research opportunities about historical artifacts, artworks, and sites.
Restoration and reconstruction	Digital twins assist in the restoration and reconstruction of damaged or lost artifacts, allowing experts to study and recreate the original appearance and context of cultural heritage objects.
Exhibition and display enhancement	Digital twins enhance the exhibition experience by offering additional information, interactive elements, and virtual tours, enriching visitors' understanding and engagement with cultural artifacts.
Data visualization and analysis	Digital twins enable the visualization and analysis of complex data related to cultural heritage, facilitating research, conservation efforts, and the identification of patterns or trends.
Risk assessment and disaster management	Digital twins assist in risk assessment and disaster management by simulating scenarios and evaluating potential risks to cultural heritage sites, enabling proactive measures to be taken for their protection.
Collaboration and cultural exchange	Digital twins facilitate collaboration among museums, researchers, and cultural institutions, promoting cultural exchange and the sharing of knowledge and resources in a virtual environment.
Virtual repatriation and cultural Revival	Digital twins support virtual repatriation efforts, allowing cultural artifacts and heritage to be digitally returned to their places of origin, contributing to cultural revival and preservation.

aimed to fuse education and entertainment to create engaging and informative experiences (Hutson & Olsen, 2022a).

From 2001 to 2010, there was a notable increase in the adoption of digital cultural heritage preservation among museums. Examples of these initiatives include The Museum of Pure Form (Loscos et al., 2004) and The Virtual Museum of Sculpture (Carrozzino et al., 2008). These museums specifically designed their VR experiences to cater to the general public, who typically had limited exposure to complex hardware setups (Carrozzino & Bergamasco, 2010). Unlike VR experiences in medical or

Fig. 5.3 REACTOR, The Foundation of the Hellenic World (FHW). (May 28, 2001)

scientific fields that could be more extensive, museum-focused experiences were intentionally kept brief to ensure a smooth flow of visitors within the physical space (Falk, 2016).

Likewise, The Kremer Museum has redefined the concept of a museum by existing entirely in the virtual realm (Brooks, 2019). Unlike traditional museums with physical galleries, The Kremer Museum is a fully immersive virtual reality experience that transports visitors into a world of seventeenth-century Dutch and Flemish Old Masters (https://www.thekremercollection.com/the-kremer-museum/). With over 70 selective artworks, this digital collection offers a unique opportunity to appreciate and explore the beauty and intricacies of these masterpieces (Fig. 5.4). Each artwork is meticulously rendered in stunning detail, allowing viewers to examine brushstrokes, textures, and colors up close. The absence of a physical existence for the museum challenges the traditional notions of accessibility and conservation, while simultaneously revolutionizing the way art is experienced and shared (Sylaiou et al., 2018). The Kremer Museum opens

Fig. 5.4 After Frans Hals, *Portrait of a Man*. (Kremmer Collection, between 1627 and 1630)

up new possibilities for art enthusiasts worldwide, transcending physical limitations and offering a captivating journey through art history in the realm of virtual reality.

Virtual museums are increasingly being recognized as powerful platforms for cultural representation and inclusivity. One notable example is the unveiling of a VR museum dedicated to the LGBTQ+ community at the annual festival organized by Tribeca Productions (Meyer, 2021). The creative team behind this innovative project aimed to address the need for a dedicated sexual and gender minority community museum in the metaverse, filling a gap in the preservation and celebration of queer history (Welbon & Juhasz, 2018).

The virtual museum provides a unique space for collecting and preserving personal histories of individuals within the queer community. By harnessing the immersive power of VR technology, the museum offers an engaging and interactive experience that transcends geographical boundaries and traditional limitations. Visitors can navigate through virtual exhibitions, explore artifacts, and delve into the rich cultural heritage of the gender and sexual diversity community (Anoll, 2019).

This virtual museum not only serves as a repository of queer history but also as a platform for storytelling and education. It allows for the amplification of marginalized voices and the representation of diverse perspectives, fostering a sense of belonging and empowerment within the LGBTQ+ community. Through digital exhibits, interactive narratives, and multimedia presentations, the virtual museum invites visitors to immerse themselves in the lived experiences, struggles, triumphs, and contributions of these individuals throughout history (Dick, 2021).

By embracing virtual technology, this museum in the metaverse opens up new avenues for engagement and access. It transcends the limitations of physical spaces, enabling individuals from all around the world to explore and connect with sexual and gender minority history and culture. It serves as a testament to the power of virtual platforms in promoting inclusivity, education, and the preservation of cultural heritage.

The emergence of virtual museums dedicated to specific communities, like the LGBTQ+ community, reflects a growing recognition of the importance of representation and the need to fill historical gaps. As technology continues to advance, we can anticipate further development and expansion of virtual museums, providing immersive and accessible experiences that celebrate the diverse cultural tapestry of humanity (De Valck, 2016).

As technology continued to advance, fully virtual museums started to emerge. Notable examples include The Exploratorium, a public science museum, and The CREATE project, an EU-funded initiative that allows users to reconstruct archaeological sites (Hutson & Olsen, 2022b). In parallel, efforts were made to digitize entire collections and museums for immersive realities, including augmented reality (AR) and VR. In such examples, visitors are able to navigate through the virtual city, exploring its streets, buildings, and landmarks, and witnessing the city's evolution over time. Through interactive features, such as the ability to toggle between different time periods or access additional historical information, visitors gained a deeper understanding of the city's history and cultural significance. In 2006, the Center for the Art of East Asia (CAEA) at the University of Chicago developed technology to digitize, archive, and view East Asian painting and sculpture collections. Projects like The Scroll Paintings Project and The Chinese Buddhist Caves Temple Projects (Fig. 5.5) aimed to increase accessibility to art-historical resources and facilitate collaboration and scholarship on works that were often difficult to access (Christou, 2010).

Fig. 5.5 Buddhist paintings from the important silk-road temples of Dun Huang

In recent years, the use of virtual learning environments (VLEs) to deliver cultural heritage content has experienced significant growth. This has been achieved through the digitization of physical museums or the creation of computer-generated versions. A significant milestone in this development occurred in 2011 with the introduction of Google's Arts & Culture platform, which allowed smartphone users to embark on virtual visits to museums. The subsequent release of Google Cardboard in 2014 further democratized the technology, enabling users to engage with head-mounted displays for more immersive experiences (Zhang, 2020).

Various Virtual Learning Environments (VLEs) have been created to enable virtual tours of both physical and virtual museums, offering opportunities for the reconstruction and preservation of damaged or lost heritage sites (Barrado-Timón & Hidalgo-Giralt, 2019). For instance, the National Archaeological Museum of Marche in Ancona, the Gyeongju VR Museum in South Korea, and the Rijksmuseum in Amsterdam have all implemented virtual tour experiences (Favro, 2006; Clini et al., 2018). In addition to VLEs, game engines such as Unreal Engine and Unity have been employed to develop virtual museums for educational purposes. An example of this is a project designed for art history students at the Universidad Nacional de San Agustin de Arequipa in Peru (Huaman et al., 2019). These initiatives demonstrate the increasing use of technology to create immersive virtual museum experiences, allowing for broader access, educational opportunities, and the preservation of cultural heritage.

The COVID-19 pandemic presented unprecedented challenges to the museum industry, leading many renowned institutions to adapt and find innovative ways to connect with audiences (Giannini & Bowen, 2022). One significant response to this shift was the digitization of collections, enabling greater access to art and culture beyond the physical confines of museums (Mihelj et al., 2019). The resulting production of digital twins of works of art and monuments has been a watershed moment for global cultural heritage (Table 5.4). For instance, in 2021, the Louvre digitized over 480,000 pieces from its collections, providing access to these treasures through their online platform (Fai, 2021). The same year, The National Gallery in London embarked on an ambitious endeavor to bring the collections of the National Gallery, National Portrait Gallery, and Royal Academy of Arts to the public through an augmented reality experience (Dragicevic & Bagarić, 2019; Prokop et al., 2021). Leveraging the power of technology and the ubiquity of smartphones, visitors could activate the artworks using a dedicated app. By scanning QR codes

Table 5.4 Examples of digital twins in museums and cultural heritage

Example	Description
British Museum's Digital Twin Project	The British Museum created a digital twin of the Rosetta Stone, a famous artifact with inscriptions in multiple languages. The digital twin allows visitors to explore the stone virtually and view detailed 3D models and accompanying information.
Louvre Abu Dhabi's Digital Twin	The Louvre Abu Dhabi developed a digital twin of their museum, providing an immersive virtual experience for users to explore the museum's galleries and artworks from anywhere in the world.
National Museum of Natural History	The National Museum of Natural History in Washington, D.C., created a digital twin of their dinosaur exhibits. Visitors can access the digital twin to explore the exhibits, view interactive content, and learn about dinosaur fossils and their history.
Virtual Angkor	The Virtual Angkor project created a digital twin of the ancient Angkor Wat temple complex in Cambodia. This digital twin allows users to explore the temples virtually, learn about their history, and experience the grandeur of the site.
Smithsonian Open Access	The Smithsonian Institution launched the Open Access initiative, providing access to digital twins of thousands of artworks, specimens, and cultural artifacts from their collections. Users can explore these digital twins and access accompanying information.

strategically placed on busy streets in central London, users were transported into the virtual world, where they could engage with and appreciate the masterpieces that define the rich artistic heritage of the city (Wu & Din, 2014). This innovative approach not only expanded the reach of these esteemed institutions but also encouraged exploration, discovery, and engagement with art in a new and accessible way. By breaking down the barriers of physical space, the AR experience offered a glimpse into the world-class art scene, empowering individuals to become active participants in their cultural surroundings (Ronchi, 2009).

A notable recent undertaking that exemplifies the increasing recognition of the potential of digital technologies in enhancing accessibility and engagement with cultural heritage is the project undertaken by UNESCO from 2017 to 2020. This project focused on the creation of extensive virtual tours showcasing World Cultural Heritage Sites, demonstrating the power of digital technology to bring these sites to a global audience (El-Said & Aziz, 2022). Through the use of immersive technologies such as virtual reality and 360-degree panoramic views, the project aimed to provide virtual access to cultural heritage sites that may be geographically distant or physically inaccessible to many people. By leveraging digital tools and platforms, UNESCO sought to overcome barriers such as travel limitations, physical disabilities, and preservation concerns to enable individuals from around the world to explore and engage with these significant sites (Kumar et al., 2023).

The virtual tours created as part of this project offered users a unique and immersive experience, allowing them to virtually navigate through the cultural heritage sites, explore their architectural and historical features, and learn about their cultural significance. Users could virtually walk through ancient ruins, admire intricate details of artworks, and gain a deeper understanding of the rich history and cultural context of these sites (Stacchio et al., 2022).

One of the key advantages of these virtual tours was their ability to enhance accessibility. By leveraging digital technologies, the project aimed to provide inclusive experiences for individuals with physical disabilities or mobility limitations, enabling them to virtually visit and experience these heritage sites from the comfort of their own homes. This approach democratized access to cultural heritage, ensuring that individuals who may not have the opportunity to visit these sites in person could still engage with and appreciate their historical and cultural value (Jiexin & Ying, 2022).

Moreover, the project demonstrated the potential for digital technologies to augment the educational value of cultural heritage sites. Through interactive features, informative annotations, and multimedia content, the virtual tours provided educational insights and contextual information about the sites. Users could access historical narratives, view high-resolution images, and listen to expert commentary, enriching their understanding and appreciation of the cultural heritage being showcased (Banfi, 2021).

The project also highlighted the importance of preservation and documentation. By creating comprehensive digital replicas of the World Cultural Heritage Sites, the virtual tours contributed to the preservation and documentation of these sites for future generations. In the face of natural disasters, human conflicts, or deterioration, the digital representations can serve as valuable records and references, ensuring that the cultural heritage is preserved and accessible for years to come. Thus, the UNESCO digital twin project exemplifies the increasing recognition of the potential of digital technologies in enhancing accessibility and engagement with cultural heritage on a global scale.

Building on these examples, museums are increasingly embracing the concept of creating digital twins of their spaces and collections, offering visitors innovative and immersive experiences (Menaguale, 2023). One notable example is the collaboration between The Metropolitan Museum of Art in New York City and Verizon, resulting in the launch of the Met Unframed, an immersive virtual art and gaming experience. While not every single image from the museum's vast collection is included, nearly 50 carefully selected pieces have been given the augmented reality (AR) treatment (Doğan & Jelinčić, 2023).

The Met Unframed allows visitors to explore digital galleries that have been meticulously rendered using high-quality AR scans. By visiting themetunframed.com, museum-goers can access these digital galleries and enjoy an up-close encounter with the Met's artworks. What sets this experience apart is the integration of gaming elements that unlock additional features within the AR-rendered versions of the art, encouraging playful exploration and deeper engagement (Kaplan, 2022). And another notable aspect of this project is that it leverages the latest digital communications protocols, including the power of 5G technology. While 5G offers an enhanced viewing experience, it's important to note that visitors with 4G devices can still access all the features and content.

The creation of digital twins allows museums to transcend physical limitations and provide a unique opportunity for visitors to engage with art and cultural artifacts in new and dynamic ways. By blending technology, art, and gaming, museums like The Met are redefining the boundaries of traditional museum experiences and reaching broader audiences beyond the physical confines of their galleries. As technology continues to evolve, we can expect to see more museums embracing digital twins to offer immersive, interactive, and accessible encounters with art and culture.

The advent of the COVID-19 pandemic has accelerated the adoption of digital twin technologies in the preservation of cultural heritage, with notable implementations taking place across different regions worldwide. Bevilacqua et al. (2022) provide a comprehensive account of various applications of virtual reality (VR) in the realm of cultural heritage. These include the utilization of reconstructive digital modeling and the development of a prototype VR application that recreates the interior space of the now-nonexistent provisional hall of the First Italian Parliament, allowing visitors to experience Palazzo Carignano in Turin. These examples underscore the expanding possibilities for immersive experiences and digital reconstructions in the realm of cultural heritage.

Another noteworthy instance involves the development of a digital twin for the Charterhouse of Pisa in Calci. This virtual environment showcases a meticulous 3D reconstruction of the illusory spaces depicted in quadraturist frescoes, as well as a comprehensive representation of the cloister's layout during its significant historical periods. Similar to the UNESCO-led initiatives, the creation of these digital twins initially aimed to enhance tourism experiences. However, their impact extends beyond that, providing valuable resources for researchers worldwide (Shahzad et al., 2022; Zhao et al., 2022).

The expanding literature on digital twins for the preservation of cultural heritage reveals a wide array of methods and approaches being employed across different regions. European scholars, for instance, have utilized specific processes to recreate and reconstitute architectural wonders. In contrast, Asian researchers, as exemplified by Tan et al. (2022), have embraced different techniques. Their study on Xiegong, a unique feature of Chinese historic buildings, highlights the urgency within the field of archaeology to capture and safeguard the physical attributes of these structures before succumbing to the detrimental effects of erosion and decay. Through a combination of archaeological data, historical records, and advanced visualization techniques, digital twins enable visitors to virtually step back in time and experience these lost heritage sites in their original form. This reconstruction not only preserves cultural heritage but also offers opportunities for research, education, and virtual tourism. Moreover, digital twins have the potential to facilitate remote access to cultural heritage. Such diverse endeavors underscore the importance of interdisciplinary collaborations and the continuous exploration of innovative methodologies in digital cultural heritage preservation.

In order to accomplish this objective, Tan et al. devised a methodology that integrates digital twin technology with the study of forms, employing a multi-faceted approach that incorporates laser scanning, oblique photogrammetry, and BIM. Their investigation on Xuanluo Hall in Sichuan, China, serves as an exemplar to validate this approach, ensuring the alignment between 2D and 3D representations in terms of geometry and semantics. The outcomes of their methodology, alongside corroborating studies (Rosa, 2022; Wang et al., 2022), affirm the feasibility of employing digital twin technology for archaeological research and the preservation of deteriorating structures.

The development of digital twins for cultural heritage sites necessitates collaborative efforts among technicians and scholars from diverse fields of expertise. As the utilization of digital twins continues to gain momentum, it becomes increasingly important to explore and refine the methodologies and approaches employed in their creation. This exploration is crucial to maximize their potential in preserving our shared history and enabling novel forms of research and engagement.

Building upon the advancements and successes of digital twin technology in cultural heritage preservation, the next section delves into the realm of wearable devices. These devices offer a unique and immersive way to engage with cultural heritage by incorporating interactive and sensory experiences. By examining the design and implementation of wearable devices in heritage contexts, we explore the potential of these technologies to enhance visitor experiences, foster deeper connections with cultural heritage, and open up new avenues for research and exploration. Through case studies and examples, we will uncover the transformative power of wearable devices in the realm of cultural heritage.

5.4 Wearables, Neuroscience, and Exhibition Design

Along with immersive environments and historical recreations, the use of wearable technology in heritage contexts allows for even more engaging experiences. Such technology includes the design and implementation of wearable device-based heritage experiences, which can include smart glasses, haptic feedback devices, and other wearables that enhance the visitor experience through augmented reality, navigation assistance, or sensory feedback (Allal-Chérif, 2022; Young et al., 2023). Through case studies of wearable device-based heritage projects, the chapter showcases the potential of this technology to create immersive, accessible, and engaging experiences that cater to the diverse needs of visitors in cultural heritage institutions.

Wearables and Exhibition Design

In 2018, the National Gallery of Prague introduced an innovative VR experience called *Touching Masterpieces*. This groundbreaking initiative was specifically designed to enable visually impaired and blind visitors to engage with some of the museum's most renowned sculptures, including iconic artworks like the Bust of Nefertiti (Fig. 5.6) and Michelangelo's

Fig. 5.6 Bust of Nefertiti, Neues Museum, Berlin

David (Montusiewicz et al., 2022). Developed in collaboration with Geometry Prague, NeuroDigital, and the Leontinka Foundation for the blind and visually impaired, this virtual reality experience incorporates haptic Manus VR gloves (Lannan, 2019). These gloves provide users with three-dimensional feedback, simulating the sensation of touch and allowing visitors to "feel" the intricate details and textures of the sculptures within the virtual environment. By leveraging cutting-edge technology, the National Gallery of Prague has successfully created a transformative experience that fosters inclusivity and opens up new avenues for sensory engagement for individuals with various sensory processing conditions (Schwind et al., 2019).

One recent development demonstrates the use of technology for accessibility in education in holographic technologies (Fig. 5.7). The holographic cube or Holo-cube, developed by Merge, is an innovative and interactive object that seamlessly integrates with a mobile app to create engaging AR experiences (Hayes et al., 2021). The six-sided object, resembling a weighted and squishy stress ball, offers users the ability to interpret it as a variety of dynamic visual representations. With the Holocube, users can transform the object into a spinning globe, a beating heart, a weapon, or even explore digital specimens of animals.

One of the key advantages of AR learning solutions like the Holocube is its ability to provide immersive augmented reality experiences without the need for wearable devices. Unlike headsets or goggles, the Holocube offers a more accessible and inclusive approach to augmented reality. Set

Fig. 5.7 Holocube, DLR German Aerospace Center

up requires minimal facilitation, allowing users to easily interact with the object and unlock its various visual interpretations, while this ease of use encourages social interaction and collaboration, as multiple users can gather around the cube and share in the augmented reality experiences together. Additionally, the design allows for a larger flow of users, making it suitable for busy museum environments or interactive installations where a high volume of visitors can engage with the technology.

By incorporating immersive examples such as the Holo-cube into museum exhibits or interactive displays, museums can create engaging and interactive experiences that captivate visitors of all ages. The versatility of the Holocube allows for a range of educational and entertaining applications, from showcasing geographical information on a spinning globe to providing a visual representation of the human cardiovascular system. This interactive object not only sparks curiosity and imagination but also encourages social interaction and collaboration among visitors, fostering a sense of shared experience and discovery. Such AR solutions exemplify the potential of immersive learning to transform museum experiences by offering a tangible and interactive medium for engaging visitors. Its unique design and functionality make it an exciting tool for museums seeking to enhance their exhibits with immersive and interactive elements (Shehade & Stylianou-Lambert, 2020).

Another added benefit to such interactables in exhibitions is to support mental health. In fact, utilizing museum objects to enhance mental health and well-being has been recognized as a valuable approach. Ander et al. (2013) argue that incorporating museum objects into interventions can positively impact the well-being of service users in mental health and neurological rehabilitation settings. Research conducted using mixed methods has shown promising results, demonstrating the benefits of museum object handling sessions in hospitals and care homes. Patients and clients participating in these sessions reported increased well-being, happiness, and a sense of distraction from clinical surroundings. Furthermore, engaging with museum objects improved communication with staff, caregivers, and family members, fostering meaningful connections.

The healthcare strategy in Britain has acknowledged the significance of multi-agency approaches and creative interventions, including cultural activities, in promoting well-being and reducing the need for medical interventions (Liddle & Addidle, 2023). Museum objects have been successfully integrated into mental health services and residential care to trigger memories and facilitate reminiscence activities (Malafouris, 2019).

These interventions have shown to enhance socialization, orientation, and validation of life experiences among participants (Cowan et al., 2019). Occupational therapy recognizes the importance of individuals' interaction with objects and the associated meaning they hold (Lobban & Murphy, 2020). While some objects may be too fragile or not readily accessible, the potential for digitizing objects and creating digital copies opens up possibilities for their use in various care facilities (Javaid et al., 2021).

Engaging with novel objects during object handling sessions has been found to stimulate new perspectives on clients' lives and aid in their mental recovery. It fosters a sense of privilege and uniqueness when handling certain objects, such as Egyptian replicas, contributing to a positive emotional experience. Incorporating a diverse range of unfamiliar objects in these sessions provides a challenging yet achievable environment for participants, promoting confidence building (Rushton et al., 2020). The availability of a wide variety of objects is contingent upon the size and nature of the museum collection. However, some museums have loan collections specifically designed to provide greater variety for educational opportunities.

Object handling sessions have emerged as a valuable approach in promoting well-being and enhancing the experiences of individuals participating in occupational therapy and neurological rehabilitation programs (Innes et al., 2021). These sessions involve actively engaging with museum objects, fostering a sense of connection and eliciting positive emotions. By incorporating museum objects into mental health interventions, healthcare professionals and occupational therapists can harness the power of cultural engagement to support individuals' mental well-being and contribute to their recovery journey (Camic et al., 2014).

Research has outlined a notable trend among neurodiverse individuals who tend to anchor themselves to reality. This means that they often make concrete associations between objects and events that are already familiar to them in order to construct meaning (Giaconi & Rodrigues, 2014). Individuals ASC may exhibit a heightened adherence to details, which can sometimes distract them from understanding the broader meaning of a situation. This can result in a confused perception of their environment and potential misunderstandings of verbal messages, facial cues, relationship dynamics, as well as social and environmental rules. The cognitive overload experienced by individuals, along with difficulties in filtering sensory stimuli, underscores the importance of designing interventions that address their specific needs and provide appropriate support (Giaconi & Rodrigues, 2014). By recognizing these challenges and tailoring object handling sessions to accommodate the sensory preferences and cognitive processes of neurodiverse individuals, museums and healthcare professionals can create meaningful and impactful experiences that support their well-being.

But the future of museums will not be defined by any one technology. Instead, the combination of different use cases for different outcomes will be more deliberately harnessed (Simon, 2010; Winesmith & Anderson, 2020). Therefore, the future of accessibility will combine the resources and technology listed above. Sensory maps represent an educational tool to prepare those with ASC to engage with new situations and/or in new environments (McLean, 2019). The multisensory approach used to create sensory maps ensures that whether over- or under-stimulated, visitors will be prepared for the visit and to benefit from the educational materials provided (Li et al., 2023). They currently exist in the form of handouts provided by an institution that takes into consideration how people perceive interacting with a space (Fig. 5.8). Social stories, on the other hand, use a narrative approach to both deliver content and to address situational awareness for those, especially with autism (Garzotto et al., 2018). Taken together, the proposed combined "storymap" can now be transformed into a digital expression and experience. Digital storytelling strategies can be used and experienced with various XR wearable devices. This *immersive storymap* can provide support prior to the visit, onsite, and engage diverse audiences with personalized, story-driven narratives of museum collections, while supporting adaptive, multisensory experiences (Hutson & Hutson, 2023).

Multisensory Experiences
Multisensory experiences hold great significance for neurodiverse individuals, as they can trigger rich memory associations, satisfaction, and pleasure by forging connections between life experiences and technologies. Tactile, olfactory, and auditory stimuli play key roles in facilitating these multisensory engagements (Lester & Nusbaum, 2021). To enhance tactile experiences, incorporating touch-sensitive technology, such as a touchscreen with a tactile map overlay, can provide individuals the opportunity to explore and interact with spatial information. This interactive approach allows for the triggering of verbal audio cues or vibrations when identifying points of interest, enabling a multisensory understanding of the

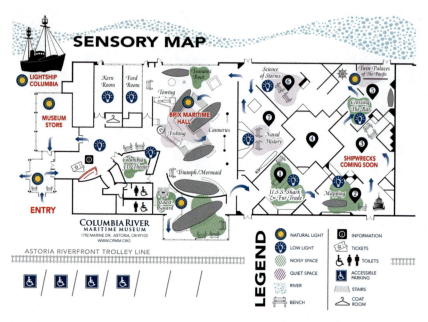

Fig. 5.8 Sensory Map, Columbia River Maritime Museum, Astoria

environment. It is essential to ensure that surfaces are sufficiently large to accommodate at least two fingers, allowing individuals to perceive and differentiate various volumes and textures (Taylor et al., 2016).

Gustatory perception, or the sense of taste, can also be integrated into multisensory experiences for individuals with ASC. Connecting gustatory experiences with regional foods, historic recipes, and cultural infusions local to the area not only adds a culinary dimension but also aids in memory formation. Incorporating tastings as part of locomotion training, where individuals explore the city and taste different foods, can create memorable associations, and enhance spatial cognition (Ward & Simner, 2020).

Spatial relationships can be better understood through the use of three-dimensional maps and multiple layered objects (Kwan, 2000). These tangible representations provide a hands-on approach to comprehending spatial concepts, such as the layout of buildings and cities. Layered maps can illustrate historical transitions over time, enabling individuals to visualize and understand how environments have evolved (Ben-Joseph et al.,

2001; de Abreu Santos & van der Borg, 2023). Furthermore, olfactory and gustatory modalities can be harnessed as tools for reflective learning and memorization. Utilizing scents and tastes associated with specific contexts or experiences can evoke memories and enhance cognitive processes. By incorporating pleasant aromas or tastes relevant to the learning environment, individuals on the spectrum can strengthen their associative memory and deepen their understanding of the subject matter (Bond & Bozdog, 2022).

Using the benefits of both sensory maps and social stories with VR, especially, enables those with sensory processing conditions, and other cognitive difficulties, to feel more comfortable in the museum space. Social stories can capitalize on existing avatar creators that are cross-platform and interoperable, such as Ready Player Me (https://readyplayer.me/) for a more immersive, enjoyable, and personalized experience. The use of avatars selected and created by a neurodiverse individual improves inclusivity through their use in virtual environments to better understand social contacts that may/will occur onsite, familiarizing them with the facilities prior to visiting, and the rewarding recognition of accomplishment by completing a visit. As noted, the benefits of using head-mounted displays (HMD) and VR include improved focus and attention span as these remove the distractions of the outside world, which can be overwhelming for those with stimuli sensitivity (Howard & Lee, 2020).

There are several use cases already available that demonstrate the efficacy of integrating emerging immersive technologies into cultural heritage institutions. One such example is *A Dip in the Blue* (2022), an application (app) developed for museum visitors with ASC to provide a clear visual agenda along with additional accessibility resources (Varriale et al., 2022). The app uses a social story that is inspired by the experience of an archeologist discovering a tomb in Naples. After the experience, a survey gathers data on the emotional reaction and sensory feedback experienced as part of the tour. Additional services and functional features within the app include a dashboard management panel, a live virtual tour scheduling system, a media library dedicated to storing documents, textual and multimedia contact like audio and video tours. There is additional socializing functionality built in with the ability to broadcast live streams of virtual tours.

Another example that uses interactive technologies, including mixed-reality, provides an interactive cultural visit of the church of Roncesvalles at the beginning of the popular tourist destination of Camino de Santiago

(Olaz et al., 2022). The inclusion of avatars provides the ability for natural social interactions to further enhance the visit. The church is experienced onsite through the use of a three-dimensional projection mapping, while an agent generating conversation acts as a storyteller for visitors. The avatar of the storyteller uses the techniques of storytelling while exhibiting emotional reactions during their narration of local stories of the objects in the room. Therefore, the storytelling experience is supported by the engagement with actual objects in the environment and the emotional conversation avatar thus bridging the real and virtual. But what makes this experience unique is the considerations of mapping the senses.

Moving beyond merely the visual, future cultural experiences will include multisensory interactions. An example can be found at the Van Abbemuseum where a comprehensive approach to accessibility has been taken by designing multi-sensory experiences for visitors with disabilities (Veerman, 2021). Through multi-sensory tours, sign language tours, and specialized opening hours, the museum has catered to diverse audiences, including those with visual impairments, hearing impairments, aphasia, dementia, and other conditions. The TIK-TIK app, developed as an outcome of this research, provides indoor navigation and audio descriptions for blind visitors, enhancing their engagement with the artworks (Buono et al., 2022). Additionally, the use of the Smartify app at the Van Abbemuseum allows visitors to explore multiple layers of storytelling and engage with artworks in a personalized and intuitive manner (Witter et al., 2022).

In 2010, Ferens Art Gallery embarked on a groundbreaking initiative to create a truly multisensory museum experience for visually impaired individuals (McColl, 2020). With funding from the Museums, Libraries, and Archive Council, the gallery developed a new type of tour that aimed to establish a meaningful connection between visitors and the artworks. Going beyond audio descriptions, Ferens Art Gallery incorporated tactile prints of the paintings, allowing visitors to feel the texture and form of the artworks. Replicas of objects depicted in the scenes were also made available for touch, enabling a more immersive understanding of the artwork. To further enhance the sensory experience, the museum strategically engaged other senses. Visitors could listen to sounds that evoked the atmosphere of the scenes, bringing the paintings to life through audio. Additionally, scents were introduced to capture the olfactory elements depicted in the artworks, adding another layer of sensory engagement. By engaging multiple senses, Ferens Art Gallery aimed to provide a comprehensive and rich experience that allowed visually impaired visitors to form a complete mental image of the paintings, fostering a deeper appreciation and connection with the art (Gray, 2012).

The importance of all of the senses for a truly immersive experience has been well-documented (Gallace et al., 2012; Melo et al., 2020). As such, a 2016 report of the Workshop in Cologne sought to understand how to map the senses and listed three steps (El-Sayyad, 2019). The first step includes a researcher mapping a specific urban space to be recreated. The second includes the subjective experiences of visitors by capturing the emotions and feelings of the citizens connected to the location. And, finally, the third is the connection of the researcher to the local community. These steps shed light on the soundscape and smellscape that compliment a visual imagery of a place. Smells often provide a memory which helps identify a place and the effects of climate should be considered. For instance, cold weather reduces the expansion of smells whereas warm weather expands them (Quercia et al., 2015). Creating an adaptive experience that can not only change based upon the environment represented, but also react to the physical and emotional states of visitors will become ever more important in crafting compelling virtual experiences.

In order to enhance accessibility for individuals with visual impairments, various technologies and tools have been developed to cater to their unique needs. One such innovative solution is Microsoft Soundscape, which has provided further support for the way individuals with visual impairments can navigate and interact with their surroundings. The solution is a mobile application that utilizes 3D audio technology to create a detailed audio map of the surrounding environment. It provides real-time audio cues and information about nearby landmarks, points of interest, intersections, and street names, allowing individuals with visual impairments to have a better understanding of their surroundings and navigate with greater confidence (McGill et al., 2020).

The audio map generated by Microsoft Soundscape offers a rich and immersive experience, providing spatial audio cues that mimic the way a sighted person perceives their environment. Using a combination of binaural audio, GPS positioning, and augmented reality, the app creates a three-dimensional auditory landscape that helps users build a mental map of the world around them (Clemenson et al., 2021).

Through the use of stereo headphones, individuals with visual impairments can perceive sounds from different directions and distances, allowing them to orient themselves and navigate more effectively. For example, the app can provide audio cues such as "turn left at the next intersection" or "approaching a coffee shop on your right," helping users make informed decisions and reach their desired destinations (Edler et al., 2019). Another key feature is the ability to provide "audio beacons," which are virtual markers that individuals with visual impairments can place in specific locations. These audio beacons serve as personalized points of interest and can be used to mark important locations, such as home, work, or frequently visited places. When the user approaches these locations, the app will provide custom audio cues, making it easier for individuals with visual impairments to navigate familiar areas.

Another significant advancement is the development of braille e-readers, such as the BraiBook, which conveniently fits into the palm of one's hand. Unlike conventional e-readers for blind users, which are often large and stationary, Braille e-readers offer greater mobility and flexibility. They allow individuals to read Braille text on the go, without the need for a table or specific conditions. This portability and ease of use greatly enhance the reading experience for individuals with visual impairments (Herzberg et al., 2017).

While audio books have been a popular choice for individuals with visual impairments, they do have limitations in terms of availability and the ability to multitask (Dali & Brochu, 2020). Blind users often require tools that enable them to engage in multiple activities simultaneously. They rely on their other senses to compensate for the lack of sight, such as using a cane for mobility and relying on sound feedback from the environment, such as traffic lights and vehicles. Therefore, it is crucial to design assistive technologies that do not distract or intrude upon these essential auditory cues, providing a seamless and efficient experience for individuals with visual impairments (Stern, 2011).

Designing for individuals with visual impairments poses unique challenges, as it requires careful consideration of their specific needs and the integration of technologies that facilitate multitasking and promote independent navigation. By leveraging soundscapes, audio maps, and portable braille e-readers, designers can create inclusive experiences that empower individuals with visual impairments to engage with their environment and access information with greater ease and efficiency.

Sound also plays a crucial role in creating inclusive and accessible environments within cultural institutions. It not only enhances the overall visitor experience but also provides essential support for individuals with sensory sensitivities or hearing impairments. The Shedd Aquarium is a prime example of an institution that recognizes the importance of sound accessibility. They offer sound reducing headphones at the front desk, theater, and amphitheater for visitors to check out for free on a first-come, first-served basis, ensuring that individuals can control their auditory environment and reduce noise distractions (Clark et al., 2016).

In addition to sound reducing headphones, the Shedd Aquarium provides a dedicated quiet room designed to accommodate individuals who may need a peaceful and calming space. This room features comfortable seating, adjustable lighting, a weighted lap pad, sound reducing headphones, and even a prayer rug to cater to diverse needs. By offering a designated quiet area, the Shedd Aquarium acknowledges the importance of providing a sensory-friendly environment where individuals can find respite from overstimulation and actively participate in their museum experience (Schwartzman & Knowles, 2022).

Furthermore, the Shedd Aquarium incorporates the use of the Aira app to facilitate wayfinding and enhance accessibility for visitors. Aira connects users with highly trained sight agents through video calls, allowing them to receive real-time assistance with navigating the museum, finding specific areas of interest, and accessing detailed information about exhibits. This technology empowers individuals with visual impairments to independently explore the aquarium, ensuring they have equal opportunities to engage with the exhibits and make informed choices about their visit (Melfi et al., 2020).

In the pursuit of improving the accessibility of exhibits and promoting universal design in aquariums, researchers at Georgia Tech have conducted studies on real-time interpretive sound as a strategy for translating visual aspects of marine animal exhibits. Initially focusing on designing soundscapes for individuals with visual impairments, the project aimed to convey informational aspects such as animal type, location, and movement, as well as the affective aspects of the exhibit, such as the mood or atmosphere perceived by visitors (Maple, 2021).

The goal of this approach is not only to enable visitors with vision impairments to experience the exhibit, but also to create a shared experience where visitors with and without visual impairments can discuss and engage with the exhibit on a deeper level. To achieve this, researchers collaborated with musicians to explore the translation of animal movement into musical patterns, enabling the development of sonification algorithms. Through this process, embodied interaction using "interactive soundification" has proven to be effective in various learning and training domains (Nadri et al., 2022).

Soundification is a technique that has been extensively studied to explore the relationship between sound and visualization. Researchers have discovered that by manipulating different attributes of sound, such as pitch, volume, and waveform, it is possible to create auditory representations that correspond to their visual counterparts. One example of soundification is the Soundview application, which allows users to interact with a colored surface using a pointing device. In this application, the characteristics of colors, including hue, saturation, and brightness, are mapped into soundscapes. As users explore the colored surface, they are able to perceive and experience the visual attributes of color through auditory feedback (Janbuala & Lindborg, 2021).

The concept of soundification opens up new possibilities for enhancing multisensory experiences in various domains, including museums and cultural heritage settings. By utilizing soundification techniques, museums can provide visitors with alternative ways of perceiving and understanding visual information. For individuals with visual impairments or those who prefer auditory experiences, soundification can bridge the gap and offer a rich and immersive experience by translating visual attributes into meaningful sounds. Furthermore, the approach can be used as a tool for artistic expression and creativity. By manipulating sound to correspond with visual elements, artists and designers can explore the intersection of sensory modalities, creating unique and engaging experiences for audiences. This approach not only allows for the accessibility and inclusivity of exhibits, but also promotes innovative and interactive forms of storytelling (Gupfinger & Kaltenbrunner, 2019).

The sound design engine used in the Georgia Tech project is built on max/MSP, with data being passed onto Reason software via the musical instrument digital interface channels. To provide a visual interface for the project, the researchers utilized the 3D animation program Maya to create virtual fish that users can observe. This visual representation showcases how the movement of fish in an aquarium drives the creation of music, which can then be heard through headphones. Each iteration and implementation of the technology resulted in new sounds and music that better represented the behaviors and characteristics of each fish in the virtual tank (Weinberg et al., 2020).

This technology has the potential to be adapted to a static setup with the use of tracking hardware, allowing for the creation of a psychological and cognitive correlation between visual aquarium stimuli and mood and emotional modification. By incorporating sound as an integral part of the exhibit experience, aquariums can enhance the accessibility and engagement for visitors with diverse sensory needs, facilitating a deeper understanding and connection with marine life.

The research conducted by Georgia Tech exemplifies the importance of sound design in creating inclusive and immersive experiences within aquariums. By harnessing the power of sound, museums and cultural institutions can provide a multi-sensory approach that caters to a wide range of visitors, including those with visual impairments. This integration of sound not only facilitates access to information but also enhances emotional and affective engagement with the exhibits, fostering a more inclusive and enriched cultural experience for all visitors.

As demonstrated through the examples above, adaptive content and interactive storytelling will revolutionize museum experiences. In order to make such experiences possible, the collection of biometrics of visitors will be required. Furthermore, adaptive content that adjusts to the needs of diverse audiences through new paradigms of interaction will provide accessible digital content to a wide range of visitors (Pietroni & Adami, 2014). Researchers will need to use the following strategies to collect data to personalize avatars to craft custom-made experiences associated with museum visits (Table 5.5).

Museums can leverage various methods to enhance visitor experiences through data collection and personalization. Biometric data collection

Table 5.5 Methods for personalized museum experiences

Methods	Description
Biometric data collection	Collection of facial features, body measurements, and voice samples to create 3D avatars for VR and AR experiences.
Surveys and questionnaires	Gathering information about visitors' preferences, interests, and background to tailor the museum experience.
Tracking and monitoring	Utilizing technologies like RFID tags and cameras to track visitors' movements and interactions for personalized insights.
Social media integration	Incorporating data from visitors' social media profiles to personalize the museum experience based on their interests.
Personalized recommendations	Providing customized suggestions for exhibits, activities, and tours based on visitors' data and preferences.
Feedback	Gathering feedback from visitors to improve and refine personalized experiences in the future.

involves capturing facial features, body measurements, and voice samples to create 3D avatars for virtual and augmented reality experiences (Goodenough et al., 2010; Noehrer et al., 2021). Surveys and questionnaires allow museums to gather information about visitors' preferences and interests, enabling tailored content and activities (O'Hagan, 2021). Tracking technologies like Radio-Frequency Identification (RFID) tags and cameras help monitor visitors' movements and interactions, providing insights into behavior and personalizing the experience. Integrating social media profiles allows museums to utilize data to suggest exhibits or activities aligned with visitors' interests. Personalized recommendations can be generated based on collected data, offering tailored tours, augmented reality experiences, or exhibit suggestions (Kamruzzaman et al., 2023).

Gathering visitor feedback helps museums refine and improve personalized experiences for future visitors. These approaches enable museums to create more engaging and individualized experiences for their visitors. Examples of this in practice can already be seen in research projects like CHESS (Cultural Heritage Experiences through Socio-personal interactions and Storytelling). CHESS (https://chess.diginext.fr/) applies constant adaptable and personalized content to enhance the experience of the Acropolis Museum, Athens (Pujol et al., 2012). The onsite engagement with objects in the museum personalizes interactive stories for each visitor. The project was created to further enhance a visit by personalizing an engaging and interactive storytelling experience by adapting information about cultural artifacts for each individual visitor.

Neuroscience and Museums

The latest generation of state-of-the-art museum programming seeks to create cultural adventures that are driven by stories and narratives, aiming to provide immersive and engaging experiences for visitors. Through the use of multimodal interfaces, these experiences involve users in various roles within a scenario, enabling them to interact with exhibits and content in dynamic ways. The incorporation of localization systems and real-time adaptive capabilities further enhances the educational experience, tailoring it to the individual visitor's interests and preferences. With the advancement of virtual connectivity, these experiences are no longer limited to physical museum spaces but can also be accessed and enjoyed from the comfort of one's home using various devices.

This shift towards user-centered approaches and the convergence of space and time through virtual connectivity have paved the way for museums to explore new avenues of engagement and accessibility. By embracing the intersection of neuroscience and museum exhibition design, institutions can unlock exciting possibilities for creating more compelling and impactful experiences for visitors (Table 5.6). Insights from neuroscience provide valuable understanding of how the brain functions in active social environments, shedding light on the cognitive and emotional processes that shape our interactions with art and cultural artifacts.

By incorporating findings from neuroscience, museums can design exhibitions and interactive experiences that tap into the human brain's natural inclinations and responses. This integration allows for a deeper exploration of the nature of the human experience, bridging the gap between art and science. Understanding how the brain processes sensory stimuli, forms memories, and engages with narratives can inform the

Table 5.6 Neuroscience and museums

Element	Description
Personalized experiences	Museums can leverage insights from neuroscience to create personalized experiences that cater to individual preferences, interests, and learning styles.
Multisensory engagement	Understanding how the brain processes and responds to different sensory stimuli can inform the design of exhibits and programs that engage multiple senses.
Emotional impact and memory	Neuroscience can inform the creation of exhibits and narratives that evoke emotional responses, leading to enhanced memory retention and meaningful experiences.
Social interaction and connection	Museums can incorporate social elements, such as group activities and shared experiences, to stimulate social interaction and foster a sense of connection among visitors.
Attention and focus	Insights from neuroscience can guide the design of exhibits and interactive experiences that capture and maintain visitors' attention and promote focused engagement.
Neurodiversity and inclusion	Neuroscience research can inform inclusive design practices that accommodate the diverse cognitive and sensory needs of all visitors, including those with neurodiverse conditions.
Learning and cognitive development	Understanding how the brain processes information and acquires knowledge can inform the design of exhibits and educational programs that optimize learning outcomes.
Stress reduction and well-being	Neuroscience can inform strategies to create museum environments that promote relaxation, reduce stress, and enhance overall visitor well-being.

development of exhibits that resonate on a cognitive and emotional level, leaving a lasting impression on visitors.

Neuroscience can also offer insights into the role of emotions in learning and memory formation, allowing museums to design experiences that evoke powerful emotional responses and enhance visitors' connections to the exhibited content. By creating environments that engage multiple senses, trigger emotional responses, and facilitate social interactions, museums can create rich and immersive experiences that leave a lasting impact on visitors' perceptions and understanding (Banzi, 2022).

One avenue for employing neuroscience in exhibition design is through the utilization of existing data from laboratory studies, as well as generating new data within the museum context. Various techniques can be employed, such as eye tracking (previously referred to as gaze tracking) to monitor attention, biometric measurements to assess physiological responses of emotions, and self-reporting methods like exit surveys and interviews to analyze visitors' perception of time spent in the exhibition space and the construction of memory (Stangl et al., 2023).

Stimulating the sensory processing pathways and transmitting signals back to the brain, exhibitions can elicit mental reactions in cognition, memory, and emotional responses. Neural signals can also travel down the spinal cord, modulating motor behavior and physiology, providing insight into emotional responses. Each output of neural function contributes to the sensations and experiences visitors feel (Berntson & Khalsa, 2021).

Biometrics and sensor trackers have emerged as valuable tools to track the emotional responses of museum visitors, providing insights into their engagement and experiences. These sensors can be categorized into three main groups based on biological functions: thermoreceptors for thermal sensing, nociceptors for pain sensing, and mechanoreceptors for mechanical stimuli and skin deformation (Fig. 5.9). In the context of assistive devices for the blind, tactile displays for fingertips and palms have been developed to provide a substitute sense of touch. These displays often utilize vibrators or movable pins to simulate tactile sensations and allow individuals to perceive information through touch (Dwivedi et al., 2022).

One example of a communication interface for the blind is the wearable finger braille interface, which enables real-time communication with others. Finger braille involves tapping specific finger combinations to transmit verbal information, with each combination corresponding to a braille digit. This method allows individuals to receive information while

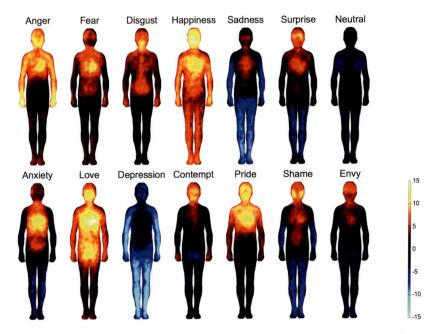

Fig. 5.9 Topographical organization of human emotions in the body from Nummenmaa et al. (2020 Proceedings of the National Academy of Sciences of the United States of America (PNAS))

simultaneously listening in real time, enhancing their access to information and communication (Ranasinghe et al., 2021).

Glove-style interfaces have proven to be the most suitable design for finger braille interfaces as they are easy to wear and provide coverage for the palm or fingertip, which are areas of the hand with high tactile sensitivity. These glove-based systems have been developed since the 1970s, and various designs and iterations have been proposed to optimize their functionality and user experience (Hirose & Amemiya, 2003). By incorporating biometric sensors and tactile interfaces, museums can gather data on visitors' emotional responses and engagement levels. This information can be valuable for understanding the impact of exhibits, identifying areas of interest or disinterest, and tailoring future experiences to enhance visitor satisfaction. Additionally, these technologies can provide new avenues for communication and interaction, allowing individuals to actively participate in the museum experience and engage with the content in a personalized and meaningful way.

In academic applications, emotions can also be measured along two dimensions: arousal and valence. A higher level of emotional arousal is associated with a greater likelihood of constructing a memory of the experience, whether it is positive or negative. Biometrics, such as Galvanic Skin Response (GSR), can be used to measure sweat production, which is regulated by the brain and provides an indirect indicator of emotional responses (Alsharif et al., 2021).

The pioneering work of Alfred Yarbus, a psychologist in the 1960s, highlighted how viewers' goals and viewing behavior impact their perception and engagement with images. Visitors who receive prompts or textual information in labels exhibit changes in their eye tracking patterns, shifting from free-viewing to more focused concentration guided by curator influence (Shields, 2023). AI algorithms can now analyze eye tracking data and identify the task or purpose of the viewer, providing valuable insights into their viewing behavior (Fig 5.10) (Sharma et al., 2020).

Studies have demonstrated that viewers exhibit instinctual bias towards the center of an image (Ahmed et al., 2021; Denson, 2020; Salam, 2021). Those who engage in free viewing, often prompted by historical content text, maintain a center bias (Hutchinson & Eardley, 2021). In contrast, viewers with searching tasks lose center bias early on in their viewing. Different viewers extract different content from the same image

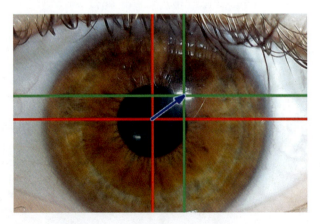

Fig. 5.10 Eye-tracking algorithm using visible light

depending on their purpose. Judgement task prompts, where visitors are asked to relate themselves to the work, have been found to be particularly effective in increasing engagement (Diamond et al., 2016).

The Default Mode Network (DMN) in the brain is activated by emotionally moving aesthetic experiences (Fig. 5.11) (Van Elk et al., 2019). Conversely, non-inspiring images suppress activity in this area. The DMN tends to be suppressed when attention is externally focused and activated when attention is internally directed towards introspection and self-referential thinking (Vessel et al., 2019). A study at the PEM (Peabody Essex Museum) exploring the work of T.C. Cannon, a Native American artist, found that activation of this network facilitates self-referential thinking and may be a critical component in creating a moving aesthetic experience. The study initially intended to use an app with question prompts at specific geolocation spots but resorted to providing physical visual information instead (Deloria, 2019).

Another important aspect to consider is the "exit effect," where attention rates decline over the course of a museum visit, with visitors spending more time with initial exhibits encountered compared to those near the exit (Taylor, 1993). Strategies to compensate for this reduction in attention could include limiting the number of works in the last gallery or selecting works that require less viewing time but still engage visitors (Görel, 2019). Slowing down the pace of visitors can also be achieved by incorporating viewing tasks that encourage slow looking and facilitate emotional engagement with art (Hutchinson & Eardley, 2021).

Across various datasets, a consistent theme emerges: design elements that foster interpersonal connections result in higher levels of engagement

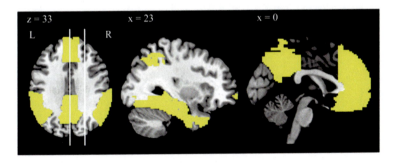

Fig. 5.11 Anatomically defined default mode network (DMN)

(Mujtaba et al., 2018; Peppler et al., 2022). This connection can manifest in introspection, a connection to another human through the artist as a knowledge archetype, and a personal connection to the subject matter (Vaughan, 2022). Therefore, integrating neuroscience into exhibition design holds immense potential for museums to create transformative and engaging experiences.

Institutions have a wide range of resources available to them to enhance visitor experiences and effectively manage their museums. One such resource is DeFrame, a software as a service (SaaS) platform specifically designed for museums (http://www.deframeart.com/). Such solutions offer a comprehensive suite of tools, including visitor engagement features and exhibit analytics (De la Prieta et al., 2015). With DeFrame, museums can create interactive maps that guide visitors through their buildings, enriching the experience with virtual content that enhances engagement at each exhibit. The platform also provides valuable insights into visitor behavior and preferences, allowing museums to better understand how guests interact with their exhibits and ultimately improve guest satisfaction ratings. By leveraging such solutions for engagement management capabilities, museums can not only enhance the visitor experience but also fuel the future of their marketing efforts, ensuring a memorable and impactful museum visit for all.

By leveraging techniques such as eye tracking, biometrics, and exit surveys, museums can gain valuable insights into visitor behavior and emotional responses. This knowledge can inform the design of exhibitions that stimulate the senses, elicit emotional engagement, and foster connections between visitors, artworks, and cultural heritage. By embracing these neuroscience-informed strategies, museums can ensure their exhibitions are not only intellectually enriching but also emotionally resonant, inviting visitors to explore the depths of the human experience through art and culture.

5.5 Artificial Intelligence and Museums

Artificial intelligence (AI) has become an increasingly prevalent and transformative force across various industries, including the field of cultural heritage. There are, in fact, many ways in which AI can be used holistically across museums (Table 5.7). The use of AI to enhance accessibility has gained significant attention and funding in recent years (Pisoni et al., 2021; Wamba-Taguimdje et al., 2020). Microsoft's AI for Accessibility

Table 5.7 Artificial intelligence and museums

Element	Description
Data analysis and insights	AI can analyze large amounts of data collected by museums, providing valuable insights for exhibition planning, visitor engagement, and more.
Personalized experiences	AI algorithms can customize museum experiences based on visitor preferences, creating tailored tours, recommendations, and interactive content.
Virtual and augmented reality	AI-powered VR and AR technologies can enhance museum experiences by creating immersive, interactive, and lifelike virtual environments.
Chatbots and virtual assistants	Museums can employ AI chatbots and virtual assistants to provide visitor information, answer questions, and offer personalized recommendations.
Language processing and translation	AI can facilitate multilingual experiences by providing real-time translation services, enabling visitors to access information in their preferred language.
Collection management and curation	AI algorithms can assist in cataloging and curating museum collections, automating tasks such as image recognition, metadata tagging, and preservation.
Visitor behavior analysis	AI can analyze visitor behavior patterns, such as navigation paths, interactions, and preferences, to understand engagement levels and improve museum offerings.
Accessibility and inclusion	AI technologies can support accessibility initiatives, providing solutions such as image recognition for visually impaired visitors or captioning for deaf visitors.
Predictive analytics and forecasting	AI can predict visitor trends, attendance patterns, and exhibit popularity, enabling museums to optimize resource allocation and plan for future exhibitions.
Conservation and restoration	AI technologies, such as machine learning and computer vision, can aid in the conservation and restoration of artworks, detecting damages and providing restoration guidance.

program, launched in 2019, exemplifies this commitment. With an initial investment of $25 million, the program supports startups that drive innovation and aim to amplify human capacity for individuals with disabilities. Microsoft continues to actively seek new projects to support through its grant program, recognizing the transformative potential of AI in improving accessibility (de Laat, 2021).

In addition to financial support, AI technologies are also being employed to analyze public sentiment through social media platforms. Sentiment analysis algorithms can identify content that mentions emotions related to museum exhibitions, providing valuable insights into the cultural ethos surrounding these experiences. By leveraging AI sentiment analysis, museums can gain a deeper understanding of visitors' emotional responses and preferences, allowing them to tailor their exhibitions and offerings to better meet the needs and expectations of diverse audiences (Qian et al., 2022).

This increased focus on utilizing AI for accessibility reflects a growing recognition of the importance of inclusive design and equal access to cultural and educational experiences. By harnessing the power of AI and investing in innovative projects, organizations like Microsoft are paving the way for a more inclusive and accessible future, where individuals with disabilities can fully participate and engage in all aspects of society, including the rich and diverse world of museums and cultural heritage (Berube, 2023).

In this section, we delve into the intersection of AI and museums, exploring how this technology can enhance and revolutionize the museum experience. However, it is important to approach AI with a critical lens, recognizing its potential to perpetuate and amplify biases. The focus should not be on making technology more human-like, but rather on designing technology that embraces and enhances our human qualities. By considering cognition and human needs as the starting point, we can harness the power of AI to create more inclusive, engaging, and meaningful museum experiences.

The first consideration is to ensure bias is reduced in AI systems (Table 5.8). Reducing bias in AI is crucial for creating fair and equitable systems (Ferrara, 2023). Open source data science can play a significant role in addressing bias and promoting ethical AI development. By adopting an open and collaborative approach, it becomes possible to mitigate bias and work towards a more inclusive and representative AI (Bondi et al., 2021). Bias in AI occurs when machine outputs consistently differ for different groups of people, often reflecting societal biases related to race, gender, nationality, or age, as seen most prevalently in algorithmic culture through algorithmic bias (Kordzadeh & Ghasemaghaei, 2022). Facial recognition technology and healthcare systems have been examples where biases have been observed due to incomplete or unrepresentative training data (Leslie et al., 2021).

However, bias in AI is ultimately a human problem given that humans design and develop AI algorithms, and their biases can inadvertently be embedded in the systems. To address algorithmic bias, two main issues

Table 5.8 Reducing bias with AI systems in museums

Element	Description
Diverse data collection	Ensuring that AI systems are trained on diverse and representative datasets to minimize bias and avoid reinforcing existing social or cultural biases.
Bias detection and mitigation	Implementing techniques to detect and mitigate biases in AI algorithms, such as bias audits, fairness metrics, and algorithmic transparency measures.
Ethical and inclusive AI design	Incorporating ethical considerations and inclusive design principles in the development of AI systems to promote fairness, transparency, and accountability.
User feedback and iterative improvement	Collecting user feedback to continuously evaluate and refine AI systems, addressing potential biases, and improving the accuracy and fairness of outcomes.
Regular evaluation and auditing	Conducting regular evaluations and audits of AI systems to identify and rectify any biases or unintended consequences that may arise during their deployment.
Collaboration with diverse stakeholders	Engaging a diverse range of stakeholders, including communities, experts, and users, in the design and development of AI systems to ensure diverse perspectives and mitigate biases.
Continuous learning and training	Providing ongoing training and education to AI developers and museum staff on bias awareness, fairness considerations, and responsible AI practices.
Transparency and explainability	Ensuring transparency in AI decision-making processes, making efforts to explain how AI systems work, and providing clear information on data usage and algorithms.
Regular ethics review	Conducting regular ethics reviews of AI systems, involving experts and stakeholders to evaluate potential biases and ethical implications of their deployment.
Accountability and responsibility	Taking responsibility for the impact of AI systems, being accountable for biases that may arise, and proactively addressing biases to promote equitable and inclusive museum experiences.

need to be tackled: data and the definition of success. Ensuring that the available data is complete and representative of all people is essential to mitigate bias in AI predictions (Coeckelbergh, 2020).

One approach is to consider open source data science as a solution to reducing bias in AI. By opening up models and the data they are trained on, the field of data science can benefit from collaboration and community contributions. This approach has been successfully employed by companies like Hugging Face, which democratizes machine learning through open-source models. In an open source data science environment, companies working on similar tasks can collaborate on common projects. For example, in face recognition, multiple companies can contribute code and data to create a more robust and unbiased solution. This collaborative effort not only saves time and resources but also brings diverse perspectives and expertise to improve the models (Gibney, 2022).

Open source data science also encourages collaboration and contribution from data scientists outside of specific companies. They can identify bugs, inefficiencies, and biases in the datasets and propose alternative models to prioritize different metrics for various use cases. Collaborative platforms and initiatives enable data scientists to showcase their skills, improve their portfolios, and actively contribute to creating fairer and more reliable AI systems (Tunstall et al., 2022).

Moreover, reducing bias in AI is of utmost importance for cultural heritage institutions, as they hold the responsibility of preserving and showcasing diverse cultural artifacts, artworks, and historical records (Taurino, 2023). These institutions play a vital role in promoting inclusivity, challenging historical imbalances, and providing a comprehensive representation of cultural heritage. With the increasing integration of AI technologies in various aspects of cultural heritage, such as digitization, curation, and interpretation, it is crucial to ensure that these AI systems are free from bias and uphold ethical standards (Giannini & Bowen, 2022).

Cultural heritage institutions strive to create an inclusive environment where diverse narratives and perspectives are respected and celebrated. By addressing bias in AI, these institutions can actively contribute to this goal. One significant aspect is ensuring inclusive representation through AI-powered digitization and curation processes (Huang & Liem, 2022). By reducing bias in these systems, cultural heritage institutions can accurately represent the wide range of cultural backgrounds, experiences, and histories present in their collections. This enables a more holistic understanding of cultural heritage and challenges the dominant narratives that may have overlooked marginalized voices.

Moreover, cultural heritage institutions need to be cautious about the reinforcement of stereotypes through AI applications. Recommendation systems and content generation tools should be carefully designed to avoid perpetuating biased narratives or promoting harmful stereotypes (Cheuk, 2021). By actively addressing bias, institutions can ensure that AI systems provide accurate and unbiased interpretations, contributing to a more balanced and authentic representation of cultural heritage.

Another critical consideration is the engagement of underrepresented communities. Cultural heritage institutions have the opportunity to reach out to communities that have been historically marginalized or underrepresented (Lemke et al., 2022). AI systems used in interpretation and interactive experiences must be designed to be free from bias and inclusive in their approach. This creates a welcoming environment for visitors from diverse backgrounds, fostering greater participation, and enabling a deeper connection with cultural heritage.

By prioritizing the reduction of bias in AI, cultural heritage institutions not only uphold ethical standards but also contribute to a more inclusive and equitable representation of cultural heritage. These institutions can actively challenge historical imbalances, promote diverse narratives, and engage a broader audience in the appreciation and preservation of cultural heritage. Through their commitment to unbiased AI applications, cultural heritage institutions play a vital role in shaping a more inclusive academic discourse and fostering a greater understanding of our shared cultural legacy.

With these considerations regarding bias, we can now approach the use of AI in use cases for museums. In the rapidly evolving digital landscape, museums and cultural organizations are seeking innovative ways to enhance visitor experiences, streamline operations, and drive engagement. One avenue that holds immense potential is the use of AI, with ChatGPT at the forefront of this transformative technology (Table 5.9). In the digital era, content plays a crucial role in attracting and engaging audiences (Femenia-Serra et al., 2022). Large language models (LLM) like ChatGPT, Bard, Llama, and others, can revolutionize content creation for museums by generating ideas, synthesizing written material, detecting popular themes, and optimizing online visibility. By analyzing audience engagement and preferences, museums can ensure that ChatGPT generates tailored content that resonates with their target audience, resulting in increased engagement, museum visits, and membership growth (Morse, 2020).

Diversifying communication channels is vital for effective member engagement. These AI tools can enable museums to drive engagement through personalized text message marketing. By generating concise, relevant content, ChatGPT can create event reminders, exhibition highlights, membership perks, and exclusive offers tailored to individual preferences. This personalized approach captures attention, fosters

Table 5.9 Use cases of ChatGPT for museums

Use case	Description
Visitor information and assistance	ChatGPT can serve as a virtual assistant to provide visitors with information about museum exhibits, hours of operation, ticketing, directions, and more.
Interactive guided tours	ChatGPT can offer interactive guided tours, providing visitors with a personalized and immersive experience, answering questions, and offering additional insights.
Artwork interpretation and historical context	ChatGPT can provide detailed interpretations and historical context for artworks, enhancing visitors' understanding and appreciation of the museum's collection.
Virtual exhibitions and virtual reality (VR)	ChatGPT can be integrated into virtual exhibitions or VR experiences, allowing users to interact with virtual artworks and receive information and guidance in real-time.
Language translation and multilingual support	ChatGPT can assist in providing language translation services, offering multilingual support to visitors who may have language barriers or prefer to communicate in their native language.
Educational and interactive games	ChatGPT can be incorporated into educational games and interactive experiences, engaging visitors in quizzes, challenges, and storytelling adventures related to museum exhibits.
Curator insights and behind-the-scenes access	ChatGPT can provide curator insights, sharing behind-the-scenes stories, archival information, and exclusive details about the museum's collections and exhibitions.

interaction, and ultimately boosts overall engagement with members and visitors.

Museums strive to make their exhibits and resources accessible to a diverse audience. Generative AI's ability to generate human-like text in multiple languages can significantly aid in this endeavor. By automatically translating museum content, such as exhibit labels, descriptions, and educational resources, AI-powered multilingual translations can make exhibits and resources accessible to a wider range of visitors, including those who may not be fluent in the local language (Wang et al., 2023). It is crucial to ensure that AI systems are unbiased and provide accurate translations to avoid any potential discrimination or exclusion. This not only enhances visitor engagement and accessibility but also promotes cultural exchange and understanding.

Additionally, these tools can assist with driving engagement. Events play a crucial role in driving museum attendance and engagement (Abkarian et al., 2022). ChatGPT can serve as a virtual assistant, providing event information, answering inquiries, sending reminders, and offering personalized recommendations. By generating compelling content for event invitations, social media posts, and email newsletters, ChatGPT creates an immersive experience that sparks curiosity and encourages participation.

At the same time, today's audiences expect highly personalized experiences. Generative AI enables museums to create customized visitor journeys by analyzing interests and preferences. By suggesting personalized tours, providing tailored information and recommendations, and offering interactive experiences such as quizzes, games, or augmented reality, museums can deliver engaging and immersive encounters that resonate with individual visitors (Rani et al., 2023).

Along the same lines, to ensure a seamless visitor experience, museums can utilize ChatGPT as a virtual assistant. ChatGPT can assist visitors by answering inquiries, providing event information, and offering personalized support through a conversational interface. This 24/7 availability enhances visitor satisfaction, reduces staffing costs, and improves overall member engagement and retention. However, training the LLM will be necessary and personnel considerations to ensure this information is up to date will be necessary.

AI-powered tools like ChatGPT can process vast amounts of qualitative data, providing museums with valuable insights. By analyzing visitor feedback, social media posts, and other unstructured data sources, museums can gain a deeper understanding of their audience, optimize resources, and enhance impact and relevance. ChatGPT's ability to identify patterns in visitor experiences, preferences, and expectations enables museums to make data-driven decisions for exhibit content, visitor services, and targeted marketing campaigns.

Finally, fundraising is a critical aspect of sustaining museum operations and driving growth (Demartini et al., 2021). AI tools can assist museums in this area by generating persuasive, tailored content for various donor segments. From engaging donation appeals and impact stories to personalized acknowledgments and informative updates, ChatGPT empowers museums to strengthen donor relationships, boost donations, and reach fundraising targets. In all, by harnessing the power of AI and ChatGPT, museums can unlock new opportunities for engaging visitors, personalizing experiences, and optimizing operations. These transformative technologies pave the way for a dynamic and immersive future, where museums can thrive in the digital age while preserving and promoting our cultural heritage.

But AI can also assist with the curation of exhibitions, as well. AI has been playing an increasingly significant role in museum curation, challenging the boundaries of traditional practices (Choi & Kim, 2021). With the emergence of AI-generated art, artists are using programs like DALL-E to create unique and compelling artworks. However, the process goes beyond simply pressing a button, as artists are actively involved in selecting outputs and engineering prompts, which becomes an act of aesthetic expression in itself (Hutson & Cotroneo, 2023).

Generative models, a subclass of computer vision algorithms, are at the center of AI art. These models are trained on large datasets of images, learning to encode statistically salient features. After training, they can generate new images based on text prompts, producing results that were not present in the original dataset. Recent advancements in image generation technology, such as OpenAI's DALL-E 2, have improved the coherence and detail of AI-generated images. Artists can now specify desired styles and even imitate famous artists, resulting in remarkably consistent and relevant images (Cahyadi et al., 2023).

AI art introduces new dimensions to the curation process. Firstly, there is the curation of outputs. Generative algorithms can produce an infinite number of images, but not all of them possess artistic merit. Similar to photographers curating their shots, AI artists need to select and promote specific outputs as artworks, expressing their intentions and artistic sensibility (Hutson & Lang, 2023).

Secondly, curation extends to the process of crafting datasets for training AI algorithms. The quality and biases of the dataset can significantly influence the performance and results of the generative model. Dataset curation becomes an essential step to ensure the network learns the desired features and avoids perpetuating harmful biases.

Lastly, AI art introduces a new form of curation through the design and collection of text prompts. Artists can describe their desired results in natural language, guiding the generative algorithm to produce images. Prompt engineering becomes a creative skill, akin to alchemy, as artists experiment with different combinations of words to unlock specific styles or subjects. The curation of prompts allows artists to develop their personal artistic style and adds an interpretive layer to the resulting artworks.

These curatorial aspects of AI art have the potential to influence traditional curatorial practices in museums and digital exhibitions. Institutions exhibiting AI art may need to provide information about the training datasets and prompts used, offering relevant context for understanding the artworks. The blurring of boundaries between artists and curators opens up new possibilities for cross-pollination and collaboration, as curators can integrate AI-generated art into their exhibitions and explore novel forms of digital curation. As AI continues to advance, it will undoubtedly have a profound impact on artistic creation and curation, fostering new forms of creativity and pushing the boundaries of traditional practices.

In this chapter, we have explored the fascinating world of immersive technologies and their impact on various domains, including education, entertainment, and cultural heritage. Immersive technologies, such as virtual reality (VR), augmented reality (AR), and mixed reality (MR), have revolutionized the way we perceive and interact with the digital world, blurring the boundaries between the physical and virtual realms.

Throughout the chapter, we have witnessed the immense potential of immersive technologies in enhancing learning experiences, creating engaging entertainment content, improving healthcare outcomes, and preserving cultural heritage. VR and AR have proven to be powerful tools for education, allowing students to explore virtual environments, visualize complex concepts, and participate in immersive simulations that enhance their understanding and retention of information. In the entertainment industry, immersive technologies have opened up new frontiers for storytelling, enabling users to become active participants in captivating narratives and immersive gaming experiences.

Furthermore, immersive technologies have made significant contributions to the healthcare sector, facilitating medical training, improving patient outcomes, and enhancing the delivery of care. From simulating surgical procedures to providing virtual therapy sessions, these technologies have demonstrated their potential in revolutionizing healthcare practices and reducing the barriers to accessing quality healthcare services.

Cultural heritage institutions have also embraced immersive technologies to preserve and showcase diverse artifacts, artworks, and historical records. VR and AR applications have allowed visitors to explore virtual museums, engage with interactive exhibits, and experience historical events firsthand. These technologies have expanded access to cultural heritage, transcending geographical boundaries and enabling a broader audience to connect with their shared history and heritage.

However, as we have delved into the realm of immersive technologies, we have also encountered challenges and ethical considerations. Issues such as privacy concerns, content moderation, and the potential for addiction and escapism require careful attention and regulation. It is crucial that developers, researchers, and policymakers work hand in hand to ensure that immersive technologies are developed and deployed responsibly, with a focus on user safety, inclusivity, and the preservation of human values.

Looking ahead, the future of immersive technologies holds great promise. As these technologies continue to evolve and become more accessible, we can expect to witness further advancements in their capabilities and applications. The potential for collaboration, interdisciplinary research, and innovation is vast. With responsible development and thoughtful integration, immersive technologies have the potential to transform industries, enrich our lives, and open up new avenues for human creativity and exploration.

In conclusion, immersive technologies have the power to reshape the way we learn, entertain, receive healthcare, and experience our cultural heritage. As we navigate this exciting frontier, it is essential to strike a balance between technological advancements and ethical considerations, ensuring that immersive technologies serve as tools for human empowerment, understanding, and connection. By harnessing the potential of immersive technologies while addressing their challenges, we can pave the way for a future where the digital and physical worlds coexist harmoniously, enriching our lives and pushing the boundaries of human experience.

References

Abkarian, H., Tahlyan, D., Mahmassani, H., & Smilowitz, K. (2022). Characterizing visitor engagement behavior at large-scale events: Activity sequence clustering and ranking using GPS tracking data. *Tourism Management*, *88*, 104421.

Ahmed, T., Tahir, M., Low, M. X., Ren, Y., Tawfik, S. A., Mayes, E. L., et al. (2021). Fully Light-controlled memory and neuromorphic computation in layered black phosphorus. *Advanced Materials, 33*(10), 2004207.

Al-Bahri, M. A. H. M. O. O. D. (2023). Smart system based on augmented reality for displaying cultural heritage in Oman. *Artificial Intelligence & Robotics Development Journal, 3*, 229–247.

Allal-Chérif, O. (2022). Intelligent cathedrals: Using augmented reality, virtual reality, and artificial intelligence to provide an intense cultural, historical, and religious visitor experience. *Technological Forecasting and Social Change*, *178*, 121604.

Alsharif, A. H., Salleh, N. Z. M., Baharun, R., Hashem, E. A. R., Mansor, A. A., Ali, J., & Abbas, A. F. (2021). Neuroimaging techniques in advertising research: Main applications, development, and brain regions and processes. *Sustainability, 13*(11), 6488.

Altundas, S., & Karaarslan, E. (2023). Cross-platform and personalized avatars in the metaverse: Ready player me case. In *Digital twin driven intelligent systems and emerging metaverse* (pp. 317–330). Singapore.

Ander, E., Thomson, L., Noble, G., Lanceley, A., Menon, U., & Chatterjee, H. (2013). Heritage, health and well-being: Assessing the impact of a heritage focused intervention on health and well-being. *International Journal of Heritage Studies, 19*(3), 229–242.

Andersen, M. S., Klingenberg, S., Petersen, G. B., Creed, P. A., & Makransky, G. (2023). Fostering science interests through head-mounted displays. *Journal of Computer Assisted Learning, 39*(2), 369–379.

Anoll, C. H. (2019). Mobilizing youth: Engaging young people in making community change. National Neighborhood Indicators Partnership (NNIP) https://www.neighborhoodindicators.org/sites/default/files/publications/Mobilizing%20Youth%20Brief.pdf.

Apollonio, F. I., Fantini, F., Garagnani, S., & Gaiani, M. (2021). A photogrammetry-based workflow for the accurate 3D construction and visualization of museums assets. *Remote Sensing, 13*(3), 486.

Arnold-de-Simine, S., & Arnold-de Simine, S. (2013). *Mediating memory in the museum: Trauma, empathy, nostalgia*. Springer.

Banfi, F. (2021). The evolution of interactivity, immersion and interoperability in HBIM: Digital model uses, VR and AR for built cultural heritage. *ISPRS International Journal of Geo-information, 10*(10), 685.

Banzi, A. (Ed.). (2022). *The Brain-friendly Museum: Using Psychology and Neuroscience to Improve the Visitor Experience*. Taylor & Francis.

Barbara, J., Bellini, M., Koenitz, H., Makai, P. K., Sampatakou, D., & Irshad, S. (2022). The Sacra Infermeria—A focus group evaluation of an augmented reality cultural heritage experience. *New Review of Hypermedia and Multimedia, 28*(3–4), 143–171.

Barrado-Timón, D. A., & Hidalgo-Giralt, C. (2019). The historic city, its transmission and perception via augmented reality and virtual reality and the use of the past as a resource for the present: A new era for urban cultural heritage and tourism? *Sustainability, 11*(10), 2835.

Baumann, U., & Guesnet, F. (2019). Kristallnacht–pogrom–state terror: A terminological reflection. *New Perspectives on Kristallnacht: After 80 Years, the Nazi Pogrom in Global Comparison, 17*, 1.

Bekele, M. K., & Champion, E. (2019). A comparison of immersive realities and interaction methods: Cultural learning in virtual heritage. *Frontiers in Robotics and AI, 6*, 91.

Ben-Joseph, E., Ishii, H., Underkoffler, J., Piper, B., & Yeung, L. (2001). Urban simulation and the luminous planning table: Bridging the gap between the digital and the tangible. *Journal of planning Education and Research*, *21*(2), 196–203.

Berntson, G. G., & Khalsa, S. S. (2021). Neural circuits of interoception. *Trends in neurosciences*, *44*(1), 17–28.

Bertrand, S., Vassiliadi, M., Zikas, P., Geronikolakis, E., & Papagiannakis, G. (2021). From readership to usership: Communicating heritage digitally through presence, embodiment and aesthetic experience. *Frontiers in Communication*, *6*, 676446.

Berube, P. (2023). *Towards a more inclusive museum: Developing multi-sensory approaches to the visual arts for visually impaired audiences* (Doctoral dissertation, Carleton University).

Bevilacqua, M. G., Russo, M., Giordano, A., & Spallone, R. (2022). 3D reconstruction, digital twinning, and virtual reality: Architectural heritage applications. In *2022 IEEE conference on Virtual Reality and 3D User Interfaces Abstracts and Workshops (VRW)* (pp. 92–96). IEEE. https://doi.org/10.1109/VRW55335.2022.00031

Birbragher, F. (2022). Felipe Mujica: Pérez Art Museum Miami, PAMM. *Art Nexus: el nexo entre América Latina y el resto del mundo*, *118*, 35.

Bond, E., & Bozdog, M. (2022). The smells and tastes of memory: Accessing transnational pasts through material culture. In *Memory, mobility, and material culture* (pp. 191–207). Routledge.

Bondi, E., Xu, L., Acosta-Navas, D., & Killian, J. A. (2021, July). Envisioning communities: A participatory approach towards AI for social good. In *Proceedings of the 2021 AAAI/ACM conference on AI, Ethics, and Society* (pp. 425–436).

Bornmann, M. P. (2022). *Augmented reality character companions in theme parks: A speculative design project*. Drexel University.

Bozzelli, G., Raia, A., Ricciardi, S., De Nino, M., Barile, N., Perrella, M., et al. (2019). An integrated VR/AR framework for user-centric interactive experience of cultural heritage: The ArkaeVision project. *Digital Applications in Archaeology and Cultural Heritage*, *15*, e00124.

Braverman, I. (2020). Fleshy encounters: Meddling in the lifeworlds of zoo and aquarium veterinarians. *University at Buffalo School of Law Legal Studies Research Paper*, (2020-012), 49–75.

Brooks, J. (2019). Promises of the virtual museum. *XRDS: Crossroads, The ACM Magazine for Students*, *25*(2), 46–50.

Buono, M., Capece, S., Chivăran, C., Gerbino, S., Giugliano, G., Greco, A., et al. (2022). Multisensory fruition between cultural heritage and digital transformation. In *Perspectives on design and digital communication III: Research, innovations and best practices* (pp. 329–355). Springer International Publishing.

Cahyadi, M., Rafi, M., Shan, W., Moniaga, J., & Lucky, H. (2023). Accuracy and fidelity comparison of Luna and DALL-E 2 diffusion-based image generation systems. *arXiv preprint arXiv:2301.01914.*

Camic, P. M., Tischler, V., & Pearman, C. H. (2014). Viewing and making art together: A multi-session art-gallery-based intervention for people with dementia and their careers. *Aging & Mental Health, 18*(2), 161–168.

Carrozzino, M., & Bergamasco, M. (2010). Beyond virtual museums: Experiencing immersive virtual reality in real museums. *Journal of Cultural Heritage, 11*(4), 452–458.

Carrozzino, M., Evangelista, C., Scucces, A., Tecchia, F., Tennirelli, G., & Bergamasco, M. (2008, September). The virtual museum of sculpture. In *Proceedings of the 3rd international conference on Digital Interactive Media in Entertainment and Arts* (pp. 100–106).

Chen, J. C., & Kent, S. (2020). Task engagement, learner motivation and avatar identities of struggling English language learners in the 3D virtual world. *System, 88,* 102168.

Cheuk, T. (2021). Can AI be racist? Color-evasiveness in the application of machine learning to science assessments. *Science Education, 105*(5), 825–836.

Choi, B., & Kim, J. (2021). Changes and challenges in museum management after the COVID-19 pandemic. *Journal of Open Innovation: Technology, Market, and Complexity, 7*(2), 148.

Christou, C. (2010). Virtual reality in education. In A. Tzanavari & N. Tsapatsoulis (Eds.), *Affective, interactive and cognitive methods for e-learning design: Creating an optimal educational experience* (pp. 228–243). IGI Global. https://doi.org/10.4018/978-1-60566-940-3.ch012

Chung, H. J. (2015). The reanimation of the digital (un)dead, or how to regenerate bodies in digital cinema. *Visual Studies, 30*(1), 54–67.

Clark, M., Ensminger, D., Incandela, C., & Moisan, H. (2016). Reflections on museums as effective field sites for teacher candidates. *Journal of Museum Education, 41*(4), 329–340.

Clemenson, G. D., Maselli, A., Fiannaca, A. J., Miller, A., & Gonzalez-Franco, M. (2021). Rethinking GPS navigation: Creating cognitive maps through auditory clues. *Scientific Reports, 11*(1), 1–10.

Clini, P., Ruggieri, L., Angeloni, R., & Sassob, M. (2018). Interactive immersive virtual museum: Digital documentation for interaction. *The International Archives of the Photogrammetry, Remote Sensing and Spatial Information Sciences, XLII-2,* 251–257. https://doi.org/10.5194/isprs-archives-XLII-2-251-2018

Coeckelbergh, M. (2020). *AI ethics.* MIT Press.

Cowan, B., Laird, R., & McKeown, J. (2019). *Museum objects, health and healing: The relationship between exhibitions and wellness.* Routledge.

Dali, K., & Brochu, L. K. (2020). The right to listen: A not so simple matter of audiobooks. *Library Resources & Technical Services, 64*(3), 106–119.

Dawley, L., & Dede, C. (2014). Situated learning in virtual worlds and immersive simulations. In *Handbook of research on educational communications and technology* (pp. 723–734). Springer.

de Abreu Santos, V. Á., & van der Borg, J. (2023). Cultural mapping tools and co-design process: A content analysis to layering perspectives on the creative production of space. *Sustainability, 15*(6), 5335.

De la Prieta, F., Barriuso, A. L., Corchado, J. M., & de Colsa, L. E. C. (2015). Security services as cloud capabilities using MAS. *Actas de las primeras Jornadas Nacionales de Investigación en Ciberseguridad: León, 14*, 15–16.

de Laat, P. B. (2021). Companies committed to responsible AI: From principles towards implementation and regulation? *Philosophy & Technology, 34*, 1135–1193.

de Leon, B. (2017). *Analysis of the application of universal design principles at National Park Service facilities* (Doctoral dissertation, Indiana University).

De Valck, M. (2016). Introduction: What is a film festival? How to study festivals and why you should. In *Film festivals* (pp. 1–12). Routledge.

Deloria, P. J. (2019, October). TC Cannon's Guitar. In *Arts* (Vol. 8, No. 4, p. 132). MDPI.

Demartini, P., Marchegiani, L., Marchiori, M., & Schiuma, G. (2021). Connecting the dots: A proposal to frame the debate around cultural initiatives and sustainable development. In *Cultural initiatives for sustainable development: Management, participation and entrepreneurship in the cultural and creative sector* (pp. 1–19). https://doi.org/10.1007/978-3-030-65687-4_1

Denson, S. (2020). *Discorrelated images*. Duke University Press.

Diamond, J., Horn, M., & Uttal, D. H. (2016). *Practical evaluation guide: Tools for museums and other informal educational settings*. Rowman & Littlefield.

Dick, E. (2021). *Current and potential uses of AR/VR for equity and inclusion*. Information Technology and Innovation Foundation.

Doğan, E., & Jelinčić, D. A. (2023). Changing patterns of mobility and accessibility to culture and leisure: Paradox of inequalities. *Cities, 132*, 104093.

Doukianou, S., Daylamani-Zad, D., & Paraskevopoulos, I. (2020). Beyond virtual museums: Adopting serious games and extended reality (XR) for user-centred cultural experiences. In *Visual computing for cultural heritage* (pp. 283–299). Springer.

Dragicevic, M., & Bagarić, A. (2019). Virtual technology in museums and art galleries business practice–The empirical research. In *7th International OFEL conference on Governance, Management and Entrepreneurship: Embracing Diversity in Organisations, April 5th–6th, 2019, Dubrovnik, Croatia* (pp. 175–183). Governance Research and Development Centre (CIRU).

Dwivedi, Y. K., Hughes, L., Baabdullah, A. M., Ribeiro-Navarrete, S., Giannakis, M., Al-Debei, M. M., et al. (2022). Metaverse beyond the hype: Multidisciplinary perspectives on emerging challenges, opportunities, and agenda for research, practice and policy. *International Journal of Information Management, 66,* 102542.

Edler, D., Kühne, O., Keil, J., & Dickmann, F. (2019). Audiovisual cartography: Established and new multimedia approaches to represent soundscapes. *KN-Journal of Cartography and Geographic Information, 69,* 5–17.

El-Said, O., & Aziz, H. (2022). Virtual tours a means to an end: An analysis of virtual tours' role in tourism recovery post COVID-19. *Journal of Travel Research, 61,* 528–548. https://doi.org/10.1177/0047287521997567

El-Sayyad, N. (2019, April). Role of sensory maps in cultural planning to shape the future of deteriorated heritage sites. In *8th International conference "ARCHCAIRO8:" Building the Future "Now"–Rights to Better Living, Architecture and Contexts* (pp. 8–10).

Fai, C. Y. (2021). Making sense of digital portraits of clinical data. *Hong Kong College of Paediatricians Hong Kong Paediatric Society, 26*(4), 185–186.

Falk, J. H. (2016). *Identity and the museum visitor experience.* Routledge.

Favro, D. (2006). In the eye of the beholder: VR models and academia. In L. Haselberger & J. Humphrey (Eds.), *Imaging ancient Rome: Documentation, visualization, imagination: Proceedings of the Third Williams Symposium on Classical Architecture* (pp. 321–334). Journal of Roman Archaeology.

Femenia-Serra, F., Gretzel, U., & Alzua-Sorzabal, A. (2022). Instagram travel influencers in# quarantine: Communicative practices and roles during COVID-19. *Tourism Management, 89,* 104454.

Ferrara, E. (2023). Fairness and bias in artificial intelligence: A brief survey of sources, impacts, and mitigation strategies. *arXiv preprint arXiv:2304.07683.*

Foster, J. K., McLelland, M. A., & Wallace, L. K. (2022). Brand avatars: Impact of social interaction on consumer–brand relationships. *Journal of Research in Interactive Marketing, 16*(2), 237–258.

Gallace, A., Ngo, M. K., Sulaitis, J., & Spence, C. (2012). Multisensory presence in virtual reality: Possibilities & limitations. In *Multiple sensorial media advances and applications: New developments in MulSeMedia* (pp. 1–38). IGI Global.

Garibay, C. (2004). *Museums and community outreach: A secondary analysis of a museum collaborative program.* Saybrook University.

Garzotto, F., Matarazzo, V., Messina, N., Gelsomini, M., & Riva, C. (2018, October). Improving museum accessibility through storytelling in wearable immersive virtual reality. In *2018 3rd Digital Heritage International Congress (DigitalHERITAGE) held jointly with 2018 24th International Conference on Virtual Systems & Multimedia (VSMM 2018)* (pp. 1–8). IEEE.

Giaconi, C., & Rodrigues, M. B. (2014). Organização do espaço e do tempo na inclusão de sujeitos com autismo. *Educação e Realidade, 39*(03), 687–705.

Giannini, T., & Bowen, J. P. (2022). Museums and digital culture: From reality to digitality in the age of COVID-19. *Heritage, 5*(1), 192–214.

Giariskanis, F., Kritikos, Y., Protopapadaki, E., Papanastasiou, A., Papadopoulou, E., & Mania, K. (2022, June). The augmented museum: A multimodal, game-based, augmented reality narrative for cultural heritage. In *ACM International conference on Interactive Media Experiences* (pp. 281–286).

Gibney, E. (2022). Open-source language AI challenges Big Tech's Models. *Nature, 606*(7916), 850–851.

Gobira, P., & de Oliveira Silva, E. (2019). About reality: Relations between museums and virtual reality. *Virtual Creativity, 9*(1–2), 63–72.

Gonzaga, E. (2019). Precarious nostalgia in the tropical smart city: Transmedia memory, urban informatics, and the Singapore golden jubilee. *Cultural Studies, 33*(1), 147–169.

Goodenough, A. E., Stafford, R., Catlin-Groves, C. L., Smith, A. L., & Hart, A. G. (2010, October). Within-and among-observer variation in measurements of animal biometrics and their influence on accurate quantification of common biometric-based condition indices. In *Annales Zoologici Fennici* (Vol. 47, No. 5, pp. 323–334). Finnish Zoological and Botanical Publishing Board.

Görel, B. (2019). *The influence of using QR codes as an information delivery method to increase user engagement in exhibition spaces* (Doctoral dissertation, Bilkent Universitesi (Turkey)).

Gorman, M. J. (2020). *Idea colliders: The future of science museums.* MIT Press.

Gray, L. (2012). Sydney Pavière and the Harris Museum and Art Gallery, Preston. In *Museums and biographies: Stories, objects, identities* (pp. 45–57). Boydell Press.

Gröppel-Wegener, A., & Kidd, J. (2019). *Critical encounters with immersive storytelling.* Routledge.

Gupfinger, R., & Kaltenbrunner, M. (2019, November). Animal-centred sonic interaction design: Musical instruments and interfaces for grey parrots. In *Proceedings of the sixth international conference on Animal-Computer Interaction* (pp. 1–11).

Hallam, R. (2022). *The evolution of human cleverness.* Routledge.

Hayes, A., Daughrity, L. A., & Meng, N. (2021). Approaches to integrate virtual reality into K-16 lesson plans: An Introduction for teachers. *TechTrends, 65*, 394–401.

Hayes, C. (2023). Museum exhibits brought to life. *Engineering & Technology, 18*(2), 48–51.

Herzberg, T. S., Rosenblum, L. P., & Robbins, M. E. (2017). Teachers' experiences with literacy instruction for dual-media students who use print and braille. *Journal of Visual Impairment & Blindness, 111*(1), 49–59.

Hirose, M., & Amemiya, T. (2003, June). Wearable finger-braille interface for navigation of deaf-blind in ubiquitous barrier-free space. In *Proceedings of the HCI International* (Vol. 4, pp. 1417–1421).

Howard, M. C., & Lee, J. (2020). Pre-training interventions to counteract seductive details in virtual reality training programs. *Human Resource Development Quarterly, 31*(1), 13–29.

Huaman, E. M. R., Aceituno, R. G. A., & Sharhorodska, O. (2019). Application of virtual reality and gamification in the teaching of art history. In *Learning and Collaboration Technologies. Ubiquitous and Virtual Environments for Learning and Collaboration: 6th international conference, LCT 2019, Held as Part of the 21st HCI international conference, HCII 2019, Orlando, FL, USA, July 26–31, 2019, Proceedings, Part II 21* (pp. 220–229). Springer International Publishing.

Huang, H. Y., & Liem, C. C. (2022, June). Social inclusion in curated contexts: Insights from museum practices. In *2022 ACM conference on Fairness, Accountability, and Transparency* (pp. 300–309). Association for Computing Machinery.

Hutchinson, R., & Eardley, A. F. (2021). Inclusive museum audio guides: 'Guided looking' through audio description enhances memorability of artworks for sighted audiences. *Museum Management and Curatorship, 36*(4), 427–446.

Hutson, J. & Cotroneo, P. (2023). Generative AI tools in art education: Exploring prompt engineering and iterative processes for enhanced creativity. *Metaverse.* Special Issue: The Art in the Metaverse Special Issue, *4*(1): 1–14. https://doi.org/10.54517/m.v4i1.2164

Hutson, J., & Hutson, P. (2023). Museums and the metaverse: Emerging technologies to promote inclusivity and engagement. https://doi.org/10.5772/intechopen.110044

Hutson, J., & Lang, M. (2023). Content creation or interpolation: AI generative digital art in the classroom. *Metaverse.* Special Issue: The Art in the Metaverse Special Issue, *4*(1), 1–14. https://doi.org/10.54517/m.v4i1.2158

Hutson, J., & Olsen, T. (2022a). Virtual reality and art history: A case study of digital humanities and immersive learning environments. *Journal of Higher Education Theory and Practice, 22*(2), 10.33423/jhetp.v22i2.5036.

Hutson, J., & Olsen, T. (2022b). Virtual reality and learning: A case study of experiential pedagogy in art history. *Journal of Intelligent Learning Systems and Applications, 14*, 57–70.

Ings, S. (2019). Dinosaurs rule! *New Scientist, 241*(3221), 44.

Innes, A., Scholar, H. F., Haragalova, J., & Sharma, M. (2021). 'You come because it is an interesting place': The impact of attending a heritage programme on the well-being of people living with dementia and their care partners. *Dementia, 20*(6), 2133–2151.

Janbuala, K., & Lindborg, P. (2021). Sonification of Glitch-Video: Making and evaluating audiovisual art made from the betta fish. In *International Computer Music Conference 2021* (pp. 255–259). International Computer Music Association, Inc.

Javaid, M., Haleem, A., Singh, R. P., & Suman, R. (2021). Industrial perspectives of 3D scanning: Features, roles and it's analytical applications. *Sensors International, 2*, 100114.

Jiexin, Z., & Ying, L. (2022). The impediments of intangible cultural heritage inheritance and conversation and the path breakthrough in the context of digital survival [J]. *Academic Journal of Humanities & Social Sciences, 5*(19), 101–105.

Jones, J. P., Thomas-Walters, L., Rust, N. A., & Veríssimo, D. (2019). Nature documentaries and saving nature: Reflections on the new Netflix series Our Planet. *People and Nature, 1*(4), 420–425.

Joseph, B. (2023). *Making dinosaurs dance*. American Alliance of Museums.

Kalantari, S., & Neo, J. R. J. (2020). Virtual environments for design research: Lessons learned from use of fully immersive virtual reality in interior design research. *Journal of Interior Design, 45*(3), 27–42.

Kamruzzaman, M. M., Alanazi, S., Alruwaili, M., Alshammari, N., Elaiwat, S., Abu-Zanona, M., et al. (2023). AI-and IoT-assisted sustainable education systems during pandemics, such as COVID-19, for smart cities. *Sustainability, 15*(10), 8354.

Kaplan, A. (2022). *Artificial intelligence, business and civilization: Our fate made in machines*. Routledge.

Karuzaki, E., Partarakis, N., Patsiouras, N., Zidianakis, E., Katzourakis, A., Pattakos, A., et al. (2021). Realistic virtual humans for cultural heritage applications. *Heritage, 4*(4), 4148–4171.

King, L., Stark, J. F., & Cooke, P. (2016). Experiencing the digital world: The cultural value of digital engagement with heritage. *Heritage & Society, 9*(1), 76–101.

Kordzadeh, N., & Ghasemaghaei, M. (2022). Algorithmic bias: Review, synthesis, and future research directions. *European Journal of Information Systems, 31*(3), 388–409.

Kumar, A., Kumar, A., Raja, L., & Singh, K. U. (2023). Rediscovering the traditional UNESCO world heritage Hawamahal through 3D Animation and Immersive Technology. *ACM Journal on Computing and Cultural Heritage, 15*(4), 1–34.

Kwan, M. P. (2000). Interactive geovisualization of activity-travel patterns using three-dimensional geographical information systems: A methodological exploration with a large data set. *Transportation Research Part C: Emerging Technologies, 8*(1–6), 185–203.

Lannan, A. (2019). A virtual assistant on campus for blind and low vision students. *Journal of Special Education Apprenticeship, 8*(2), n2.

Lemke, A. A., Esplin, E. D., Goldenberg, A. J., Gonzaga-Jauregui, C., Hanchard, N. A., Harris-Wai, J., et al. (2022). Addressing underrepresentation in genomics research through community engagement. *The American Journal of Human Genetics, 109*(9), 1563–1571.

Leslie, D., Mazumder, A., Peppin, A., Wolters, M. K., & Hagerty, A. (2021). Does "AI" stand for augmenting inequality in the era of covid-19 healthcare? *BMJ, 372*.

Lester, J. N., & Nusbaum, E. A. (Eds.). (2021). *Centering diverse bodyminds in critical qualitative inquiry*. Routledge.

Li, H., Li, M., Zou, H., Zhang, Y., & Cao, J. (2023). Urban sensory map: How do tourists "sense" a destination spatially? *Tourism Management, 97*, 104723.

Liddle, J., & Addidle, G. (2023). 12. Reframing 'place leadership': An analysis of leadership in responding to the wicked issue of county lines and criminality within a context of post-pandemic public health policing. *Research handbook on public leadership: Re-imagining public leadership in a post-pandemic paradigm*, 222. https://doi.org/10.4337/9781786439673.00021

Lobban, J., & Murphy, D. (2020). Military museum collections and art therapy as mental health resources for veterans with PTSD. *International Journal of Art Therapy, 25*(4), 172–182.

Loscos, C., Tecchia, F., Frisoli, A., Carrozzino, M., Widenfeld, H. R., Swapp, D., & Bergamasco, M. (2004, December). The museum of pure form: Touching real statues in an immersive virtual museum. In *VAST* (pp. 271–279).

Lucie, S. (2021). Teknopolis. *PAJ: A Journal of Performance and Art, 43*(3), 54–57.

Maddali, H. T., & Lazar, A. (2023, April). Understanding context to capture when reconstructing meaningful spaces for remote instruction and connecting in XR. In *Proceedings of the 2023 CHI conference on Human Factors in Computing Systems* (pp. 1–18). https://doi.org/10.48550/arXiv.2301.09492

Malafouris, L. (2019). Understanding the effects of materiality on mental health. *BJPsych bulletin, 43*(5), 195–200.

Maple, T. L. (2021). The practice of management: The ascent of women as scholars and leaders in the field of zoo biology. *The Psychologist-Manager Journal, 24*(2), 97.

Marom, A., & Hovers, E. (2017). *Human paleontology and prehistory*. Springer.

McColl, M. M. (2020). *Accessing other worlds: Engaging art* (Doctoral dissertation, University of Glasgow).

McGill, M., Brewster, S., McGookin, D., & Wilson, G. (2020, April). Acoustic transparency and the changing soundscape of auditory mixed reality. In *Proceedings of the 2020 CHI conference on Human Factors in Computing Systems* (pp. 1–16).

McLean, K. (2019). *Sensory maps*. Elsevier.

Melfi, V. A., Dorey, N. R., & Ward, S. J. (2020). *Zoo Animal Learning and Training*. John Wiley & Sons.

Melo, M., Gonçalves, G., Monteiro, P., Coelho, H., Vasconcelos-Raposo, J., & Bessa, M. (2020). Do multisensory stimuli benefit the virtual reality experience? A systematic review. *IEEE Transactions on Visualization and Computer Graphics, 28*(2), 1428–1442.

Menaguale, O. (2023). Digital twin and cultural heritage–The future of society built on history and art. In *The Digital twin* (pp. 1081–1111). Springer International Publishing.

Meyer, S. R. (Ed.). (2021). *Interactive storytelling for the screen.* Routledge.

Mihelj, S., Leguina, A., & Downey, J. (2019). Culture is digital: Cultural participation, diversity and the digital divide. *New Media & Society, 21*(7), 1465–1485.

Montusiewicz, J., Barszcz, M., & Korga, S. (2022). Preparation of 3D Models of cultural heritage objects to be recognised by touch by the blind—Case studies. *Applied Sciences, 12*(23), 11910.

Morgan, E. J. (2013). Virtual worlds: Integrating "Second Life" into the history classroom. *The History Teacher, 46*(4), 547–559.

Morowitz, L. (2022). Reviled, repressed, resurrected: Vienna 1900 in the Nazi Imaginary. *Austrian History Yearbook, 53*, 169–189.

Morse, N. (2020). *The museum as a space of social care.* Routledge.

Mujtaba, T., Lawrence, M., Oliver, M., & Reiss, M. J. (2018). Learning and engagement through natural history museums. *Studies in Science Education, 54*(1), 41–67.

Muñoz, A., & Martí, A. (2020). New storytelling for archaeological museums based on augmented reality glasses. *Communicating the Past, 85.*

Nadri, C., Anaya, C., Yuan, S., & Jeon, M. (2022). From visual art to music: Sonification can adapt to painting styles and augment user experience. *International Journal of Human–Computer Interaction*, 1–13.

Nikolakopoulou, V., Printezis, P., Maniatis, V., Kontizas, D., Vosinakis, S., Chatzigrigoriou, P., & Koutsabasis, P. (2022). Conveying intangible cultural heritage in museums with interactive storytelling and projection mapping: The case of the mastic villages. *Heritage, 5*(2), 1024–1049.

Noehrer, L., Gilmore, A., Jay, C., & Yehudi, Y. (2021). The impact of COVID-19 on digital data practices in museums and art galleries in the UK and the US. *Humanities and Social Sciences Communications, 8*(1).

Nummenmaa, T., Buruk, O., Bujić, M., Sjöblom, M., Holopainen, J., & Hamari, J. (2020, December). Space Pace: Method for creating augmented reality tours based on 360 videos. In International Conference on ArtsIT, Interactivity and Game Creation (pp. 119–138). Cham: Springer International Publishing.

O'Hagan, L. (2021). Instagram as an exhibition space: Reflections on digital remediation in the time of COVID-19. *Museum Management and Curatorship, 36*(6), 610–631.

Olaz, X., Garcia, R., Ortiz, A., Marichal, S., Villadangos, J., Ardaiz, O., & Marzo, A. (2022). An interdisciplinary design of an interactive cultural heritage visit for in-situ, mixed reality and affective experiences. *Multimodal Technologies and Interaction, 6*(7), 59.

Ondrejka, C. (2008). *Education unleashed: Participatory culture, education, and innovation in second life*. MIT Press.

Ott, M., & Pozzi, F. (2011). Towards a new era for cultural heritage education: Discussing the role of ICT. *Computers in Human Behavior, 27*(4), 1365–1371.

Pagano, A., Palombini, A., Bozzelli, G., De Nino, M., Cerato, I., & Ricciardi, S. (2020). ArkaeVision VR game: User experience research between real and virtual paestum. *Applied Sciences, 10*(9), 3182.

Pan, P. (2021). *Curating multisensory experiences: The possibilities of immersive exhibitions* (Doctoral dissertation, OCAD University).

Papathanasiou-Zuhrt, D., Thomaidis, N., Di Russo, A., & Vasile, V. (2019). Multi-sensory experiences at heritage places: SCRIPTORAMA, The Black Sea open street museum. In *Caring and sharing: The cultural heritage environment as an agent for change: 2016 ALECTOR conference, Istanbul, Turkey* (pp. 11–49). Springer International Publishing.

Partarakis, N., Zabulis, X., Antona, M., & Stephanidis, C. (2020). Transforming heritage crafts to engaging digital experiences. *Visual Computing for Cultural Heritage*, 245–262.

Patin, N. V., Pratte, Z. A., Regensburger, M., Hall, E., Gilde, K., Dove, A. D., & Stewart, F. J. (2018). Microbiome dynamics in a large artificial seawater aquarium. *Applied and Environmental Microbiology, 84*(10), e00179–e00118.

Peppler, K., Keune, A., Dahn, M., Bennett, D., & Letourneau, S. M. (2022). Designing for others: The roles of narrative and empathy in supporting girls' engineering engagement. *Information and Learning Sciences, 123*(3/4), 129–153.

Pietroni, E., & Adami, A. (2014). Interacting with virtual reconstructions in museums: The Etruscanning Project. *Journal on Computing and Cultural Heritage (JOCCH), 7*(2), 1–29.

Pisoni, G., Díaz-Rodríguez, N., Gijlers, H., & Tonolli, L. (2021). Human-centered artificial intelligence for designing accessible cultural heritage. *Applied Sciences, 11*(2), 870.

Prandi, C., Barricelli, B. R., Mirri, S., & Fogli, D. (2021). Accessible wayfinding and navigation: A systematic mapping study. *Universal Access in the Information Society*, 1–28.

Prokop, E., Han, X. Y., Papyan, V., Donoho, D. L., & Johnson, C. R., Jr. (2021). AI and the digitized photoarchive: Promoting access and discoverability. *Art Documentation: Journal of the Art Libraries Society of North America, 40*(1), 1–20.

Pujol, L., Roussou, M., Poulou, S., Balet, O., Vayanou, M., & Ioannidis, Y. (2012, March). Personalizing interactive digital storytelling in archaeological museums: The CHESS project. In *40th annual conference of Computer Applications and Quantitative Methods in Archaeology*. Amsterdam University Press (pp. 93–100).

Qi, Q., Tao, F., Hu, T., Anwer, N., Liu, A., Wei, Y., et al. (2021). Enabling technologies and tools for digital twin. *Journal of Manufacturing Systems, 58*, 3–21.

Qian, C., Mathur, N., Zakaria, N. H., Arora, R., Gupta, V., & Ali, M. (2022). Understanding public opinions on social media for financial sentiment analysis using AI-based techniques. *Information Processing & Management, 59*(6), 103098.

Quercia, D., Schifanella, R., Aiello, L. M., & McLean, K. (2015). Smelly maps: The digital life of urban smellscapes. In *Proceedings of the Future Technologies Conference (FTC) 2020, Volume 2* (pp. 740–756). Springer International Publishing.

Rahim, N. Z. A., Nasaruddin, N. I. S., Shah, N. B. A., Halim, F. H., Samah, K. A. F. A., Saman, F. I., & Rum, S. F. M. (2021, July). Aftermath of pandemic Covid-19 on tourism industry: A review on virtual tourism platform. In *AIP Conference Proceedings* (Vol. 2347, No. 1, p. 020173). AIP Publishing LLC.

Ranasinghe, N., Jain, P., Tolley, D., Chew, B., Bansal, A., Karwita, S., et al. (2021). EnPower: Haptic interfaces for deafblind individuals to interact, communicate, and entertain. In *Proceedings of the Future Technologies Conference (FTC) 2020, Volume 2* (pp. 740–756). Springer International Publishing.

Rani, S., Jining, D., Shah, D., Xaba, S., & Singh, P. R. (2023). Exploring the potential of artificial intelligence and computing technologies in art museums. In *ITM Web of Conferences* (Vol. 53). EDP Sciences.

Ratican, J., Hutson, J., & Wright, A. (2023). A proposed meta-reality immersive development pipeline: Generative AI Models and Extended Reality (XR) Content for the Metaverse. *Journal of Intelligent Learning Systems and Applications, 15*. https://doi.org/10.4236/jilsa.2023.151002

Ronchi, A. M. (2009). *eCulture: Cultural content in the digital age*. Springer Science & Business Media.

Rosa, F. (2022). Digital twin solutions to historical building stock maintenance cycles. *IOP Conference Series: Earth and Environmental Science, 1073*, Article ID: 012013. https://doi.org/10.1088/1755-1315/1073/1/012013

Rose, D. (2021). *Supersight: What augmented reality means for our lives, our work, and the way we imagine the future*. BenBella Books.

Rushton, M. A., Drumm, I. A., Campion, S. P., & O'Hare, J. J. (2020). The use of immersive and virtual reality technologies to enable nursing students to experience scenario-based, basic life support training—Exploring the impact on confidence and skills. *CIN: Computers, Informatics, Nursing, 38*(6), 281–293.

Ryding, K., & Fritsch, J. (2020, July). Play design as a relational strategy to intensify affective encounters in the art museum. In *Proceedings of the 2020 ACM Designing Interactive Systems Conference* (pp. 681–693). https://doi.org/10.1145/3357236.3395431

Salam, R. (2021). Men will be men?: Masculinities on display in the Facebook communication practices of Pakistani men. *Norma, 16*(1), 38–56.

Schwartzman, R., & Knowles, C. (2022). Expanding accessibility: Sensory sensitive programming for museums. *Curator: The Museum Journal, 65*(1), 95–116.

Schwind, V., Leusmann, J., & Henze, N. (2019). Understanding visual-haptic integration of avatar hands using a fitts' law task in virtual reality. In *Proceedings of Mensch Und Computer 2019* (pp. 211–222). https://doi.org/10.1145/3340764.3340769

Shahzad, M., Shafiq, M. T., Douglas, D., & Kassem, M. (2022). *Digital twins in built environments: An investigation of the characteristics, applications, and challenges. buildings, 12*, Article 120. https://doi.org/10.3390/buildings12020120

Sharma, K., Giannakos, M., & Dillenbourg, P. (2020). Eye-tracking and artificial intelligence to enhance motivation and learning. *Smart Learning Environments, 7*(1), 1–19.

Shehade, M., & Stylianou-Lambert, T. (2020). Virtual reality in museums: Exploring the experiences of museum professionals. *Applied Sciences, 10*(11), 4031.

Shields, J. A. (2023). Phenomenology and architecture: Examining embodied experience and graphic representations of the built environment. In *Horizons of phenomenology: Essays on the state of the field and its applications* (pp. 285–304). Springer International Publishing.

Simon, N. (2010). *The participatory museum.* Museum 2.0.

Skalska-Cimer, B., & Kadłuczka, A. (2022). Virtual museum. Museum of the future? *Technical Transactions, 119*(1), 1–6.

Stacchio, L., Angeli, A., & Marfia, G. (2022). Empowering digital twins with eXtended reality collaborations. *Virtual Reality & Intelligent Hardware, 4*(6), 487–505.

Stangl, M., Maoz, S. L., & Suthana, N. (2023). Mobile cognition: Imaging the human brain in the 'real world'. *Nature Reviews Neuroscience*, 1–16.

Stern, C. (2011). The role of audiobooks in academic libraries. *College & Undergraduate Libraries, 18*(1), 77–91.

Styliani, S., Fotis, L., Kostas, K., & Petros, P. (2009). Virtual museums, a survey and some issues for consideration. *Journal of cultural Heritage, 10*(4), 520–528.

Sultana, R., & Hawken, S. (2023). Reconciling nature-technology-child connections: Smart cities and the necessity of a new paradigm of nature-sensitive technologies for today's children. *Sustainability, 15*(8), 6453.

Sundar, S. S., Go, E., Kim, H. S., & Zhang, B. (2015). Communicating art, virtually! Psychological effects of technological affordances in a virtual museum. *International Journal of Human-Computer Interaction, 31*(6), 385–401.

Sylaiou, S., Kasapakis, V., Dzardanova, E., & Gavalas, D. (2018, September). Leveraging mixed reality technologies to enhance museum visitor experiences. In *2018 International conference on Intelligent Systems (IS)* (pp. 595–601). IEEE.

Tan, J., Leng, J., Zeng, X., Feng, D., & Yu, P. (2022). *Digital Twin for Xiegong's architectural archaeological research: A case study of Xuanluo Hall, Sichuan, China*. Buildings, 12, Article 1053. https://doi.org/10.3390/buildings12071053

Taurino, G. (2023). Algorithmic art and cultural sustainability in the museum sector. In *The ethics of artificial intelligence for the sustainable development goals* (pp. 327–345). Springer International Publishing.

Taylor, B., Dey, A., Siewiorek, D., & Smailagic, A. (2016, October). Customizable 3D printed tactile maps as interactive overlays. In *Proceedings of the 18th International ACM SIGACCESS Conference on Computers and Accessibility* (pp. 71–79).

Taylor, R. (1993). The influence of a visit on attitude and behavior towards nature conservation. *Visitor Studies: Theory, Research and Practice, 6*.

Theodoropoulos, A., & Antoniou, A. (2022). VR games in cultural heritage: A systematic review of the emerging fields of virtual reality and culture games. *Applied Sciences, 12*(17), 8476.

Tunstall, L., Von Werra, L., & Wolf, T. (2022). *Natural language processing with transformers*. O'Reilly Media, Inc..

Tzortzaki, D. (2001). Museums and virtual reality: Using the CAVE to simulate the past. *Digital Creativity, 12*(4), 247–251.

Underberg, N. M., & Zorn, E. (2013). *Digital ethnography: Anthropology, narrative, and new media*. University of Texas Press.

Van Elk, M., Arciniegas Gomez, M. A., van der Zwaag, W., Van Schie, H. T., & Sauter, D. (2019). The neural correlates of the awe experience: Reduced default mode network activity during feelings of awe. *Human Brain Mapping, 40*(12), 3561–3574.

Varriale, L., Cuel, R., Ravarini, A., Briganti, P., & Minucci, G. (2022). Smart and inclusive museums for visitors with autism: The app case "A Dip in the Blue". In *Sustainable digital transformation: Paving the way towards smart organizations and societies* (pp. 133–152). Springer International Publishing.

Vaughan, A. G. (2022). On Jung, archetypes, aesthetics, and culture in the art from the African Diaspora. *Jung Journal, 16*(3), 38–70.

Veerman, J. (2021). Entangled: The synesthetic art museum.

Vessel, E. A., Isik, A. I., Belfi, A. M., Stahl, J. L., & Starr, G. G. (2019). The default-mode network represents aesthetic appeal that generalizes across visual domains. *Proceedings of the National Academy of Sciences, 116*(38), 19155–19164.

Viñals, M. J., Gilabert-Sansalvador, L., Sanasaryan, A., Teruel-Serrano, M. D., & Darés, M. (2021). Online synchronous model of interpretive sustainable guiding in heritage sites: The avatar tourist visit. *Sustainability, 13*(13), 7179.

Wamba-Taguimdje, S. L., Fosso Wamba, S., Kala Kamdjoug, J. R., & Tchatchouang Wanko, C. E. (2020). Influence of artificial intelligence (AI) on firm performance: The business value of AI-based transformation projects. *Business Process Management Journal, 26*(7), 1893–1924.

Wang, L., Lyu, C., Ji, T., Zhang, Z., Yu, D., Shi, S., & Tu, Z. (2023). Document-level machine translation with large language models. *arXiv preprint arXiv:2304.02210*.

Wang, P., Ma, X., Fei, L., Zhang, H., Zhao, D., & Zhao, J. (2022). When the digital twin meets the preventive conservation of wooden cultural heritages. Available at SSRN 4211559. https://doi.org/10.2139/ssrn.4211559

Wang, S. (2023). A bodies-on museum: The transformation of museum embodiment through virtual technology. *Curator: The Museum Journal, 66*(1), 107–128.

Ward, J., & Simner, J. (2020). Synesthesia: The current state of the field. In *Multisensory perception* (pp. 283–300). Academic Press.

Weinberg, G., Bretan, M., Hoffman, G., & Driscoll, S. (2020). *Robotic musicianship: Embodied artificial creativity and mechatronic musical expression* (Vol. 8). Springer Nature.

Welbon, Y., & Juhasz, A. (Eds.). (2018). *Sisters in the life: A history of out African American lesbian media-making*. Duke University Press.

Wiehl, A. (2021). The body and the eye—The I and the other: Critical reflections on the promise of extended empathy in extended reality configurations. In *Augmented and mixed reality for communities* (pp. 20–37). CRC Press.

Wills, J. (2019). *Gamer nation: Video games and American culture*. Johns Hopkins University Press.

Winesmith, K., & Anderson, S. (2020). *The digital future of museums: Conversations and provocations*. Routledge.

Witter, M., de Rooij, A., van Dartel, M., & Krahmer, E. (2022). Bridging a sensory gap between deaf and hearing people–A plea for a situated design approach to sensory augmentation, *Frontiers in Computer Science, 4*.

Wu, S. W. P., & Din, H. W. H. (Eds.). (2014). *Digital heritage and culture: Strategy and implementation*. World Scientific.

Yilmaz, M., Hacaloğlu, T., & Clarke, P. (2022, August). Examining the use of non-fungible tokens (NFTs) as a trading mechanism for the metaverse. In *Systems, Software and Services Process Improvement: 29th European Conference, EuroSPI 2022, Salzburg, Austria, August 31–September 2, 2022, Proceedings* (pp. 18–28). Springer International Publishing.

Young, G. W., O'Dwyer, N., & Smolic, A. (2023). Volumetric video as a novel medium for creative storytelling. In *Immersive video technologies* (pp. 591–607). Academic Press.

Zhao, J., Guo, L., & Li, Y. (2022). Application of digital twin combined with artificial intelligence and 5G Technology in the art design of digital museums. *Wireless Communications and Mobile Computing*, Article ID: 8214514. https://doi.org/10.1155/2022/8214514

Zhang, A. (2020). The narration of art on Google arts and culture. *Johns Hopkins University, 1*(1).

Ziker, C., Truman, B., & Dodds, H. (2021). Cross reality (XR): Challenges and opportunities across the spectrum. *Innovative learning environments in STEM higher education: Opportunities, challenges, and looking forward*, 55–77.

CHAPTER 6

Conclusion: Future Directions for Neuro-inclusivity in Museums and Heritage Sites

This concluding chapter summarizes the key insights and findings from the preceding chapters, highlighting effective strategies for promoting neuro-inclusivity in museums and heritage sites. Digital storytelling techniques, personal narratives, community engagement, and immersive technologies have been identified as powerful tools for engaging neurodiverse audiences and enhancing their cultural heritage experiences. These approaches foster a sense of belonging, challenge stereotypes, and provide meaningful experiences for individuals with diverse sensory and cognitive abilities. The future of neuro-inclusive smart museums lies in emerging technologies, collaborations, and best practices that prioritize accessibility and inclusivity. By creating more accessible environments and embracing the diversity of human experiences, the heritage sector can drive positive change and ensure that cultural heritage is enjoyed by all visitors.

6.1 Apprenticeships and Residencies

Creating inclusive smart museums and designing multimodal exhibitions supported by emerging technology is a crucial first step towards enhancing accessibility and engagement for neurodiverse populations in art and cultural heritage settings (Varriale et al., 2022). These advancements have the potential to break down barriers and provide immersive, interactive experiences that cater to diverse sensory needs and learning styles. However, technology alone is not enough to ensure true inclusivity. The

© The Author(s), under exclusive license to Springer Nature Switzerland AG 2024
J. Hutson, P. Hutson, *Inclusive Smart Museums*,
https://doi.org/10.1007/978-3-031-43615-4_6

next step is to bridge the skills gap and divide that exists between the art and cultural heritage sector and the neurodiverse population (Kirby & Smith, 2021). By offering tailored solutions and opportunities such as apprenticeships, artist residencies, and skills training programs, we can empower neurodiverse individuals to fully participate in and contribute to the arts, fostering a more inclusive and diverse cultural landscape.

As such, the implementation of apprenticeships and artist residencies has emerged as one of the most effective ways to support and empower neurodiverse populations within the arts (Heddon, 2020). These programs provide invaluable opportunities for individuals to bridge the gap between traditional schooling and meaningful careers, fostering their creative skills, independence, and self-expression (Istance & Paniagua, 2019).

To ensure a more inclusive and diverse arts sector, it is crucial to advocate for the expansion and accessibility of various supportive initiatives that provide opportunities for neurodivergent artists. One such initiative is the establishment of apprenticeships, which can offer valuable training and hands-on experience under the guidance of experienced artists (Luttin, 2022). By participating in apprenticeship programs, neurodivergent artists can enhance their skills, develop their artistic voice, and gain practical knowledge of the industry (Armstrong, 2012).

Artist residencies are another important avenue for supporting neurodivergent artists. These programs provide dedicated time and space for artists to focus on their creative practice, offering opportunities for experimentation, collaboration, and professional growth (Gold, 2021). By providing neurodivergent artists with access to artist residencies, they can benefit from the resources, networks, and mentorship provided, fostering their artistic development and exposure.

Commissions play a significant role in supporting neurodivergent artists by offering them the opportunity to create artwork specifically for a particular project or exhibition. Commissions not only provide financial support but also help neurodivergent artists gain visibility and recognition for their work. Through commissions, artists can explore their unique perspectives and contribute their creativity to the cultural landscape (Marstine, 2017).

Internships are invaluable for neurodivergent artists as they provide practical experience within arts organizations or cultural institutions. These internships can encompass various roles, including curation, arts administration, event planning, or education. By participating in internships, neurodivergent artists can gain firsthand knowledge of the inner workings of the arts sector, develop professional skills, and build networks within the industry (Krzeminska & Hawse, 2020).

It is essential that these initiatives are designed with inclusivity in mind. Providing appropriate training, mentorship, and accommodations for neurodivergent artists ensures that they can fully participate and thrive in these programs. This may involve implementing neurodiversity training for staff, creating accessible environments and communication methods, and offering flexible accommodations tailored to individual needs (Ortiz, 2020).

One of the significant challenges lies in the successful rollout of creative apprenticeships that cater to the specific needs of neurodivergent individuals. Organizations like Screenskills at Pinewood Studios in the UK have been piloting apprenticeship models within the context of the creative sectors, aiming to create inclusive pathways for aspiring artists. These initiatives recognize the importance of providing tailored support, accommodations, and accessible learning environments to ensure the success and well-being of neurodivergent apprentices (McElroy et al., 2019).

Efforts are being made to address the accessibility of apprenticeships for autistic individuals and those with learning disabilities. In November 2017, a parliamentary group convened to discuss ways to make apprenticeships more accessible and inclusive. Supported internships, such as those offered by Ambitious about Autism, play a vital role in providing work-based learning opportunities and helping individuals with autism and learning disabilities transition into the workforce (Ashworth et al., 2023).

Moreover, the Art Apprenticeship Network, led by the Shumka Centre for Creative Entrepreneurship at Emily Carr University of Art + Design, has embarked on a three-year initiative to provide students with real-world, hands-on experiences in various artistic settings. These immersive opportunities, including work in studios, production spaces, and exhibition venues, offer neurodiverse individuals the chance to develop their skills, collaborate with professionals, and gain practical insights into their chosen artistic fields (Somers et al., 2022).

In addition to apprenticeships, the Hart Club serves as a community arts organization dedicated to championing neurodiversity within the arts. Through commissioning original artwork and content that celebrates the intersection of ideas and differences in artistic approaches, the Hart Club provides a platform for neurodiverse artists to gain creative and financial recognition for their work. With its gallery, design studio, print studio, ceramics studio, and art store, the Hart Club fosters an inclusive and supportive environment that encourages conversation and appreciation of diversity (Moraru, 2023).

By actively supporting and promoting apprenticeships, artist residencies, commissions, internships, and other initiatives, we can empower neurodivergent artists to thrive in the arts sector. These opportunities not only foster artistic growth but also contribute to the diversity and vibrancy of the artistic landscape. It is through these collaborative efforts and a continued commitment to inclusivity that we can create a truly inclusive and enriching environment that values and embraces the talents and contributions of all individuals, regardless of their neurodiversity.

6.2 Looking Ahead

Museums and heritage sites are constantly adapting and embracing emerging technologies to ensure accessibility for all visitors. Among these visitors, neurodiverse populations play a crucial role in driving innovation and the adoption of technological advancements. The integration of digital storytelling techniques, immersive technologies, and wearable devices has opened up new possibilities for engaging neurodiverse audiences and enhancing their cultural heritage experiences (Martinez-Conde et al., 2019).

Digital storytelling strategies, supported by immersive and wearable devices, have the potential to provide personalized, story-driven narratives of museum collections. These narratives can be tailored to support adaptive, multisensory experiences both before and during a visit. By combining narrative and storytelling in virtual environments, visitors can engage with a given space intellectually and physically (Rosli & Kamaruddin, 2020). This approach not only enhances understanding but also enables visitors to visualize and interact with historical and cultural heritage in meaningful ways.

The use of digital storytelling in museums is inherently multimedia, encompassing various mediums and methodologies. Through interactive events and experiences, digitized objects and virtual reconstructions enable visitors to connect with the culture and history of a location or subject on a deeper level. The narrative-driven approach allows visitors to shape their own stories and visits, creating personal meaning and context (Okanovic et al., 2022). Additionally, evolving systems can establish emotional connections with visitors, adapting storytelling activities based on visitor preferences and age-specific content. Mini games and avatars can further encourage interaction and investment in the historical significance of objects (Chu, 2004; Doukianou et al., 2020; Othman et al., 2021; Pearce, 2008).

As the digital landscape evolves, the concept of the metaverse and interconnected virtual realms holds great potential for museums. Portals can be created to link museum collections with similar content, allowing for expanded and immersive experiences with art and culture (Uddin et al., 2023). These metaverses enable visitors to traverse multiple museums and heritage sites seamlessly, creating a more comprehensive understanding of cultural heritage. The metaverse concept also opens doors to digital reconstructions and digital embodiment, providing visitors with a unique perspective and immersive encounters with historical contexts (Cesário et al., 2023).

The integration of immersive technologies and digital storytelling techniques in museums and heritage sites has the power to foster neuro-inclusivity and enhance cultural heritage experiences for all visitors. The utilization of wearable devices, virtual environments, and immersive narratives can create personalized and adaptive encounters, allowing neurodiverse audiences to engage with cultural heritage on their own terms (Hutson & Hutson, 2023). The potential for future research and advances in the field is vast, with opportunities for interdisciplinary collaborations, best practices, and the continued exploration of emerging technologies. These efforts can have broader implications on policy and practice within the heritage sector, emphasizing the importance of creating accessible and inclusive environments for all visitors.

Institutions need not start from scratch with these efforts when looking to be more inclusive. Regardless of budget, there are numerous resources to assist. The commitment to inclusivity extends to museums around the world, and there are several notable resources available to support their efforts (Giannini & Bowen, 2022; Meng et al., 2023; Johnson & Thomas, 1998; Topaz et al., 2019). One company leading the way in this regard is Infiniteach, based in Chicago (Bell, 2015). Infiniteach has been at the forefront of developing innovative technology to help individuals with autism, and their work has had a significant impact on several museums, including the Shedd Aquarium and Field Museum in Chicago (Keskinova et al., 2021). These museums have partnered with Infiniteach to offer free-to-download apps, available for both Apple and Android devices, to enhance the museum experience for individuals on the autism spectrum (https://free.infiniteach.com/apps/). The Infiniteach apps are tailored specifically for each museum, such as The Chicago Children's Museum, The Field Museum, and The Shedd Aquarium, providing social guides, games, tips, and maps that highlight quiet areas, tactile spaces, and sensory trigger points within the museum (Schwartzman & Knowles, 2022). One particularly valuable feature of the app is the visual schedule, which helps visitors with autism navigate and comprehend the museum by providing a structured checklist of areas to explore. This resource not only supports individuals with autism but also empowers museums to create a more inclusive and welcoming environment for all visitors (Keskinova et al., 2021).

Another resource can be found in the example of the Domus platform, which serves as an exemplary resource for museums seeking to enhance accessibility and inclusivity. This digital network of museum collections in Spain provides valuable insights and evaluations on the use of technologies in museums and exhibitions worldwide. Domus focuses on studying and comparing different experiences to guide the design and implementation of facilities and digital media that can improve the visitor experience, particularly for individuals with disabilities. By showcasing successful examples and best practices, Domus offers inspiration and guidance for museums looking to create more inclusive and accessible spaces for all visitors (Llamazares De Prado & Arias Gago, 2020).

To highlight best practices in the field, an example should be noted. In recognition of their dedication to diversity, equity, accessibility, and inclusion, the Field Museum in Chicago was honored with the Diversity, Equity, Accessibility, and Inclusion award by the American Alliance of Museums in 2017. This recognition acknowledged the collaborative efforts of the museum and Infiniteach in enhancing accessibility for individuals with autism. The museum's "Field For All" app (https://apps.apple.com/us/app/field-museum-for-all/id1171510231) has played a pivotal role in providing a personalized and inclusive experience for visitors. The app offers features that help families plan their visit, including exhibition previews, an interactive schedule, and a sensory-friendly map. Communication tools such as tap-to-talk buttons are integrated into the app, enabling users to ask questions, express their needs, and engage in dialogue about their museum experience. Additionally, educational games within the app are designed to spark interest and curiosity among visitors. Practical information about available facilities and their locations is provided, and the sensory map highlights areas where lighting and sound levels may differ, ensuring visitors can navigate the museum with greater ease and comfort. The Field Museum's commitment to accessibility through technology exemplifies their dedication to creating an inclusive environment where individuals of all abilities can engage with the museum's rich offerings.

In this comprehensive exploration of promoting inclusivity in cultural heritage institutions, we have uncovered valuable insights and strategies that can guide the path towards a more equitable and accessible future. Cultural heritage institutions hold a significant responsibility in addressing bias and ensuring inclusivity in their practices (Huang & Liem, 2022). By harnessing the power of emerging technologies, such as immersive storytelling, wearable devices, and virtual environments, these institutions can revolutionize the way visitors engage with and experience cultural heritage. These technologies offer unprecedented opportunities to create personalized narratives, adaptive interactions, and multisensory experiences, empowering neurodiverse populations and diverse audiences to connect with their heritage in profound and inclusive ways.

Openness and collaboration emerge as vital pillars in the pursuit of bias reduction and inclusivity. Through the adoption of open-source data science approaches, cultural heritage institutions can actively contribute to the development of unbiased AI algorithms while sharing resources and knowledge with a broader community of stakeholders. This collaborative mindset enables the creation of robust solutions, optimizes the utilization of data scientists' expertise, and facilitates the elimination of biases ingrained in datasets. Moreover, fostering interdisciplinary collaborations and establishing partnerships with technology experts, researchers, and communities can fuel progress, innovation, and the advancement of inclusive practices within the cultural heritage sector.

To effect lasting change, cultural heritage institutions must prioritize diversity, inclusion, and accessibility as core principles. By actively engaging with diverse communities and listening attentively to their unique needs and perspectives, institutions can ensure that their offerings are representative of the diverse tapestry of humanity. Initiatives such as co-creation projects, community storytelling endeavors, and participatory design processes empower individuals to shape their own narratives and experiences, creating a more inclusive and empowering environment for all visitors.

The journey towards reducing bias in AI and promoting inclusivity in cultural heritage institutions necessitates concerted efforts from all stakeholders involved (Chakravorty et al., 2022). By embracing emerging technologies, nurturing openness and collaboration, and placing diversity and inclusion at the heart of their practices, cultural heritage institutions can create transformative and meaningful experiences that celebrate the richness and diversity of our shared cultural heritage. In order to create more inclusive and innovative museum experiences, cultural heritage institutions are encouraged to take action through the following recommendations (Table 6.1).

First, institutions should embrace open-source data science by actively engaging in open-source projects and contributing their expertise and resources. By participating in these initiatives, museums can help develop unbiased AI algorithms and promote fairness in AI systems. This will ensure that the technology used in their exhibits and interactions is inclusive and equitable for all visitors.

Second, fostering collaboration and partnerships is essential. Institutions should establish collaborative relationships with technology experts, researchers, and communities to foster innovation and exchange best practices. By working together, museums can leverage collective knowledge and expertise to create more inclusive experiences for diverse audiences.

Third, prioritizing diversity and inclusion should be central to the policies and practices of cultural heritage institutions. By involving diverse communities in decision-making processes and co-creating experiences, museums can ensure that their offerings are representative and meaningful

Table 6.1 Recommendations for action

Recommendation	Description
Embrace open-source data science	Cultural heritage institutions should actively engage in open-source data science projects to develop unbiased AI algorithms and promote fairness.
Foster collaboration and partnerships	Establish collaborative partnerships with technology experts, researchers, and communities to foster innovation and exchange best practices.
Prioritize diversity and inclusion	Make diversity, inclusion, and accessibility central to policies and practices, involving diverse communities in decision-making and co-creation.
Embrace emerging technologies	Explore and invest in emerging technologies like immersive storytelling, wearables, and virtual environments for inclusive and engaging experiences.

to all visitors. This includes considering the needs and perspectives of individuals from different backgrounds, abilities, and identities.

Lastly, institutions should embrace emerging technologies to provide more inclusive and engaging experiences. By exploring and investing in technologies such as immersive storytelling, wearable devices, and virtual environments, museums can transcend traditional barriers and create unique opportunities for individuals with diverse abilities and backgrounds. By following these recommendations, cultural heritage institutions can play an active role in shaping a more inclusive and accessible future for museums. This will ensure that all visitors, regardless of their backgrounds or abilities, can engage, learn, and connect with the rich cultural heritage preserved within these institutions.

Furthermore, integrating neuroscience-informed strategies into exhibition design goes beyond enhancing the experiences of neurotypical visitors. It also holds significant implications for accessibility and inclusivity, supporting a broader range of visitors in engaging with and appreciating cultural heritage.

Considering the needs of neurodiverse populations, such as individuals on the spectrum, ADHD, or sensory processing sensitivities, can greatly enhance their ability to access and enjoy museum exhibits. Neuroscientific insights can inform exhibition design in ways that accommodate sensory sensitivities, minimize overwhelming stimuli, and create a more inclusive environment. By providing options for adjustable lighting, reducing auditory distractions, and incorporating sensory-friendly spaces, museums can ensure that individuals with diverse neurological profiles can fully participate in and benefit from the museum experience.

Moreover, the application of neuroscience principles in exhibition design can extend to individuals with cognitive disabilities or learning differences. By incorporating clear and concise information, intuitive navigation, and interactive elements, museums can support comprehension and engagement for individuals who may have difficulties with traditional modes of communication. The use of visual aids, multisensory experiences, and interactive technologies can facilitate understanding, foster memory retention, and promote active learning.

By embracing these considerations for accessibility, museums not only support neurodiverse populations but also benefit the general public. Accessibility features designed with neurodiversity in mind create a more welcoming and inclusive environment for all visitors. Exhibitions that incorporate sensory-friendly elements, clear communication, and interactive experiences offer a more enriching and engaging encounter with cultural heritage for everyone, regardless of their neurological profile.

Moreover, by recognizing the value of inclusivity and accessibility, museums demonstrate a commitment to equitable access to knowledge and cultural experiences. They become spaces that promote diversity, celebrate different ways of perceiving and experiencing the world, and foster a sense of belonging for all visitors. In this way, museums become agents of social change, advocating for inclusivity and challenging societal barriers that limit participation in cultural activities.

The integration of neuroscience-informed strategies in exhibition design not only enhances the experiences of neurotypical visitors but also supports accessibility and inclusivity for a broader audience. By accommodating the needs of neurodiverse populations and creating inclusive environments, museums ensure that cultural heritage is accessible to all individuals, regardless of their neurological profiles. By embracing these considerations, museums foster a more inclusive society and contribute to the democratization of knowledge and cultural experiences. It is through these efforts that museums can truly fulfill their role as public institutions that enrich and engage the entire community.

References

Armstrong, T. (2012). *Neurodiversity in the classroom: Strength-based strategies to help students with special needs succeed in school and life*. ASCD.

Ashworth, M., Heasman, B., Crane, L., & Remington, A. (2023). *Evaluating the impact of an online autism training on employers' autism knowledge and commitment to inclusion in the workplace*. OSF Preprints.

Bell, B. (2015). The issues index: Expanded opportunity through an issues. In *Public interest design practice guidebook* (pp. 195–198). Routledge.

Cesário, V., Freitas, J., & Campos, P. (2023). Empowering cultural heritage professionals: Designing interactive exhibitions with authoring tools. *Museum Management and Curatorship*, 1–15.

Chakravorty, N., Sharma, C. S., Molla, K. A., & Pattanaik, J. K. (2022). Open Science: Challenges, possible solutions and the way forward. *Proceedings of the Indian National Science Academy, 88*(3), 456–471.

Chu, K. C. (2004). *Gender reactions to games for learning among fifth and eighth graders*. Michigan State University. Department of Telecommunication, Information Studies and Media.

Doukianou, S., Daylamani-Zad, D., & Paraskevopoulos, I. (2020). Beyond virtual museums: Adopting serious games and extended reality (XR) for user-centred cultural experiences. *Visual Computing for Cultural Heritage*, 283–299. https://doi.org/10.1007/978-3-030-37191-3_15

Giannini, T., & Bowen, J. P. (2022). Museums and digital culture: From reality to digitality in the age of COVID-19. *Heritage, 5*(1), 192–214.

Gold, B. (2021). Neurodivergency and interdependent creation: Breaking into Canadian disability arts. *Studies in Social Justice, 15*(2), 209–229.

Heddon, D. (2020). Professional development for live artists: Doing it yourself. *Theatre, Dance and Performance Training, 11*(2), 145–161.

Huang, H. Y., & Liem, C. C. (2022, June). Social inclusion in curated contexts: Insights from museum practices. In *2022 ACM conference on Fairness, Accountability, and Transparency* (pp. 300–309).

Hutson, J., & Hutson, P. (2023). Museums and the metaverse: Emerging technologies to promote inclusivity and engagement. *Faculty Scholarship*, 452.

Istance, D., & Paniagua, A. (2019). *Learning to leapfrog: Innovative pedagogies to transform education*. Center for Universal Education at The Brookings Institution.

Johnson, P., & Thomas, B. (1998). The economics of museums: A research perspective. *Journal of Cultural Economics, 22*, 75–85.

Keskinova, A., Troshanska, J., Ramadani Rasmini, T., & Georgievski, P. (2021). Accessible museums. In *International scientific and practical conference "Current trends and prospects of international tourism"*, Macedonia, pp. 27–35.

Kirby, A., & Smith, T. (2021). *Neurodiversity at work: Drive innovation, performance and productivity with a neurodiverse workforce*. Kogan Page Publishers.

Krzeminska, A., & Hawse, S. (2020). Mainstreaming neurodiversity for an inclusive and sustainable future workforce: Autism-spectrum employees. In *Industry and higher education: Case studies for sustainable futures*, 229–261.

Llamazares De Prado, J. E., & Arias Gago, A. R. (2020). Education and ICT in inclusive museums environments. *International Journal of Disability, Development and Education, 70*(1), 1–15.

Luttin, S. (2022). Arts project Australia: Raising the bar through collaborative partnerships. *Artlink, 42*(2), 84–91.

Marstine, J. (2017). *Critical practice: Artists, museums, ethics*. Taylor & Francis.

Martinez-Conde, S., Alexander, R. G., Blum, D., Britton, N., Lipska, B. K., Quirk, G. J., et al. (2019). The storytelling brain: How neuroscience stories help bridge the gap between research and society. *Journal of Neuroscience, 39*(42), 8285–8290.

McElroy, R., Noonan, C., McElroy, R., & Noonan, C. (2019). Building a sustainable labour force. In *Producing British television drama: Local production in a global era* (pp. 97–121). Springer.

Meng, Y., Chu, M. Y., & Chiu, D. K. (2023). The impact of COVID-19 on museums in the digital era: Practices and challenges in Hong Kong. *Library Hi Tech, 41*(1), 130–151.

Moraru, C. (2023). The cultural category of neurodiversity: Art spaces for creating identities and understanding neurominorities. *Espace, 133*, 6–16.

Okanovic, V., Ivkovic-Kihic, I., Boskovic, D., Mijatovic, B., Prazina, I., Skaljo, E., & Rizvic, S. (2022). Interaction in extended reality applications for cultural heritage. *Applied Sciences, 12*(3), 1241.

Ortiz, L. A. (2020). Reframing neurodiversity as competitive advantage: Opportunities, challenges, and resources for business and professional communication educators. *Business and Professional Communication Quarterly, 83*(3), 261–284.

Othman, M. K., Aman, S., Anuar, N. N., & Ahmad, I. (2021). Improving children's cultural heritage experience using game-based learning at a living museum. *Journal on Computing and Cultural Heritage (JOCCH), 14*(3), 1–24.

Pearce, C. (2008). The truth about baby boomer gamers: A study of over-forty computer game players. *Games and Culture, 3*(2), 142–174.

Rosli, H., & Kamaruddin, N. (2020). A conceptual framework of digital storytelling (Dst) elements on information visualisation (Infovis) types in museum exhibition for user experience (Ux) enhancement. *International Journal of Academic Research in Business and Social Sciences, 10*(9), 185–198.

Schwartzman, R., & Knowles, C. (2022). Expanding accessibility: Sensory sensitive programming for museums. *Curator: The Museum Journal, 65*(1), 95–116.

Somers, E., Beugh, K., Chung, M., Crawford, G., Creery, C., Diab, A., ... & Schneider, S. (2022). *Student job postings: Looking through the lens of disability justice.* https://doi.org/10.35010/ecuad:17928

Topaz, C. M., Klingenberg, B., Turek, D., Heggeseth, B., Harris, P. E., Blackwood, J. C., et al. (2019). Diversity of artists in major US museums. *PloS One, 14*(3), e0212852.

Uddin, M., Manickam, S., Ullah, H., Obaidat, M., & Dandoush, A. (2023). Unveiling the metaverse: Exploring emerging trends, multifaceted perspectives, and future challenges. *IEEE Access, 11*, 87087–87103.

Varriale, L., Cuel, R., Ravarini, A., Briganti, P., & Minucci, G. (2022). Smart and inclusive museums for visitors with autism: The app case "A Dip in the Blue". In *Sustainable digital transformation: Paving the way towards smart organizations and societies* (pp. 133–152). Springer International Publishing.

Index

A
Accessibility maps, 23
Acropolis Museum, 196
Acropolis Museum Chess app, 109, 110
Active aids, 92
Active touch, 91
Adaptive extended reality, 40, 153–165
Ajman University, 94
   United Arab Emirates, 94
Algorithmic bias, 204
Ambitious About Autism Youth Patrons, 37
American Civil War, 111
American Museum of Natural History, 129, 131, 160
Analytics tools, 54
Apprenticeships, 229–232
Apps, 22, 35, 36, 56, 59, 60, 74, 75, 90, 93, 94, 105, 109, 110, 156–160, 177, 184, 189–193, 201, 233, 234
Artful Practices for Well-Being, 75

Artificial intelligence (AI), 51, 94, 134, 164, 200, 202–212, 235, 236
Artists, 54, 101, 158, 194, 201, 202, 210, 211, 230–232
Asperger's Syndrome, 13
Attention deficit disorder (ADD), 5
Attention deficit hyperactive disorder (ADHD), 5, 6, 13, 237
Audio narration, 50
Augmented reality (AR), 3, 4, 40, 56, 58, 60, 63, 70, 90, 93–95, 131, 135, 139–141, 144, 146, 153–158, 160, 163–165, 175, 177, 178, 180, 182, 184, 185, 191, 196, 209, 211
Australian State Library of New South Wales Oral History and Sound Collection project, 65
Autism, 5, 6, 13, 23, 25–30, 68–70, 75, 86, 95, 96, 102, 106, 187, 231, 233, 234
Autism Awareness for Museum Professionals, 34

© The Author(s), under exclusive license to Springer Nature Switzerland AG 2024
J. Hutson, P. Hutson, *Inclusive Smart Museums*,
https://doi.org/10.1007/978-3-031-43615-4

The Autism Society, 32, 33
Autism spectrum condition (ASC), 5,
    6, 22, 24–35, 54, 61, 67–70, 92,
    93, 186–189
Autism spectrum disorders (ASD),
    5, 13, 26
Automatic Museum Guide, 74
Avatar, 40, 144, 153, 165–171, 189,
    190, 195, 196, 233

B
Bard, 207
Binoculars, 89
Biodiversity, 111, 140, 163
Biometric measurements, 198
Biometrics, 195, 198–200, 202
Bluetooth, 56, 94, 95
Booth, Sally, 101
Boston Athenaeum, 59
Boston Children's Museum,
    30, 31, 69
BraiBook, 192
    braille, 192
Braille, 99–102, 192, 198, 199
Brandywine Museum of Art, 68
British Gallery, 99
British Library's Turning the
    Pages, 145
British Museum, 58, 88, 99, 105,
    131, 141
Building information modeling
    (BIM), 181
Bust of Nefertiti, 182, 183

C
Canadian Museum for Human
    Rights, 72, 73
Case studies, 37, 39, 40, 49, 50, 62,
    64–67, 127, 137, 153, 166,
    171, 182

Cave automatic virtual environment
    (CAVE), 2, 171
Center for Brooklyn History, 72
Center for Disease Control and
    Prevention (CDC), 5, 27
Center for the Art of East Asia
    (CAEA), 176
Charterhouse of Pisa, 181
ChatGPT, 207–209
Chicago Children's Museum, 69, 234
Children's Council, 131
The Children's Museum of
    Indianapolis, 30
Children's Museum of Pittsburgh, 29
Children's museums, 28–32
The Children's World of the Jewish
    Museum Berlin (ANOHA), 131
Chinese Buddhist Caves Temple, 176
Civilization III, 128
Civil Rights History Project
    (CRHP), 64
Civil Rights Movement, 64
Collective narratives, 39, 74
Color book, 139, 140
Color symbolism, 98
Communication card, 37, 87, 88
Community engagement, 38, 49, 50,
    63, 70, 75, 76, 111, 229
Community storytelling, 38–39, 49,
    70–76, 235
Conservation, 54, 111, 112,
    140, 173
Council for Museums, Archives, and
    Libraries, 6
COVID-19, 1, 2, 107, 177, 180
    pandemic, 1–5, 36, 177, 180
CREATE project, 175
Cultural Heritage Experiences through
    Socio-personal interactions and
    Storytell-ing (CHESS), 196
Curators, 54, 74, 100, 200, 211
Curio, 62

D
Default Mode Network (DMN), 201
DeFrame, 202
Deus Ex, 131
Digital audio guides, 35
Digital communication, 50, 51, 180
Digital Guide System, 56
Digital labeling, 53
Digital storymap, 61
Digital storytelling, 36, 38, 39, 49–63, 74, 127, 142–146, 166, 187, 229, 232, 233
Digital tour guides, 56, 59
Digital twin, 1–4, 36, 40, 153, 171–182
A Dip in the Blue, 189
Diversity, equity, accessibility, and inclusion (DEAI), 5, 23, 234
Dysgraphia, 12
Dyslexia, 5, 6, 12, 35
Dyslexic Design, 35, 36

E
Edutainment, 2, 171
Elder Scrolls, 131
Emerging technologies, 1, 2, 4, 40, 51, 59, 63, 76, 229, 232, 233, 235–237
Environmental noise control, 62
The Euan's Guide Access Survey, 7, 8
Eugene Science Center, 69
Exhibition design, 92, 93, 99, 100, 102, 182–202, 237, 238
Exit effect, 201
Exploratorium, 142, 175
Extended reality (XR), 1–4, 40, 51, 153–165, 187
Eye tracking, 198, 200, 202

F
Facebook, 3
  Meta, 3
Family guide, 139, 140
Ferens Art Gallery, 190
Fidget toys, 29, 86, 88, 89, 114
Find It, 101
First Italian Parliament, 180
5G technology, 180
Foresight Augmented Reality (FAR), 94
Foundation of the Hellenic World (FHW), 171, 173
4G devices, 180
Free-viewing, 200
Front-of-house staff, 2, 37

G
Galactic Golf, 155
Galvanic skin response (GSR), 200
Game-based learning, 39, 127–132, 135–137, 145, 146
Gamification, 39–40, 127–146
General sensory overload, 104
Geolocation, 59, 60, 201
Geometry Prague, 183
Georgia Tech, 193–195
A Gift for Athena, 58
Ginley, Barry, 99–101
Global positioning system (GPS), 90, 93, 94, 100, 191
Glove-based systems, 199
God of War Ragnarök, 134
Google's Arts & Culture, 177
Great Barrier Reef, 111–113
  Great Barrier Reef Marine Park Authority, 111
Guidebooks, 87
Gustatory perception, 188

H

Hall of Northwest Coast Indians, 139
Haptic controller feedback, 134
Haptic feedback devices, 40, 182
haptics, 40, 134, 182, 183
Head-mounted display (HMD), 3, 177, 189
Heritage sites, 2, 40–41, 49, 51, 61, 62, 66, 70, 71, 74–76, 85, 87–89, 109, 112, 114, 127, 139, 167, 168, 171, 177–179, 181, 229–238
Historical narratives, 4, 49, 63, 142, 158, 161, 166, 179
Holocube, 184, 185
Hugging Face, 205
Hypermedia-supported tools, 51
Hypersensitivity, 104, 106
Hyposensitivity, 104, 105

I

Identity-first language, 27, 28
Immersive storymaps, 39, 76, 85, 108–115, 187
Immersive technologies, 2, 40, 59, 69, 153–212, 229, 232, 233
Inclusive design elements, 53
Indian Memory Project, 72
Interactables, 185

J

Journey through Hallowed Ground, 111, 114
National Park Service, 111

K

Kremer Museum, 173

L

Large language models (LLM), 207, 209
Last of Us Part II, 134
Leontinka Foundation, 183
LGBTQ+, 72, 174, 175
Libraries, 6, 59, 60, 102, 189, 190
Library of Congress, 65
Llama, 207
Location-aware technologies, 60
London Natural History Museum, 88
Louvre, 2, 141, 177
Lowell Milken Center, 65

M

Magnifying glasses, 89
Mapping Indigenous LA, 110, 114
University of California Los Angeles, 110
Maya, 194
Memory retention, 58, 237
Merge, 184
Meta, *see* Facebook
The Metropolitan Museum of Art (The Met), 33, 180
Met Unframed, 180
The Metropolitan Museum of Art, 180
Michelangelo's *David*, 182
MicroRangers, 140
Microsoft Soundscape, 191
Missouri History Museum, 100
Mixed reality (MR), 3, 4, 40, 154, 155, 165, 211
Mobile apps, 22, 36, 59, 60, 159, 184
Mobile game, 58, 140
Mobile Tour App, 56
Mobility-enhancing systems, 51
Monitor attention, 198
Monströös, 131
Morningstar Access Program, 30
Multilingual translations, 208

Multimodal interfaces, 196
Multisensory engagement, 187
Museum of English Rural Life
 (MERL), 107, 108
The Museum of Modern Art
 (MoMA), 75
Museum of New Zealand Te Papa
 Tongarewa, 145
Museum of Pure Form, 2, 172
Museum of Science and Industry
 (MSI), 34, 88
Museum of Vancouver, 74
Museums, Libraries, and Archive
 Council, 190
My Story, My Tattoo, 66

N
National Archaeological Museum of
 Marche, 177
National Autistic Society
 (NAS), 32–34
National Gallery
 London, 177
 Prague, 182, 183
National Portrait Gallery, 177
National Zoo, 2
Neue Galerie, 59
Neural mechanisms, 4
NeuroDigital, 183
Neurodiversity, 1, 5–24, 26, 31, 32, 35,
 36, 38, 132, 146, 231, 232, 237
Neurological rehabilitation, 185, 186
Neuroscience, 4, 182–202, 237, 238
Nociceptors, 198
North Carolina Museum of Art, 53

O
Occupational therapy, 23, 186
Oculus Quest, 3
 Meta Quest, 3

Open-source data, 205–207, 235, 236
Oral History project, 65, 72
Oral motor tools, 87
Oregon Trail, 130
Oticon, 92
Our Stories Live Here, 74

P
Pandemic, 1–5, 36, 177, 180
Parking, 3, 15, 16, 20, 54, 55
Park Voyagers, 154
 Shed Aquarium in Chicago, 154
Passive aids, 92
Peabody Essex Museum (PEM), 201
Pérez Art Museum Miami (PAMM), 156
Personalized content delivery, 60
Personalized learning, 60, 135
Personal narratives, 38, 49, 50, 63–68,
 75, 76, 110, 229
Person-first language, 27
Pervasive Developmental Disorder-
 Not Otherwise Specified
 (PDD-NOS), 13
Photogrammetry, 3, 181
Physiological responses, 198
Players Journey, 131
Please Touch Museum, 30
Postal Museum, 37
Post satchels, 37
 sensory kits, 37
Post-Traumatic Stress Disorder
 (PTSD), 13
Premenstrual Dysphoric Disorder
 (PMDD), 13
Preservation, 50, 54, 61–63, 65, 66,
 162, 168, 171, 172, 174, 175,
 177, 179–182, 212
Pre-visitation, 15, 16, 56
Project Gameface, 134
Proprioception, 104
Proprioceptive input, 86

Q
Quadraturist frescoes, 181
Quiet spaces, 15, 20, 22, 30, 95

R
Racing Auditory Display (RAD), 133
Radio-frequency identification tags (RFID), 131, 196
Raid, 145
   National Museum of Denmark, 145
Reader Rabbit Toddler, 101
Ready Player Me, 170, 189
Reason software, 194
Residencies, 229–232
RFID wristbands, 131
Richmond, Eric, 101
Rijksmuseum, 177
Rocky Mountain National Park, 89
Roncesvalles, 189
Royal Academy of Arts, 177
Royal National Institute for Blind People, 100

S
San Diego Natural History Museum, 68
San Francisco Exploratorium, 141
Scantech, 3
Scent containers, 89
Scroll Paintings Project, 176
Self-identification, 27
Self-regulation, 86–88
Self-reporting methods, 198
Sensor trackers, 198
Sensory backpacks, 88, 89, 108
   sensory kits, 88, 89
Sensory balls, 86
Sensory barriers, 59
Sensory days, 25–27, 54
Sensory-friendly, 8, 14, 15, 19–22, 24, 26, 29–31, 52, 54, 95–97, 193, 237

Sensory Friendly Day, 30
Sensory-friendly map, 95, 106, 234
Sensory hours, 25, 28
Sensory kits, 29–31, 39, 85–89, 114
Sensory maps, 1, 2, 4, 19, 20, 22, 24, 37, 39, 61, 68, 85, 90–108, 114, 187–189, 234
Sensory processing disorders (SPD), 61, 95, 102–104
Sensory toys, 37, 89
   sensory kits, 37, 89
Sentiment analysis, 203, 204
Shedd Aquarium, 192, 193, 233, 234
Sign language, 3, 56, 190
Smart glasses, 40, 94, 182
Smartify app, 190
Smart Museum of Art, 59
Smart museums, 34–38, 56, 59, 60, 63, 229
Smellscapes, 61, 191
Smithsonian, 2, 73
Social media, 10, 11, 35, 36, 51, 55, 196, 203, 209
Social stories, 1, 2, 4, 19, 20, 23, 24, 30, 37, 61, 67–70, 75, 76, 85, 108, 187, 189
Software as a service (SaaS), 202
Sony Interactive Entertainment, 134
Soundification, 194
Sound reducing headphones, 193
Soundscapes, 61, 62, 191–194
Spectrum Project, 68
Spotzer Digital, 59
Staff training programs, 1, 29, 31–34
Stories from Main Street, 72
StoryCorps project, 65
Storymap, 39, 61, 76, 85, 108–115, 187
Storytelling, 4, 36, 38–40, 49–76, 108–111, 127, 131, 136, 142–146, 154, 158, 159, 161, 164–166, 170, 175, 187, 190, 194–196, 211, 229, 232, 233, 235, 237

Stress balls, 87, 88, 184
  squeezy toys, 87
Swedish Library of Talking Books and Braille, 101
Swell-Touch Paper, 101, 102

T
Tactile books, 100–102
Tactile exhibits, 23, 95
Tactile globes, 99, 100
Tactile graphics, 101
Tactile guides, 99
Textured cards, 86
3D animation, 194
3D audio, 134, 191
3D models, 3, 110
360-degree videos, 154
TIK-TIK app, 190
TiM project, 101
  European Commission, 101
Tomb Raider, 131
Touching Masterpieces, 182
  National Gallery, Prague, 182
Touchscape maps, 61
Touch tours, 100–102
Tourism, 3, 181
Tower of London, 89
Treasure hunt, 39, 127, 135, 137–142, 144
Treasure Hunt Expedition, 137, 139
  Museum of Natural History, 129, 131, 137

U
UNESCO, 178, 179
UNESCO World Culture Heritage Sites, 2
UNESCO World Heritage Sites, 2
United States Holocaust Memorial Museum, 65
Universal design, 9, 28, 134, 193
Unsung Heroes Project, 65, 66
User experience, 52, 54, 199

V
Victoria and Albert Museum (V&A), 100
Van Abbemuseum, 190
Vestibular, 6, 104
Video games, 58, 131, 133, 134
Virtual assistants, 208, 209
Virtual characters, 40, 153
Virtual Learning Environments (VLEs), 177
Virtual museum (VM), 1, 2, 4, 136, 169, 174, 175, 177, 211
Virtual Museum of Sculpture, 2, 172
Virtual reality (VR), 3, 4, 59, 70, 76, 154, 155, 161–165, 172–175, 177, 178, 180, 182, 183, 189, 211
Virtual tours, 35, 108, 111, 144, 177–179, 189
Visitor experience, 7, 40, 49, 50, 54, 59, 60, 64, 66, 67, 89, 105, 127, 128, 146, 153, 156, 158, 182, 192, 195, 202, 207, 209, 234
Visually impaired, 90–92, 94, 98–102, 133, 134, 182, 183, 190, 191
Visualscapes, 61, 62
Visual schedule, 23, 29, 86, 234
  social stories, 23, 86

W
Wayfinding, 14, 90–108, 158, 193
Wearable devices, 40, 153, 182, 184, 187, 232, 233, 235, 237
  wearables, 70, 131, 153, 154, 182, 198
Wearable Immersive Virtual Reality (WIVR), 70
Wearables, 40, 70, 131, 153, 154, 182–202, 232, 233, 235, 237

Websites, 7, 15, 20, 35, 51, 58, 68, 69, 97, 100, 105, 107
Weighted lap pad, 31, 86, 114, 193
Wellington Museum in New Zealand, 66
Workshop in Cologne, 191
World Autism Awareness Day, 25, 26
World Cultural Heritage Sites, 2, 179
World Health Organization (WHO), 2

X
Xbox, 132
Xiegong, 181
Xuanluo Hall, 181
    Sichuan, China, 181

Y
Yarbus, Alfred, 200

Printed in the United States
by Baker & Taylor Publisher Services